BLACKS IN THE NEW WORLD
August Meier, Series Editor

Black over White

Black over White

Negro Political Leadership in
South Carolina during
Reconstruction

THOMAS HOLT

UNIVERSITY OF ILLINOIS PRESS

Urbana and Chicago

To my Mother and Father
and
to Nancy

Illini Books edition, 1979
© 1977 by the Board of Trustees of the University of Illinois
Manufactured in the United States of America
P   10   9   8   7   6

Library of Congress Cataloging-in-Publication Data

Holt, Thomas, 1942–
  Black over white.
    (Blacks in the New World)
    Includes index.
    1. Afro-American legislators—South Carolina.
  2. Reconstruction—South Carolina. 3. South Carolina—
  Politics and government—1865–1950. 4. Republican
  Party. South Carolina. I. Title. II. Series.
  E185.93.S7H64   975.7'004'96073   77-7513
  ISBN 0-252-00775-1

Acknowledgments

This study is a considerably revised version of my doctoral dissertation written at Yale University. In preparing this and earlier versions of the manuscript, I received the kind assistance of many people; indeed, far more than I can name here. But the contributions of some were so substantial that I must single them out. The study in its present form would not exist but for the timely assistance of C. Vann Woodward, John McCarthy, and John Blassingame. Mr. Woodward inspired the original idea for a collective biography of black Reconstruction leadership and provided advice and encouragement as it slowly took shape. Mr. McCarthy not only introduced me to quantitative analysis of historical data, without which I could not have handled the large quantities of data collected, but cheerfully gave me a great deal of technical assistance on the application of roll call procedures. Mr. Blassingame made numerous and very helpful suggestions about potential sources of biographical information; without his assistance there would have been a lot less data to analyze. No novice can begin to apply the many complicated computer routines required in this study without incurring numerous debts to technicians and experts. William Craven and Gregory King of Howard University gave generously of their time to help me with computer problems. Under their tutelage I advanced several steps beyond the novice stage in taming the "monster."

Much of the research for this study was made possible by a research fellowship in Ethnic Studies granted to me by the Ford Foundation. Two faculty research grants from the Howard University Department of History helped me with some of the computer coding in the later stages of my research and in the final preparation of the manuscript. Census data used in early stages of this project were obtained from the historical data archives at the Inter-University Consortium for Political Research.

I am grateful to staffs of the South Carolina Archives, the South Caroliniana Library, the South Carolina Historical Association, and the National Archives, who were all very helpful. I am especially indebted to James Walker, whose assistance at an early stage of my research with the military records at the National Archives was critical. A number of people have read part or all of this manuscript in various stages, shapes, and forms and have made useful suggestions. For this assistance I thank Allison Blakely, William S. McFeely, Okon Uya, Joel Williamson, William Harris, Frank Schubert, Maceo Dailey, Cassandra Smith-Parker, Michael Holt, William C. Hine, and Kai Erikson. I am indebted to August Meier for a thorough critique of the entire manuscript, which proved invaluable even when I sharply disagreed with it. A special thanks is due my typist, Mary Thomas, who cheerfully and tolerantly met all my ridiculous deadlines.

My wife Nancy has helped me think out loud about many critical problems of statistical analysis and has offered occasional words of advice. To her belongs the credit for helping me resist—even at my lowest moments—the temptation to lie with statistics. The credit for the failures is, of course, mine alone.

Harvard University   —T. H.

Contents

Introduction

Of the 487 men elected to the various state and federal offices in South Carolina between 1867 and 1876, more than half were black. This is surely a phenomenal fact in American history and has attracted more than its share of attention from both contemporary observers and historians of the Reconstruction period. Yet, although the history of South Carolina during Reconstruction probably has been studied more than that of any other state, the origins, political development, attitudes, and aspirations of the black leadership cadre remain somewhat distorted by gross errors and obscured by silly caricatures and myths. Despite a virtual deluge of printed matter, we still do not know who these men were, or very much about what they wanted, what they did, and what their role was in the successes and failures of the Reconstruction experiment.

In truth, although there are several excellent studies available, we have not progressed very far beyond the state of affairs in 1934 when W. E. B. Du Bois raised critical questions about the political history of black Republicans in South Carolina.

> The whole body of facts concerning what the Negro actually said and did, how he worked, what he wanted, for whom he voted, is masked in such a cloud of charges, exaggeration and biased testimony, that most students have given up all attempt at new material or new evaluation of the old, and simply repeated perfunctorily all the current legends of black buffoons in [the] legislature, golden spittoons for fieldhands, bribery and extravagance on an unheard of scale, and the collapse of civilization until an outraged nation rose in wrath and ended the ridiculous travesty.[1]

In the final analysis, however, even Du Bois's reach exceeded his grasp. Whatever wisdom, fresh insights, theory, and sheer moral energy he brought to bear on the problem of describing the black part of Reconstruction, he could not overcome one critical defect. Complaining of the lack of extant primary source materials on and by blacks themselves, he was forced to rely for his documentation on many of the same scholars

1. W. E. B. Du Bois, *Black Reconstruction . . . in America, 1860-80* (New York: Harcourt Brace, 1935), pp. 381-82.

he criticized. Much of his material on the numbers, roles, and social backgrounds of black politicians in South Carolina, for example, was taken from the patronizingly racist study published just two years before by Francis Simkins and Robert Woody, *South Carolina During Reconstruction.* As a result the critical questions remained unanswered. Instead Du Bois pursued the interpretation of Reconstruction, particularly in South Carolina, as the demonstration of a tendency toward the dictatorship of the proletariat and the elimination of the dominion of private capital; that it was in truth "the story of a normal working class movement, successful to an unusual degree, despite all disappointment and failure." [2]

While Du Bois's treatment of this thesis opened up some interesting new lines of inquiry, it did little to flesh out the biographical and political profiles of the black leadership. The task was left to Joel Williamson, a white native of the state, who began constructing a biographical profile of South Carolina's black leadership. Williamson has examined the role of critical institutional forces, the military, the church, and the Freedmen's Bureau, in recruiting and developing political leadership during the immediate postwar period. He has identified many of the Negro members according to their antebellum condition, nativity, literacy, and color. Yet, while Williamson's study has certainly been an inspiration and beginning point for the present one, it falls short of completing what this author has found to be an arduous and exhausting task. Furthermore, the impressive body of manuscript material that Williamson mined for his definitive treatment of the social and economic adjustments of freedmen after slavery was far less responsive to questions about the black political leadership, especially with respect to its social origins and political attitudes. Like Du Bois, Williamson found sources on black leaders scarce and was eventually forced to rely heavily on information collated from daily newspapers which were not only politically and racially biased, but notoriously inaccurate as well. [3]

Because this study is considerably narrower in focus than many of these earlier ones, it has been possible to examine a broader range of sources and to more meticulously collate this data. Then, too, the simple passage of time has brought to the fore many new facilities and conceptual approaches that have made the gathering and analysis of large quantities of data more feasible than in 1965 and certainly 1934. The most obvious influence on this study has been the development of new methodologies for the quantitative analysis of historical data, particularly the analysis

2. *Ibid.,* p. 383.

3. Williamson relies heavily on the Charleston *Mercury* and *New York Times* for biographical data. See Joel Williamson, *After Slavery: The Negro in South Carolina During Reconstruction, 1861-77* (Chapel Hill: University of North Carolina Press, 1965), p. 378.

of legislative voting behavior. To a lesser extent concepts and techniques of collective biography and political theory have also stimulated and refined the conceptual approaches taken here, although their effects are not always obvious.[4]

This study attempts to answer several key questions about the emergence and decline of black leadership in South Carolina. (1) What were the social backgrounds of the Negro political leaders? Specifically, what were their relationships to the prewar regime, and how did this influence their political development? (2) How were black leaders recruited, and what institutions were instrumental in that recruitment? (3) What was the political role of blacks? Did they dominate South Carolina politics, or were they merely the pliant tools of white Republicans? (4) What were the political attitudes and ideologies of black leaders? Were they unified in their political perspectives and interests, or were there significant differences among them? (5) How did black leaders relate to their constituents? Were they, as Du Bois suggests, harbingers of a potential dictatorship of the proletariat? (6) What caused the debacle of 1876, when black Reconstruction ended? Were the forces mainly external to the Republican party, or internal? Was it violence and intimidation, or a failure in the leadership itself? (7) Finally, why was the party's collapse so total? Why did it never revive in the 1880's as a serious political challenge?

The answers to these questions involve some basic departures from the conclusions of Du Bois and Williamson. Contrary to Williamson's findings, the results of this study do not depict Reconstruction as "a tremendous success" in which black political power "turned doubtful economic issues" in the black peasant's favor.[5] Nor does it show what Du Bois contends was "a splendid failure." [6] Rather, an analysis of the social background and voting behavior of these men reveals that the key leaders were basically bourgeois in their origins and orientation and oftener than not failed to act in the interests of black peasants. For example, the Combahee strike of rice workers on the eve of the Conservative counterrevolution dramatically exposed the Republican legislative record on labor questions to have been a failure more abject than splendid.

More of the blame for this failure must be laid at the door of Negro

---

4. For a discussion of the methods and issues of collective biography, see Dankwart Rustow, "The Study of Elites; Who's Who, When and How," *World Politics*, XVIII (July, 1966), 690; Morris Janowitz, "The Systematic Analysis of Political Biography," *World Politics*, VI (April, 1954), 411; Harold Lasswell, *The Comparative Study of Elites* (Palo Alto: Stanford University Press, 1952), pp. 11ff.

5. Williamson, *After Slavery*, p. 179.

6. Du Bois, *Black Reconstruction*, p. 708.

leaders than heretofore. Contrary to tradition, these men were not simply
the pliant tools of white Republicans, but the single most powerful segment
of the Republican party, exercising extensive influence over legislative
and political affairs. The ultimate cause of their failure to remain in
power had less to do with corruption (which scholars have unvaryingly
cited) than with the disintegration of their own party in the years and
months preceding the electoral crisis of 1876. This disintegration was
only superficially linked to the popular revulsion against the corruption
of Republican government. Certainly the cause of failure was not, as
Williamson insists, "an absence of a sense of responsibility to the whole
society, white as well as black." [7] It is doubtful that the majority of white
South Carolinians would have accepted a responsive black government
any more readily than an unresponsive one. It is much more likely that
they would have chosen to make their peace with a strong government,
responsive or not.

Indeed, one specific cause of failure was Governor Daniel H. Chamberlain's attempt to create a new party alignment of whites and conservative Negroes which contributed directly to the dismantling of South
Carolina Republicanism. Under Chamberlain's administration the flaws
of the Republican hegemony were made manifest. While blacks exercised
a great deal of political influence, the state's reconstructed constitution
had consolidated statutory control of patronage in the governor's office.
Given the divisions within the party generally and the Negro majority
in particular, and given a governor ambitious enough to challenge the
legislative leaders of his own party, the black leaders' control of their
state's political destiny was curtailed considerably.

Ultimately, it was not the black electoral majority that failed in South
Carolina; their transition from slaves to political men was unusually
successful. It was their leaders who failed. Neither the Republican party
as a whole nor the Negro leadership appears to have formulated or
manifested a clear and unifying ideology or legislative program. There
were wide differences in views on many of the more important issues
they faced; moreover, these differences appear to have been influenced
by differences in socioeconomic background more than any other factor.
The Negro leaders' inability to resolve these differences contributed significantly to the intraparty cleavages and hence to the final debacle. Confronted by a determined white minority united on one hand by a devotion
to a well-defined although crumbling social order, and on the other by
an almost religious crusade to restore white supremacy, the Republicans
lost. Furthermore, they lost so decisively that their power could not be
regained in that century.

7. Williamson, *After Slavery*, p. 381.

The Negro political leadership of South Carolina was stronger in both numbers and influence than black Republicans in any other state. If Reconstruction was to succeed anywhere, it had to succeed there. Therefore, an understanding of the failure of South Carolina Republicanism should provide some insights into the causes of the party's general destruction in the post–Civil War South. A clear portrait of the Negro politicians of that state is an essential first step in gaining that understanding.

PART ONE

THE MAKING OF A POLITICAL REVOLUTION

Chapter One

From Protest to Power: Negro Leaders on the Eve of Reconstruction

The meeting at Zion Church in Charleston during the late fall of 1865 was by all accounts unprecedented. Sensing the prospect of significant events, black Charlestonians crowded into the church's galleries to hear the daily debates and to applaud the speeches of their newly emergent, largely indigenous leadership at nightly mass meetings. The large church was too small to handle the crowd; the overflow spilled anxiously into surrounding streets, where the stench of fire damage lingered still in this war-torn city. Gnarled but enterprising old men and women with newly found economic liberties hawked peanuts and plied other sundries to black onlookers along Calhoun Street in front of the church. Inside, black men—mostly freeborn and relatively affluent—met to demand new liberties and to fashion their first major political manifesto.

Drawing on the revolutionary tradition of their century, these leaders would write a "Declaration of Rights and Wrongs" proclaiming their inalienable rights to that bourgeois triad of life, liberty, and property, and denouncing the oppression of taxation without representation. They would petition the legislature of South Carolina and the Congress of the United States for a redress of grievances. And finally, they would appeal directly to the white citizens of South Carolina for *"even-handed Justice,"* explaining their resolve to "come forward, and like MEN, speak and *act,"* secure in the knowledge that "God helps those who help themselves." [1] As if to emphasize that resolve, they established the first statewide organization of black leaders in South Carolina and provided a mechanism for reconvening their assembly should events warrant. They dramatized their resolution of self-help and independence by financing their meeting from the proceeds of a twenty-five-cent admission fee paid by audiences of the nightly mass meetings, which were partly political and part-

1. *Proceedings of the Colored People's Convention of the State of South Carolina Held in Zion Church, Charleston, November, 1865* (Charleston: South Carolina Leader Office, 1865), p. 23.

ly social.[2] These actions gave some truth to the hopeful banner headline in a recently established Republican weekly:

RECONSTRUCTION BEGUN [3]

Indeed, this announcement was too sanguine, and it was certainly premature. Reconstruction, at least in the sense of political freedom, would come almost two years after the Calhoun Street meeting and only after extensive agitation by blacks and whites in the North as well as the South. The nation was not yet ready to grant political liberties to black men in 1865. After all, it had only grudgingly conceded the military necessity of unconditional emancipation in 1863. It would be sufficient for now to continue with President Andrew Johnson's policy of reconciliation wherein most ex-Confederates were pardoned after renewing their oaths of allegiance to the Union, and the southern states would be readmitted after provisional governors were appointed to reorganize their governments, and after those new governments recognized the supremacy of the federal Union by repudiating their Confederate debts and abolishing slavery. Eventually, political necessities would alter this "politics of reconciliation" into a "politics of reconstruction" which accorded the black man full citizenship rights—but only after continuous and bitter agitation, and fully two years after Lee's surrender at Appomattox.

Of course, the major theater for this agitation was in the Congress and the constituencies of northern congressional delegations. South Carolinians, white as well as black, waited largely in the wings for their cues while a powerful faction of Republican congressional leaders resisted the presidential initiatives and condemned the policy of reconciliation as a betrayal of a war victory so costly in human sacrifice. Of course, South Carolinians did have important roles to play. Misreading the flow of events, many whites looked backward and tried to save remnants of a discredited and anachronistic social order, destroying all prospect for its redemption in the process. Sensing the revolutionary potential of the postwar situation, many blacks looked forward to a new political order which would—albeit temporarily—stand the old order on its head. While their protests and petitions during this early period probably played a minor role in bringing on that new order, it is significant that black men nevertheless assumed an unwonted political personality, long before their right to citizenship—much less to suffrage—was settled.

Even before the statewide convention in Charleston several events marked the political initiation of black South Carolinians. A delegation

2. *Ibid.*, pp. 16-17, 20. Indeed, the surplus from this fund was sufficient to pay for an oyster supper on the final day of the meetings.

3. *South Carolina Leader* (Charleston), November 25, 1865.

of Sea Islanders that had tried unsuccessfully to be seated in the national Republican convention of 1864 included four Negroes, with the ubiquitous Robert Smalls among them.[4] And soon after Union troops marched into their city, black leaders and ministers of Zion and Bethel Churches in Charleston had organized a massive parade to celebrate their day of Jubilee. A crowd of 4,000 began gathering at noon to watch two mounted black marshals wearing red and blue rosettes and blue sashes proudly lead the procession. It was a parade of the people, of butchers, carpenters, blacksmiths, and other tradesmen. They marched from Citadel Square to the Battery and back; all along the way the crowd cheered lustily for the smart black soldiers and band of the 21st U.S. Colored Infantry. They applauded the thousands of schoolchildren carrying flags and banners praising the heroes of the Union and declaring: "We know no cast[e] or color." With unaccustomed audacity, they playfully mocked the auctioneer on a spring cart towing a coffle of slaves for sale. Behind them came a hearse bearing the body of slavery.[5]

In a more serious mood, other Charleston Negroes assembled in a mass meeting on March 30, 1865, to vote public resolutions confirming their Union sentiments and gratitude.[6] The apparent organizers of this meeting were all members of the free Negro community of Charleston. Therefore, it is difficult to assess its full significance, for during the war many in the free Negro community had remained loyal to, if not actually accomplices of, the rebel regime.[7] Their forthright declaration of loyalty to the Union was commendable, nevertheless, coming at a still uncertain juncture in the war (Lee had not yet surrendered) and with rumors rampant about violent reprisals against Columbia's Negro population after Union troops left that city.[8] Indeed, their erstwhile white guardians must have been chagrined at these resolutions, since such a meeting of Negroes had been illegal in South Carolina only a scant six weeks before.[9]

A flurry of activity by Negroes continued throughout the spring and summer of 1865, culminating in the local and state conventions and petitions of the fall. In fact, the March meeting of the Charlestonians coincided with the first election held by freedmen for town officers in

4. Okon Edet Uya, *From Slavery to Public Service: Robert Smalls, 1839-1915* (New York: Oxford University Press, 1971), p. 38.

5. *Daily Courier* (Charleston), March 22, 1865.

6. *Ibid.,* April 1, 3, 1865.

7. At least one of the authors of the resolutions, Robert C. De Large, earned a tidy sum while in the employ of the Confederate Navy. *Daily Republican* (Charleston), July 7, 1870.

8. *Daily Courier,* April 3, 1865.

9. The Negro codes of the prewar period prohibited any public meeting of more than six Negroes except in the presence of a white man.

the coastal village of Mitchellville.[10] Some of these later activities were evidently organized by the army and the Freedmen's Bureau. Major Martin R. Delany and Captain O. S. B. Wall, two black Northerners attached to General Rufus Saxton's Bureau staff, were actively engaged in military recruiting and promoted political activism throughout the coastal lowlands. Reuben Tomlinson, a white Philadelphian and the Bureau's superintendent of education, was also active in encouraging freedmen to demand the right to vote. But General Saxton himself was a key spokesman for the political and economic interests of freedmen. It was undoubtedly through his auspices that Zion Church, which was under military control during this period, was made available for practically all of the mass meetings in Charleston. Moreover, Saxton forthrightly made a case for the freedmen's claim on the nation for a voice in shaping their own destinies; he practically commanded his audience to petition Congress for their rights. "If the nation asks you to help in time of war, you certainly have a right to call for the help of the nation for your rights in time of peace," he declared before a mass meeting in May, 1865. "I want the colored men in this department to petition the President of the United States and Congress for the right to exercise the elective franchise—the right to vote for those who are to rule over them." He urged further that a committee be formed at that very meeting to draw up such a petition.[11]

It would be inaccurate, however, to conclude—as generations of historians have—that the Negroes were merely the inert and unreacting political tools of northern carpetbaggers. While the encouragement and resources supplied by northern whites were desirable and possibly even essential, Negroes themselves made the initial moves toward political participation. They organized and paid for their own exclusive conventions, wrote their petitions, identified their leadership, and generally fashioned the basis for the Republican party of later years.

Indeed, an indigenous Negro leadership was necessary to the success of Republicanism. Saxton and his cohorts were active and sympathetic, but they were very few in number and very much outside the circles of power and influence then dominant within the federal bureaucracy. Indeed, Saxton's aggressive and generally uncompromising support of the freedmen would cost him his job at the year's end.[12] Excluding a few of the missionaries remaining at Port Royal, many Northerners

10. S. C. Hale to George Whipple, March 28, 1865, South Carolina, American Missionary Association Archives, Microfilm, No. 627, Amistad Research Center, New Orleans.

11. *Daily Courier,* May 13, 1865.

12. Saxton was removed early in January, 1866. See Francis L. Cardozo to George Whipple, January 27, 1866, A.M.A. Papers.

destined to become politically involved were largely engaged in "new careers" as planters during this formative period.[13] Their political involvement with the black population developed much later under the protective aegis of a congressional mandate in 1867-68. The missionary societies as organizations were largely apolitical at the local level, and the Freedmen's Bureau, always understaffed, relied on appointments from a military corps that was proverbially hostile to blacks.[14]

Indeed, while General Saxton was encouraging political activism among black Charlestonians, Quincy A. Gilmore, the commanding general, and his subordinates were actively discouraging them. General Gilmore was charged with having attempted to discourage a meeting of blacks at St. Luke's Church in June. Evidently, to resolve the difficulty, he dispatched a subordinate to a second meeting one month later. Apparently this mission was successful, since the meeting was adjourned without pressing its announced business, which was to protest grievances against the military. Probably the intercession with President Johnson by a prominent Massachusetts Republican, Judge Charles Cowley, aided the amicable settlement, since he later reported to the Negroes the president's assurance that the military had no authority to restrain the people's political activities.[15] Still, the military and local federal bureaucracy generally continued to be hostile to the political interests of the black population.[16]

An incident in Beaufort further illustrates the sometimes repressive role of some Northerners during this early period in the development of black political leadership. Major Martin R. Delany, prominent before the war among black abolitionists and emigrationists and active afterward as a political theorist, made a speech to a mass meeting of six hundred freedmen at St. Helena's Old Brick Church; his message provoked the condemnation not only of the military, but of the white missionary element as well. In his speech Delany had attempted to instill in the freedmen racial

13. Edward M. Stoeber, Daniel H. Chamberlain, and Francis E. Wilder are examples of those white Northerners who came South to make investments in planting or selling cotton during the immediate postwar period. Others (Charles P. Leslie and D. T. Corbin) came to take federal patronage jobs, and their planting investments were secondary. For an example, see Edward M. Stoeber Papers, South Caroliniana Library, University of South Carolina, Columbia.

14. See Martin Abbott, *The Freedmen's Bureau in South Carolina, 1865-72* (Chapel Hill: University of North Carolina Press, 1967), pp. 20-21.

15. *Daily Courier,* July 12, 1865; *South Carolina Leader,* November 25, 1865.

16. In an open letter to Richard H. Gleaves in 1875, former governor Robert K. Scott declared that the federal office-holders in South Carolina were generally opposed to the Reconstruction government. "Nine out of ten of those who were appointed were opposed to the State governments that had been organized." "Ex-Governor Scott and the Colored People," clipping from an unidentified newspaper dated June 12, 1875, in Reconstruction Scrapbook MSS, South Caroliniana Library, University of South Carolina, Columbia.

pride and independence of thought and action. The war would not have been won without black troops, he told them. They were not an inferior race, but an able and intelligent people. The whole nation depended upon their labor. They should be as wary and critical of those Yankees who sought to be their new masters and to impose on them wage slavery as they were of their former owners. Furthermore, they should demand their own lands and deal only with those cotton agents authorized by the government.[17]

For this speech General Gilmore sought to have Delany removed. But two other Northerners, soon to become Republican politicians in the state, also had a role in the affair. Lieutenant Edward M. Stoeber, a white Austrian immigrant who later became a planter and Republican state representative, was assigned to spy on Delany. Stoeber's report condemned Delany's behavior and served as a basis for Gilmore's attempt to have him dismissed.[18] Meanwhile, Reuben Tomlinson, scion of Pennsylvania abolitionists, journeyed hastily to the Old Brick Church to try to counteract and discredit Delany's leadership in the area.[19] It should be added, however, that General Saxton did support Delany, at least to the extent of resisting the many attempts to have him fired. Nevertheless, the incident was a clear illustration at the outset that the alliance of the blacks and northern whites would be an uneasy one, and that an independent black leadership would have to develop to some extent in spite of, not through the aid of, white Republicans.

In September, 1865, while native whites gathered in convention to reconstitute the old regime, more than a hundred blacks assembled in Charleston and an unspecified number on St. Helena Island to petition for political recognition in the state's new constitution. The constitutional convention unceremoniously ignored their petitions and their pretensions to political and civil rights. Instead, the convention and the subsequent special session of the legislature took strong measures to consign freedmen to an inferior political, economic, and social status. Shortly thereafter, on October 26, a preliminary meeting was held in Charleston preparatory to convening the first statewide meeting of the Negro leadership for the announced purpose of "deliberating upon the plans best calculated to advance the interests of our people, to devise means for our mutual protection, and to encourage the industrial interests of the State." [20]

17. Victor Ullman, *Martin R. Delany: The Beginnings of Black Nationalism* (Boston: Beacon Press, 1971), pp. 328-30.

18. *Ibid.*, p. 331.

19. Laura Towne, *Letters and Diary of Laura M. Towne, Written from the Sea Islands of South Carolina, 1862-84,* ed. Rupert Sargent Holland (Cambridge: Riverside Press, 1912), p. 165.

20. *Colored People's Convention,* p. 5.

Each district was to have as many delegates to this convention as it had representatives in the lower house of the state legislature. Under this legislative formula eighty-three delegates would have been expected to attend, but only a little more than half that number actually met at Zion Church on November 25, 1865. While representatives were probably never expected from the remoter districts with small black populations, many of the other delegations were either underrepresented (like that of Beaufort, with only one of its two delegates attending) or had far more than their share. Charleston, for example, was entitled to ten delegates by the legislative formula, but it had twenty-four representatives in attendance—two more than all the other districts combined.

The choice of the representation scheme then current in the state legislature was somewhat incongruous in any case, since that scheme was based on the suppositions that blacks were not part of the political constituency and that the wealth of Charleston warranted extra representation. Consequently, the 33,339 Negroes of Beaufort were allowed only two representatives, while the 40,912 Negroes of Charleston were alloted ten. In any event, the meeting did succeed in bringing representation from all sections of the state, including areas like Greenville in the west and Sumter and Kershaw in the midlands that had given no previous evidence of black activism.[21]

The dominant element in both numbers and influence in this convention, as in previous political activities, was the freeborn petite bourgeoisie of Charleston. While some of the delegates were only recently emancipated, at least twenty-four of the forty-six present were freeborn natives. Most were mulattoes; some were either relatively affluent themselves or scions of well-to-do families. One organizer of the convention and a prominent figure in most of the preceding political meetings in Charleston was Paul McCall Poinsett, a fifty-three-year-old mulatto barber who had real estate assessed at $1,200 in 1860. Thomas M. Holmes, the president of the convention, had been a sexton in prewar Charleston; he was listed as the owner of three slaves in 1860. E. P. Wall, a free mulatto tailor, was forty-eight years old and owned $1,500 in real estate in Charleston.[22] He had been politically active since early summer, frequently lecturing to groups such as the Ladies Patriotic Society on the Negro's claims to the elective franchise.[23] Many of the representatives from other sections

21. The districts represented were Charleston (24 delegates), Chester (1), Colleton (4), Greenville (1), Kershaw (2), Prince George Winyaw (3), Richland (4), Sumter (3), Orangeburg (3), and Beaufort (1).

22. "Tax on Property Paid by Persons of Indian Descent and Free Persons of Color," *List of Taxpayers of the City of Charleston for 1860* (Charleston, 1861), p. 329, 323, 332.

23. *Daily Courier*, June 2, 1865.

of the state also appear to have been drawn from the middle-class strata of the Negro community. Edward G. Rue was a free black clergyman from Georgetown whose property was worth $1,300 in 1870.[24] One of his colleagues was A. G. Baxter, a free mulatto carpenter.[25] Another was Edward C. Rainey, one of the officers of the convention and the older brother of Joseph H. Rainey, the first Negro to be seated in Congress. Like his brother and his father, Edward was a barber in Georgetown.[26] Almost a third of these delegates would later be elected to the state legislature or senate, while two would serve in Congress, and one would take a seat on the state's highest court. Some, like E. P. Wall, would hold elective offices in the Charleston city and county governments, while others would be found in various state and appointive offices during the coming decade. Without a doubt these men, along with some of those allowed to participate as honorary members (Martin R. Delany, Richard H. Cain, Francis L. Cardozo, Benjamin A. Bosemon, and the soon to be martyred Benjamin F. Randolph), provide a preview of the Negro leadership that would emerge during the Reconstruction era.

The discussions and resolutions produced by the convention also anticipate some of the problems, divisions, and conflicts of the subsequent period. The group was keenly self-aware and felt constrained to balance forthright assertions of their rights with some mollification of northern opinion upon which those rights ultimately depended. To some extent the discussions and language of the resolutions themselves reveal much about the nature of the differences between the goals, needs, and ambitions of the freeborn mulatto petite bourgeoisie, in contrast to those of the slave-born black peasantry.

The concern with the image of the convention, its decorum and its tone, seems almost overdrawn. Speaker after speaker counseled moderation and dignity as well as firmness in seeking their goals. Guest speakers, such as Captain O. S. B. Wall and Martin R. Delany, were particularly prone to offer such advice. At one point Delany was reported to have advised the group "to be active, but firm and conciliatory, and manifest destiny would solve the problem." [27] The unanimous adoption of the following resolution reflects the delegate's attempt to project this image of a long-suffering but conciliatory people. "*Resolved,* That as the old institution of slavery has passed away, that we cherish in our hearts no hatred or malice toward those who have held our brethren as slaves,

24. U.S. MSS Census, 1870, Population, Town of Georgetown, p. 45.

25. U.S. MSS Census, 1860, Population, Georgetown District, Parish of Prince George, p. 9.

26. *Ibid.,* p. 17.

27. *South Carolina Leader,* November 25, 1865.

but we extend the right hand of fellowship to *all,* and make it our special aim to establish unity, peace and love amongst all men." [28]

The strenuous efforts to project a conciliatory attitude toward the whites, and dignity and harmony among themselves in their deliberations, merely underscores conflicts which, though muted, did break to the surface. The record of the convention gives very little of actual debates, but pregnant phrases and fleeting glimpses of "spirited discussions" betray the general subject, if not the substance of these conflicts. The resolution quoted above was actually a substitute for an earlier version that was evidently less platitudinous and more pointedly analytical of the effects of slavery on black peoples. Given the models that the convention's writers generally adapted, the original resolution was probably a bill of particulars of the evil effects of slavery somewhat in the style of Jefferson's long list of charges against the British crown in the Declaration of Independence. In any case, when the resolution came to the floor, De Large moved to strike out the phrase, "And thereby cause us to make distinctions among ourselves." This reference appears to have been to the intraracial color prejudices that had grown up between mulattoes and blacks during slavery. The debate, which was between Robert C. De Large, Alonzo J. Ransier, and John Chestnut, all mulattoes, and Jonathan J. Wright, William Beverly Nash, and Harvey D. Edwards, all blacks, was described by the recorder, with obvious reserve and understatement, as "a trying scene to the members." [29] And well it might have been, for De Large and several other delegates including Thomas M. Holmes, the convention's president, were members of the Brown Fellowship Society, a fifty-year-old fraternal organization which strictly barred blacks from membership; in addition, Nash, a former urban slave, was not above bitter denunciations of the "mongrel" mulattoes in the heat of the political in-fighting of later years.[30] Ultimately, the resolution with its offending passage was recommitted and the more palliative substitute adopted—possibly because of a continuing concern for the convention's image and the maintenance of harmony, and possibly because the free mulatto class, which was ostensibly offended, made up a majority of the convention.

One could easily overemphasize the color aspects of this conflict; subsequent events would show that that aspect was really only the visible tip of a deeper schism in the postwar Negro leadership. There were subtle but distinct differences in emphasis and outlook between the largely mulatto bourgeoisie and the black peasantry, with the urban-based slaves and ex-slave domestics constituting something of a swing group. For

28. *Colored People's Convention,* p. 13.
29. *Ibid.,* p. 12.
30. *Beaufort Republican,* January 30, 1873.

example, although the major concern of plantation-based freedmen was reform in land distribution, that issue appears to have been pushed toward the background in the discussions and proposals of the delegates. Of the numerous "sprightly and lively" speeches made during the nightly mass meetings, only two seem to have touched on specific problems of the newly emancipated farmworker class. On the third night of the convention, the Reverend Richard H. Cain, a black A.M.E. missionary who evidenced a persistent and deep concern about the land reform issue throughout his political career, spoke extemporaneously on the topic "Free Suffrage and the Labor Question." He had been preceded by John Chestnut, a barber from the Kershaw District who was the slave-born child of a free father and slave mother. Chestnut's theme evidently was simply that the freedmen were willing to work if given the opportunity. The tenor of his remarks can be surmised from the fact that he had been praised by the conservative press for discouraging the confiscation idea among the freedmen.[31]

Furthermore, the only resolutions reported to the convention floor relative to freedmen and abandoned lands were "after some debate" indefinitely postponed—that is, killed. The initiator of the motion to scuttle these resolutions was William Beverly Nash, a Columbia hotel servant during slavery and owner of a brick factory and numerous city properties in the postwar period.[32] The absence of a record of the debate makes it difficult to ascribe precise motives for killing the resolutions, but one might infer the general sentiment from the fact that Nash, an urban businessman, later developed something of a conservative reputation for his consistent opposition to the confiscation of rebel property.

However, it is true that the land issue was addressed in the most militant of the four petitions adopted by the delegates—that sent to the U.S. Senate and House of Representatives; but the language was curiously oblique and lacking in force or specific direction. Instead of demanding validation of the "possessory" titles then held by thousands of Sea Islanders, which had been granted under General Sherman's Field Order No. 15,[33] they merely requested that "a fair and impartial consideration

31. *Colored People's Convention,* p. 14; Joel Williamson, *After Slavery: The Negro in South Carolina During Reconstruction, 1861-77* (Chapel Hill: University of North Carolina Press, 1965), p. 377.

32. *Colored People's Convention,* p. 16.

33. Sherman's field order provided for black refugees that had followed his army through Georgia by allowing them to settle on forty-acre lots along the abandoned strip of coastal land in South Carolina and Georgia. But in February, 1866, President Andrew Johnson vetoed the Freedmen's Bureau Bill (Senate 60), which would have given three-year "possessory" titles to the freedmen until some equitable redistribution scheme could be worked out. For fuller discussion, see William S. McFeely, *Yankee Stepfather: General O. O. Howard and the Freedmen* (New Haven: Yale University Press, 1968), pp. 211-36.

be given to the pledges of the government to us concerning the land question." But even as the delegates met, President Andrew Johnson was hastily pardoning dispossessed rebel planters, abrogating government pledges to freedmen, and forcing them with Union bayonets off their forty-acre patches of ground into perpetual serfdom.[34] Prompt government action to ensure their economic freedom was the critical need of the freedmen; yet the convention responded with resolutions like the ones urging "education, industry and economy," and declaring that "Knowledge is power; and an educated and intelligent people can neither be held in, nor reduced to slavery." [35]

This apparent gingerliness with the labor-land issue is perhaps merely further evidence of the constraint imposed by the attempts to maintain an image of moderation and to avoid a backlash in northern opinion. However, other facts belie such a simple explanation. The model for the phraseology of many of the documents and arguments was obviously the Declaration of Independence, but perhaps it is indicative of the orientation of the delegates that the principle seized therefrom was "no taxation without representation." This is hardly the kind of basis for an appeal that the propertyless and non-taxpaying masses could reasonably stand on. Nor would a class fresh from the debilitating effects of slavery, a class in need of positive and affirmative government action, advocate, as did this convention, an essentially laissez-faire relationship with the government, declaring: "We ask for no special privileges or peculiar favors. We ask only for even-handed Justice, or for the removal of such positive obstructions as past, and recent Legislators have seen fit to throw in our way, and heap upon us." [36]

Some of the "positive obstructions" that the delegates did object to were the Black Codes proposed during the special session of the state legislature a month earlier. These deprived Negroes of "the rights of the meanest profligate in the country—the right to engage in any legitimate business free from any restraints, save those which govern all other citizens of this State." [37] This passage—one of the most direct and forceful to come from the convention—reveals much about the essential nature of the delegates' grievances, for while the Black Codes may have restricted the newly won freedoms of the ex-slaves, they struck still harder at the more traditional privileges of the antebellum free class. Conceding all the oppressions and indignities of their "quasi-free" status under the old regime, the free Negroes had generally enjoyed an economic freedom,

34. *Ibid.*, pp. 92-96.
35. *Colored People's Convention*, p. 9.
36. *Ibid.*, pp. 24-25.
37. *Ibid.*, p. 25.

in fact if not in law, that enabled many of them to live comfortable and in some cases wealthy lives. With the liberation of the slaves, free Negroes were no longer a small minority, but—in the view of the whites—part of a threatening majority who had to be curtailed.

The temper of many white conservatives had been indicated by the resolution introduced by a Kershaw delegate at the constitutional convention, demanding that blacks be restrained by law to manual labor occupations.[38] Although this resolution was defeated, a series of laws passed by the succeeding legislature were certainly indebted to its spirit. While the Code accorded Negroes some basic rights and privileges, such as property ownership, the legitimacy of their marriages and families, and limited protection for the indigent and aged against immediate eviction, it also required Negroes to acquire special licenses, costing from ten to one hundred dollars, to engage in any employment outside agriculture or personal service. They were required to obtain special permits to sell farm produce, and violators were subject to arrest and hiring out for the use of any planter desiring labor.[39]

Therefore, while the Black Codes threatened the ex-slave with a serfdom only a notch or two above slavery, they threatened the ultimate survival of the bourgeoisie as a class. The freeborn class had carved its place in the antebellum economy by a near dominance of many of the trades—trades from which Negroes would now be either barred outright or taxed at a confiscatory rate. It was against this legislation that this convention of barbers and millwrights and carpenters and tailors and masons directed most of their wrath. This knowledge suggests a double entendre in DeLarge's statement during the fourth night's mass meeting: "The conflict of arms is past—all *that* can win for us is already won. But there is a question to be solved—a moral battle to be fought. The simple act of emancipation, if it stops there, is not worth much. We are not freemen till we attain to all the rights and privileges of freemen." [40]

Emancipation was not worth much, indeed, to men who were already free, especially if it contributed directly to erosion of rights that they had traditionally enjoyed without granting them political weapons with which to defend themselves. While insisting upon the right of suffrage, they were perfectly willing to accept any "qualifications" *except* that of

38. *New York Times,* October 1, 1865.

39. The impact of this tax might be better comprehended if one realizes that the minimum fee was equivalent to a month's wages for a fieldhand, and the maximum was more than a month's wages for many of the more lucrative federal patronage jobs, such as inspector of customs. See *Acts of the General Assembly of the State of South Carolina Passed at the Sessions of 1864-65* (Columbia: Julian A. Selby, 1866), pp. 271-304.

40. *Colored People's Convention,* p. 19.

color.[41] In other words, a government by the educated and propertied classes, the privileged of both races, was acceptable to some of them. Like an earlier mass meeting of many of these same delegates, they might well have asked that suffrage be regulated by a rule of *quid pro quo:* "if the ignorant white man is allowed to vote, that the ignorant colored man shall be allowed to vote also." [42]

Indeed, this position on the suffrage question stands in pointed contrast to that announced in the resolutions adopted by freedmen from St. Helena Island earlier that fall. The islanders demanded the right of suffrage for "every man of the age of twenty-one years, without other qualifications than that required for the whole citizens of this State." They based their claims to participate in the selection of their own rulers on their demonstrated willingness to defend the government and its Constitution. They pledged unceasing efforts "to obtain, by all just and legal means, a full recognition of our rights as citizens of the United States and this Commonwealth." And with thinly veiled innuendo they tied the continued peace and security of the state to the fulfillment of their demands: "*Resolved,* That we believe the future peace and welfare of this State depends very materially upon the protection of the interests of the colored man, and can only be secured by the adoption of the sentiments embodied in the foregoing resolutions." [43]

These sentiments were quite different from those of 103 Negroes meeting in Charleston a few days later. Many of the participants in the latter meeting—Robert Houston, Thomas M. Holmes, E. P. Wall, and Robert C. De Large—were also organizers of the November convention at Zion Church. In September they had declared that their interests were "identical" with those of the whites, as long as the latter stood on the "common ground" of "perfect equality for all men *before the Law.*" They freely admitted the inadequacies of their people and would forbear to press their claims to citizenship rights to dangerous extremes: "We know the deplorable ignorance of the majority of our people; we also are sensible of the deficiencies of those among us who have acquired some degree of education; and we ask not at this time that the ignorant shall be admitted to the exercise of a privilege which they might use to the injury of the State." But their position between the white ruling class and the black majority was a delicate one, and they tried to strike a tone of reconciliation without truckling. "We would be unmanly and uncandid did we not avow our intense joy at the course of events, which struck

41. *Ibid.,* p. 21.
42. Herbert Aptheker, "South Carolina Negro Conventions, 1865," *Journal of Negro History,* XXXI (January, 1946), 94.
43. *Ibid.,* p. 93.

from our limbs the chains of slavery, but we would be equally unmanly and uncandid did we not express our sorrow that freedom to us and our race is accompanied by the ruin of thousands of those for whom, notwithstanding the bitterness of the past, and of the present, we cherish feelings of respect and affection." The verbal balancing act was continued with a more insistent note: "Let us also assure your honorable body that nothing short of this, our respectful demand, will satisfy our people." Again they grew simultaneously submissive and threatening: "If our prayer is not granted, there will doubtless be the same quiet and *seemingly* patient submission to wrong that there has been in the past. We can bide our time. The day for which we watched & prayed came when we least expected it; the day of our complete enfranchisement will also come; and in that faith we will work and wait." [44]

Finally, the last clause expresses infinite patience, while firmly insisting that they were right and that it was the prejudiced whites who must change, who must grow and mature, who must "rise above" their encul-turated prejudices which (the implication was) they had unthinkingly adopted from their fathers. In the end their petition expresses an optimism about the mutability of racial prejudice that neither their time nor our own has yet justified: "We fully understand what prejudices & precon-ceived opinions must be overcome before our prayers can be granted; but we try to believe that the people of South Carolina are capable of rising superior to the prejudices of habit and education; and buoyed up by this hope we respectfully ask that our prayer may be granted and we will ever pray." [45]

Whatever the differences, subtle or overt, between the several petitions, all met a similar fate. The petitions of the September meetings had been tabled by the constitutional convention of 1865 without being read. The petition of the November statewide Colored People's Convention was referred to the House committee on colored population, which disclaimed jurisdiction over the issues it raised and declared that it should have gone to the constitutional convention which had adjourned two months before. [46]

In spite of the short-term disabilities they entailed, these blindly un-compromising acts of the white power structure were to prove ultimately beneficial to the masses of freedmen. After all, no compromise could possibly have helped them, while the whites' intransigency forced the mulatto bourgeoisie into a political alliance with the ex-slaves, instead of with the white ruling classes, as happened in many Caribbean societies

44. *Ibid.*, pp. 93-94, 95.
45. *Ibid.*
46. *Ibid.*, pp. 95, 97; *Daily Courier*, December 18, 1865.

during the post-emancipation period.[47]

For the white population, a free Negro majority unencumbered by ex-traordinary restrictions on their movements and actions was the ultimate antebellum nightmare come true. Thus the whites fell back on the remedies they had developed, but infrequently enforced, upon the real and ima-gined aggressions of the small free Negro population before the war. Although the issues raised in the petition of the Colored People's Conven-tion had been declared beyond its jurisdiction, the legislators felt compe-tent to enact a "Bill to regulate the domestic relations of persons of color," in which restraints were applied to travel and economic activities, appren-ticeship laws were enacted, and blacks were given the legal title of "ser-vants" and their employers were "masters." [48]

With these acts and others of incredible arrogance, South Carolina and her sister states badly misjudged the temper of the North and eventu-ally brought on repudiation of Andrew Johnson's Reconstruction policy. Even before the regular legislative session had adjourned, Congress had refused to seat the state's elected representatives and had established a joint congressional committee to investigate Johnsonian Reconstruction. The Black Codes were barely off the presses in January, 1866, before General Daniel E. Sickles demonstrated the continued supremacy of military over local authority by declaring them null and void. One month later Congress would effectively endorse General Sickles's action by passing the nation's first civil rights bill over President Johnson's veto. The Civil Rights Bill of 1866 sought to ensure freedmen the equal protection of the laws with such basic immunities as the right to sue, to be a witness in judicial proceedings, and other protections. To ensure their work against sudden shifts in political or judicial fortunes, Congress followed this act with the Fourteenth Amendment to the Constitution, which gave black men clear title to citizenship and forbade states to make or enforce laws which abridged the privileges or immunities of U.S. citizens.

James L. Orr, a reluctant secessionist, had been inaugurated as the first elected postwar governor of South Carolina in November, 1865. It was soon evident to the governor, as well as to many other conservative South Carolinians, that the attempt to reestablish the old order in essence, if not letter, was doomed to failure. Therefore Orr, who had not been the most popular choice for governor, garnered considerable support when he vetoed an act to amend the patrol laws because it smacked of indirect recognition of the laws of slavery. He did not even try to enforce the special capitation tax levies on Negroes, and when the legislature gathered

47. See Philip D. Curtin, *Two Jamaicas: The Role of Ideas in a Tropical Colony, 1830-65* (Cambridge: Harvard University Press, 1955), pp. 175-77.

48. *Acts of the General Assembly, 1864-65,* pp. 291-304.

in an extra session in September, 1866, Orr asked them to repeal the moribund Black Codes. A new bill was passed which declared that Negroes would "have full and equal benefit of the rights of personal security, personal liberty and private property, and of all remedies and proceedings for the enforcement and protection of the same as white persons now have, and shall not be subjected to any other or different punishment, pain or penalty, for the commission of any act or offence, than such as are prescribed for white persons committing like acts or offences." [49] This act effectively repealed the previous codes, except those prohibiting interracial marriages.

All in all, the legislature had not acquitted itself very well in the eyes of many constituents. Ironically, the vehement and sarcastic tone of the public's criticism prefigured that leveled at the Republican legislatures of later years. The representatives were ridiculed for laziness in being anxious to adjourn before their important business was finished; for ineptitude in passing the impractical Black Codes, only to have to repeal them the very next session; for increasing the expense of the sessions unnecessarily with showy but irrelevant debates. But most of all they were condemned for their failure to deal effectively with critical problems, such as relief of debtors and aid for the poor. When the legislature adjourned, one correspondent uttered a public sigh of relief: "To those who are disposed to be despondent in view of the present state of the country, there is some little solace found in the fact that the legislature has adjourned to meet no more, until the people shall have an opportunity of making some changes in its membership. In all the history of the State, there never has been a greater amount of useless expensive and unwise legislation than the past two years have witnessed in this State." [50]

Other South Carolinians, not constituents of this legislature, also found cause for dissatisfaction with the course of events; they expressed this discontent forcefully and sometimes violently. There were constant altercations between black and white troops, especially in the cities.[51] Even in rural areas blacks openly demonstrated their unwillingness to resume their former subordinate status. On a quiet summer Sunday three black women and one man suddenly left their seats on the "colored side" of the Spring Hall Methodist Church in Sumter to take seats among the white "ladies" and "gentlemen." The ensuing argument led to the killing of one black man and the firebombing of a white man's home.[52]

However, most of the unrest among blacks can be traced to their

49. *Daily Courier,* September 10, 22, 1866.
50. *Ibid.,* September 4, 17, 1866, January 22, 1867.
51. *Ibid.,* June 19, July 10, 1865.
52. *Ibid.,* June 29, 1866.

dissatisfaction with the evolving land tenure arrangements. President Johnson had thwarted administrative and legal efforts to validate the freedmen's claims to lands obtained during the war. Planters and military authorities had united in a campaign to cajole, convince, and finally coerce freedmen to abandon all hope of owning their own lands and to sign labor contracts with their former masters.[53] After the 1866 harvest, blacks gathered at Freedmen's Tabernacle in Sumter County to express their dissatisfaction with the one-third share of the crop that the Freedmen's Bureau and the planters had imposed upon them.[54] In January, 1867, farmworkers who had been settled by Sherman's Field Order No. 15 on the Delta plantation along the Carolina coast refused to renew their contracts for the coming year because the old one had not been fairly administered. A force of fifty Union soldiers sent to evict them was surrounded and repulsed. Only after the personal intervention of the Freedmen's Bureau commissioner, General Robert Scott, were the disgruntled freedmen convinced to sign contracts or leave the area.[55]

These unsettled conditions were new to the white power structure, and people scarcely knew how to react. In the very same message in which he urged repeal of the Black Codes, Governor Orr asked for more stringent vagrancy laws. The same legislature that repealed the Codes refused to ratify the Fourteenth Amendment. The men who had considered their state fully reconstructed in the fall of 1865 viewed the new demands of northern radicals with genuine dismay. Clearly these proposals for Negro suffrage were "the height of folly, injustice and madness," wrote former provisional Governor Benjamin F. Perry.

> The African has been, in all ages, a savage or a slave. God created him inferior to the white man in form, color, and intellect, and no legislation or culture can make him his equal. You might as well expect to make the fox the equal of the lion in courage and strength, or the ass the equal of the horse in symmetry and fleetness. His color is black; his head covered with wool instead of hair, his form and features will not compare with the Caucasian race, and it is in vain to think of elevating him to the dignity of the white man. God has created a difference between the two races, and nothing can make him equal.[56]

Surely the majority of white men in the North would see these truths and repudiate the radicals in the approaching congressional elections. There was already evidence of such a political backlash in the fact that several northern states had voted against allowing blacks the franchise

53. *Ibid.*, December 16, 1865. For a sample contract, see December 28 issue.
54. *Ibid.*, November 24, 1866.
55. *Ibid.*, January 23, 1867.
56. *Ibid.*, October 1, 1866.

in their states. Indeed, the evidence had seemed so clear and unmistakable that the overwhelming defeat of northern conservative candidates in the 1866 elections left South Carolina leaders shaken and bewildered. Certainly the southern position had been distorted. "We do not think that the schemes thus proposed [Negro suffrage] will ever be endorsed by the American people," wrote the editors of the Charleston *Daily Courier*.[57]

But a few months later the political fruits of the radical victory were ripe, and the reconstruction of South Carolina was begun anew. March 2, 1867, saw the passage of the first of a series of Reconstruction Acts which abolished the existing state regimes and established temporary military governments. These military governments would be superseded by civilian ones as soon as new state constitutions were written and the Fourteenth Amendment was ratified. The military governors would oversee referenda in each state to determine whether and by whom these constitutions would be written. Black men would have the privilege of voting on this referendum.

Thus, exactly two years after Sherman's troops invaded South Carolina and one and one-half years after the convention of colored men at Zion Church, black men were admitted to a new political relationship. They poured into mass meetings in Charleston and Columbia to celebrate, to organize, and to prepare for their new responsibilities. It was the middle of March; spring in the Palmetto State. This season of regeneration, of new beginnings, seemed appropriate to the freedmen's excitement as they looked forward to the dawn of a new era. The times seemed pregnant with hope, and summer lay just ahead. Yet, on March 15, like a portent of the winters of discontent still to come, a light snow fell on Charleston.

57. *Ibid.*, November 17, 1866.

Chapter Two

Forging a Black Majority:
The Emergence of a New Order

It was clear to the freedmen that the Reconstruction Acts only opened the door to voting and officeholding; blacks themselves would have to make these legal rights political realities by forging a constituency and developing a leadership group. The first step was to formally organize the Union Republican party of South Carolina, a task begun within days of the passage of the first Reconstruction Act. A meeting was held in Charleston on March 7, at which a committee of fourteen was appointed to draft a platform and report back at a later meeting. All but two members of the platform committee were Negro, and several had been participants in the Colored People's Convention of 1865.[1]

At a second meeting convened at Military Hall on March 21, the committee presented their platform with eleven points, several of which would become major tenets of South Carolina Republicanism. After endorsing congressional Reconstruction policy and expressing their gratitude to Union war veterans and solicitude for their widows and orphans, the delegates opposed any attempt to pay the rebel debt. They called for a universal, tax-supported education system and endorsed the concept of government aid for internal improvements such as railroads, canals, and public works. Furthermore, the contracts for these public works projects should be awarded in a way that would "give all our fellow-citizens an equal and fair chance to share in them." They opposed imprisonment for debt and corporal punishment, and favored breaking up land monopolies by encouraging the sale of unoccupied lands among the poorer classes. They demanded protection of the farm tenant from eviction and for the poor man's homestead. They wanted a revised code of state laws and reorganization of the court system, and guarantees that their newly won rights would be preserved in perpetuity. Finally, it was the govern-

1. *Daily Courier*, March 22, 1867. See also Francis B. Simkins and Robert H. Woody, *South Carolina During Reconstruction* (Chapel Hill: University of North Carolina Press, 1932), p. 82.

ment's duty to care for society's aged, sick, and poor.[2]

The convention endorsed these principles overwhelmingly and turned its attention to practical matters of perfecting the party's organization. During the immediate postwar period, the political initiatives of Republicans—black and white—had been confined largely to the environs of Charleston, Columbia, and Beaufort. The meetings held during the early spring of 1867 were no exception to this pattern, because there was sparse representation from rural, inland counties. To correct this situation, agents were dispatched to the hinterland to organize Republican clubs. Mass meetings were held—in churches, homes, and open fields—to ratify the party platform and elect delegates to the convention to be held that summer. Slowly but surely the hard work paid off, and the South Carolina countryside came alive with political activity. "Depend upon it," a Republican correspondent assured his readers, "the country is all right and will send forth such an expression of loyalty as will convince the scheming, unreconciled non-conformist, to the logic or march of events, and that old things have passed away and a new order of relations exists." [3]

The freedmen were not the only ones to sense that a revolutionary change in black-white relations, "a new order," was in the making. Some of their white neighbors in Pickens and Lexington counties gathered in mass meetings to endorse universal suffrage and the Republican party. Their actions were motivated by simple pragmatism, they admitted, for clearly "the colored vote in South Carolina outnumbers the white vote, and will inevitably defeat it, if the two should be brought into antagonism." [4] Meanwhile, in Chesterfield County a biracial mass meeting gathered at the county courthouse. Pointing out that, contrary to the statewide pattern, the white voters in Chesterfield outnumbered the blacks, they resolved nevertheless to fuse their respective slates of candidates into a common ticket "for the sake of harmony between the two races." [5] They would support black nominees for the constitutional convention and Congress, while those nominated for the state legislature would be white. An executive committee of sixteen—half black and half white—was appointed to select the nominees and conduct the campaign. But evidently the Chesterfield resolves either were never fully implemented or were amended later, for black legislators were elected to the General Assembly from that county. It may be that blacks gained sufficient political acumen to realize that the agreement was not as fair as it had appeared. Except for the convention delegate, the offices to which blacks would be nomin-

2. *Daily Courier*, March 22, 1867.
3. *Charleston Advocate*, April 27, 1867.
4. *Daily Courier*, April 27, 1867.
5. *Ibid.*, October 17, 1867.

ated were not actually within the power of the citizens of Chesterfield to bestow. The U.S. senator would be elected by the General Assembly, and the election of a congressman would depend on the votes of other counties in the congressional district.[6]

It is clear, however, that many prominent South Carolinians were having second thoughts about their heretofore intransigent positions against black political participation. Shortly before the passage of the Reconstruction Acts, Governor Orr, who had urged rejection of the Fourteenth Amendment to preserve the state's self-respect, told a mass meeting of freedmen that now he favored suffrage for literate blacks.[7] General Wade Hampton, the Confederate hero and wealthy planter, endorsed a similar compromise and made a futile effort to gain control of the ex-slaves' votes. However, others, perplexed and angered, prepared like former provisional Governor Benjamin F. Perry to assume a martyr's pose and ride out the storm.[8] With the editors of the influential Charleston *Daily Courier,* they waited for the inevitable backlash that must come when the blatant contradiction between the subordinate status of black men in the North and their proposed status in the South would break the back of the Radical cabal.[9]

To many white natives, events in the Palmetto State that spring and summer clashed sharply with fond reveries of the old regime and the people they thought they knew best. This sudden politicization of their ex-slaves was inexplicable except through some extraordinary new agencies of social control. Were not these children of Ham born to be servants? Was it not clear that they could function in civilized society only with the guidance and direction of white men? In the minds of the planters, the answers to these questions were unquestionably affirmative; hence they assumed that the Union League, or perhaps the army, had taken over their roles vis-à-vis their ex-slaves. Twentieth-century scholarship still bears traces of this "new massas" legend, as indicated by the following description of the Union League found in a reputable historical work.

> The nocturnal secrecy of the gatherings, the weird initiation ceremonies, the emblems of virtue and religion, the songs, the appeal to such patriotic shibboleths as the Declaration of Independence, the Constitution, the Flag and the Union, the glittering platitudes in the interest of social uplift—all these characteristics of the League had an irresistible appeal to a cere-

6. Two leaders of this convention, M. M. Hough and G. W. Duvall, were Democrats elected to the legislature in 1870 and 1868, respectively. A prominent black Republican, Henry J. Maxwell, was also a participant in this meeting.

7. *Daily Courier,* February 15, 1867.

8. Simkins and Woody, *South Carolina During Reconstruction,* pp. 83-85.

9. *Daily Courier,* October 11, 1867.

mony-loving, singing, moralistic, and loyal race. That the purposes of the order, when reduced to the practical, meant that the Negro had become the emotional and intellectual slave of the white Radical did not dull the Negro's enthusiasm; he was accustomed to be a slave to the white man.[10]

Actually, the army and the League have been given too much credit in the forging of South Carolina's new Republican majority in 1868. The hostility of the army to the freedmen had been demonstrated repeatedly; it was more likely to impose restrictions on the electioneering activities of the freemen than to actively encourage them. For example, during the election of convention delegates, the Democratic press credited the resultant "good order" to Major S. C. Allen, who ordered the freedmen to go directly home after voting and warned them that "he would prohibit in future all unauthorized meetings in old fields and elsewhere which have already been attended with much injury to the interest of employer and employee." [11] In another instance, during the 1868 presidential election campaign in which two Negro legislators were assassinated, Richard H. Cain alerted Governor Scott to rumors of a plot to murder several leading Republicans in Charleston. "We have no confidence in the troops stationed here," he declared. "The present police are democrats and some of them are in the *plot* to murder us." [12]

As another student of the period has pointed out, the Union League was something less than the all-powerful, pervasive organization that traditionally has been portrayed; besides, the political preferences of the new black voters are surely explicable without recourse to the mumbo-jumbo and the nocturnal incantations traditionally ascribed to the League.[13] The state president of the League, the conservative and dignified Francis L. Cardozo, was hardly the "grand dragon" type. And even the authors of the lurid passage quoted above had to admit that the Leagues were never fully organized throughout the state, and that they faded rather quickly after the first elections.[14] Discussions of the League oaths and secret paraphernalia have lost all perspective, given the widespread popularity of Masonic orders and similar organizations among all groups and classes during the period. And the transcripts of any major political convention will reveal that the Leaguers were not the only ones to indulge in "patriotic shibboleths" and "glittering platitudes." The testimony of

10. Simkins and Woody, *South Carolina During Reconstruction*, p. 75.

11. *Daily Courier*, November 25, 1867.

12. Richard H. Cain to Robert K. Scott, October 24, 1868, Robert K. Scott Papers, South Carolina Archives, Columbia.

13. Joel Williamson, *After Slavery: The Negro in South Carolina During Reconstruction, 1861-77* (Chapel Hill: University of North Carolina Press, 1965), p. 373.

14. Simkins and Woody, *South Carolina During Reconstruction*, p. 77.

some League officers at the Ku Klux Klan hearings in 1872 belies the image of their fearful hold on credulous freedmen. Cross-examined about the League oath by a hostile congressman, Henry Johnson, an ex-slave and local League president in Winnsboro, answered matter-of-factly: "We swore to stick to one another, and vote the republican ticket." [15] This was hardly more unusual than any pledge of party loyalty in that time or the present.

On the other hand, the League was undoubtedly a potent tool for self-protection and for educating the freedmen in their new political relations. The functions that had been observed by one native white writing some years later were probably more significant in wielding a black political consciousness than the mumbo-jumbo traditionally cited. The Union League gave the freedmen their first experience in parliamentary law and debating, urged them to attend courts as spectators, and encouraged jury and militia service. The freedmen became "the most irrepressible democrats it is possible to conceive," he mused. The members were active in their meetings, joining in the debate, and prone to heckle the speakers with questions and points of order.[16]

Certainly the League function that most rankled native whites was organizing the new voters for self-defense. In South Carolina, as elsewhere, one reaction to suffrage for freedmen was retaliation by white employers with threats of eviction. Lists of "proscribed" workers were circulated at the agricultural fairs. Like the acts of violence that came later, evictions appear to have been used primarily in up-country counties where black workers were often a minority. In such areas Union Leagues also appear to have been most active.[17]

The freedmen's mood was generally one of grim determination to resist coercion by the planters. Observers frequently reported the presence of rifles at political rallies, usually stacked in a clump of bushes behind the speakers platform, sometimes with the womenfolk left to guard them. And well before the Reconstruction Acts, or even the prospect of black suffrage, Francis L. Cardozo had observed the organization of leagues for self-defense and noted evidence of a new attitude of resistance among the freedmen. "When Civil Law [meaning Governor James L. Orr's regime] is fully restored," he wrote George Whipple in 1865, "I anticipate some trouble, as the colored people are formed into Leagues, and are

15. *Testimony Taken by the Joint Select Committee to Inquire into the Condition of Affairs in the Late Insurrectionary States,* Volume I: South Carolina (Washington: Government Printing Office, 1872), p. 321.

16. A South Carolinian [Belton O'Neal Townsend], "The Political Condition of South Carolina," *Atlantic Monthly,* XXXIX (February, 1877), 193.

17. *Ibid.,* pp. 185-86; Simkins and Woody, *South Carolina During Reconstruction,* p. 78.

determined not to submit so tamely as they did before the war." [18]

The new militancy undoubtedly led to overreaction at even apparent threats from whites. John W. De Forest, an up-country Bureau commissioner, reports one such incident in Pickens District, a county with a white majority. In the autumn of 1867, a League chapter made up mostly of blacks, but with a white president named Bryce, was holding a meeting with its usual armed sentries on the perimeter. When a poor white named Smith tried to enter the meeting, shots were fired; there followed a general alarm and, subsequently, a melee with a white debating club nearby. "The Negroes rushed out; Smith fled, hotly pursued, to the schoolhouse; the members of the debating club broke up in a panic and endeavored to escape; a second pistol was fired, and a boy of fourteen, named Hunnicutt, the son of a respectable citizen, fell dead. The ball entered the back of his head, showing that, when it struck him, he was flying." [19] The tragic results of the League's overreaction were further compounded as the freedmen continued to act under the impression that they had been under a general attack.

> The Negroes, unaware apparently that they had done anything wrong, believing, on the contrary, that they were re-establishing public order and enforcing justice, commenced patrolling the neighborhood, entering every house, and arresting numbers of citizens. They marched in double file, pistol in belt and gun at the shoulder, keeping step to the "hup, hup!" of a fellow called Lame Sam, who acted as drill sergeant and commander. By noon of the next day they had the country for miles around in their power, and a majority of the male whites under their guard.[20]

Shortly, a detachment of U.S. soldiers arrived to liberate the whites and arrest the freedmen. The blacks were tried by civil authorities; eighteen were found guilty of riot and sentenced to prison, but eight others were found guilty of murder in the first degree and sentenced to hang. "The Leaguers exhibited such a misguided loyalty to their order and each other," in De Forest's view, "that it was impossible to fix a charge for murder on any one person or to establish grounds for an indictment of any sort against Bryce." [21] However, before the sentences were carried out a federal marshal successfully pressured the condemned men to point out the one who had fired the shot killing Hunnicutt, and that man was hung.

18. Francis L. Cardozo to George Whipple, October 21, 1865, American Missionary Association Archives, Amistad Research Center, New Orleans.

19. John W. De Forest, *A Union Officer in the Reconstruction*, ed. James H. Croushore and David M. Potter (New Haven: Yale University Press, 1948), p. 127.

20. *Ibid.*, p. 128.

21. *Ibid.*

The apparent dictatorship of men like Bryce over some of the local Leagues of freedmen is the basis for the frequent assumption that such control by whites was general. No doubt whites did exercise considerable and inordinate control over the freedmen, individually or in groups, in some instances. But the disposition to accept white leadership was less likely to occur in those areas where Negro leadership was available. "They are too suspicious to be led by the whites," complained a white Northerner concerning the Sea Islanders.[22]

Laura Towne reported one earnest discussion among the freedmen about the nature of their relationship to white Republicans. The occasion was a Republican mass meeting in the Beaufort area during the spring of 1867 which, evidently, the northern white residents had boycotted.

> The speakers were all black men, except Mr. Hunn. The white men did not attend—they are going to have a *white* party, they say. One black man said he wanted no white men on their platform but he was taken to task by all the other speakers, who disclaimed all such feelings. It was funny to hear the arguments from the other side—such as—"What difference does skin make, my bredren, I would stand side by side a *white* man if he acted right. We mustn't be prejudiced against their color." "If dere skins is white, dey may have principle." "Come, my friends, we mustn't judge a man according to his color, but according to his acts," etc., etc.[23]

The meeting eventually agreed unanimously to "cooperate" with the whites, and to invite all colors to a second meeting. Significantly, the attitude toward whites was pragmatically keyed upon the latter's "principles" and whether they "acted right," and not on their color alone.[24]

Thus the process by which blacks arrived at their political opinions generally involved a realistic appraisal of their vital self-interests. Comparing notes with a fellow Bureau officer who had publicly maligned the freedmen's intelligence about the meaning of their ballots, John W. De Forest came to a contrary impression. "My impression is, although I can not make decisive averment in the matter, that a majority of the Greenville freedmen had a sufficiently intelligent sense of purport of the election. The stupidest of them understood that he was acting 'agin de Rebs,' and 'for de freedom.' None of them voted into the post office or into hollow trees [as the lowland officer had charged]." [25]

22. T.E.R. to C.P.W. [T. Edwin Ruggles to Charles P. Ware], May 21, 1867, in *Letters from Port Royal, 1862-1868,* ed. Elizabeth Ware Pearson (Boston: W. B. Clarke Company, 1906), pp. 328-29.

23. Laura Towne, *Letters and Diary of Laura M. Towne, Written from the Sea Islands of South Carolina, 1862-84,* ed. Rupert Sargent Holland (Cambridge: Riverside Press, 1912), pp. 182-83.

24. *Ibid.*

25. De Forest, *A Union Officer,* p. 127.

Perhaps out of deference for his low-country colleague, De Forest did not wish to generalize from his observations of Greenville freedmen to the whole state. Rather, he chose to attribute their display of common sense in the election to the fact that Greenville was an area of small farmers which allowed the former slaves to have closer and enlightening contact with the white landowners. Yet observers in areas where the Greenville conditions did not exist describe similar phenomena, wherein freedmen displayed intelligent self-interest in arriving at independent political positions.

Chaplain Noble, who conducted literacy classes for the enlisted men of the 128th United States Colored Troops in Beaufort (an infantry of native ex-slaves), related the outcome of a debate he arranged "to enliven" the class. The question was whether Negroes should be given immediate suffrage or whether they should learn to read first, with "the more intelligent" of the class clearly favoring the latter position "on the ground that you ought never to undertake a job unless you know *how* to do it." [26]

But those who learned less easily were in favor of immediate suffrage. One of the speakers—a black thick-lipped orator—commenced his speech as follows: "de chaplain say we can learn to read in short time. Now dat may be so with dem who are mo' heady. God hasn't made all of us alike. P'rhaps some *will* get an eddication in a little while. *I knows de next generation will.* But we'se a downtrodden people. We hasn't had no chance at all. De most uf us are slow and dull. We has bin kept down a *hundred years* and I tink it will take a *hundred years to get us back agin.* Dere fo' Mr. Chaplain, I tink we better not wait for eddication." [27]

Whether because of the political logic of universal suffrage for the illiterate black majority, or because the difficulties of the chaplain's lessons made suffrage based on literacy seem rather remote for some of the slow learners, the speaker's sagacity brought decisive nods of approval from the majority of the audience.

Where the Union League or logic failed, other sanctions and attractions were available. Though black women, like their white sisters, were not included in the elective franchise, they played a role in these political proceedings nevertheless. Unaccustomed at first to the political discrimination between the sexes that their countrymen practiced, they attended the Republican meetings along with their menfolk. Evidently the northern whites hastened to educate the black men as to the proper place for women and convinced them to leave their wives at their firesides, or,

26. F. K. Noble to George Whipple, September 29, 1868, A.M.A. Papers.
27. *Ibid.*

better still, to "cut grass," as one speaker impishly suggested.[28] The men's success in these arrangements is uncertain, since other observers often found the women guarding the weapons stacked behind the speakers' platform at political rallies. They appear to have also assumed a role more in keeping with their "place" as they, like the ancient Greek women of *Lysistrata*, reportedly applied the sanctions of the bedroom to whip male political defectors into conformity with "self-interest." [29] Or they took more direct action, like the wife of a starving freedman who was alleged to have struck the poor fellow with an ax when he sold his vote to Democrats in exchange for food.[30] Of course, we cannot know how widespread such actions were. But the black woman's reputation for political partisanship was undoubtedly enhanced by her frequent appearance at the head of angry Charleston mobs, like the one which wreaked havoc on the German merchants after the Republican defeat in the municipal elections of 1871.[31] In any case, women were a factor in black political life.

However, less coercive inducements than these were more apt to be applied in the election campaign. In antebellum days it had been traditional for the "gentlemen" politicians to refresh their adherents "by the barrelful" with whiskey.[32] The tradition was not neglected by Republicans—nor were the mounds of barbecued ribs and baked yams and picnics and outings. Political campaigning provided for freedmen and whites alike a source of entertainment and relief from the boredom endemic to the rural South. In Beaufort, Robert Smalls organized a brass band and led torchlight processions.[33] Nor was sentimentality neglected: the symbol placed at the top of the Republican ballot was a picture of "the Liberator," the martyred President Lincoln.

Whether sentimental, coercive, or logical, the arguments of the Republican campaign succeeded far beyond the worst fears of Democrats and possibly beyond the boldest dreams of the Negro leadership. Of the 128,056 persons registered to vote in the 1867 referendum on the convention, more than 60 percent were black. And when 124 elected delegates convened to rewrite the South Carolina Constitution, 70 were Negroes.[34]

28. Towne, *Letters and Diary*, p. 183.

29. [Townsend,] "Political Condition of South Carolina," p. 193; see also a speech by Senator Stephen A. Swails at a Georgetown rally: *Daily Republican*, July 8, 1870.

30. *Daily Republican*, October 23, 1869.

31. *Daily Courier*, August 4, 1871. See also Winthrop Brown Conrad, Jr., "Rehearsal for Redemption" (Senior thesis, Yale University, 1967), pp. 55-59.

32. De Forest, *A Union Officer*, p. 139.

33. Okon Edet Uya, *From Slavery to Public Service: Robert Smalls, 1839-1915* (New York: Oxford University Press, 1971), p. 58.

34. This figure is smaller than that accepted by most authorities, but is based on exhaustive checking and cross-checking of numerous primary sources.

A powerful and tenacious tradition has developed about these Negro delegates, created by the Democratic press and nurtured by succeeding generations of historians and publicists; they have been depicted as poor, ignorant ex-slaves ascending straight from cotton fields to legislative halls. Of course, exceptional individuals like Francis L. Cardozo and Robert B. Elliott, the former educated at seminaries in Edinburgh and the latter claiming to have studied at Eton College, have been more or less acknowledged.[35] But the traditional image has been sustained largely by our continued ignorance of those unexceptional and "ordinary" colleagues of Elliott and Cardozo, and perhaps because the image conveniently fits the rationale for the failure of the movement which these delegates began.[36]

With singular exceptions, the agreement on the nature of the delegates has been general on two points: their antebellum status and their literacy. "Of the seventy-six, two-thirds—one authority gives the number as fifty-seven—had only a few years before been slaves," declare two respected scholars. They confidently infer from this information that "it is scarcely necessary to add that illiteracy was one of their most distinguishing characteristics." [37] Actually, 44 percent of the seventy Negro convention delegates had been free before the war.[38] Furthermore, there is ample evidence that the overwhelming majority (82 percent) were literate; on the other side, there is positive evidence of illiteracy for only five men. Of the fifty-seven we know to have been literate, additional evidence for twenty-nine allows for greater differentiation of their educational attainments. Fourteen of these (20 percent of the delegates) had attained at least a common school education, five were graduates of a normal school, and a talented ten had achieved a college or professional education.[39]

The persistent generalizations which historians have made about property-holding and the general wealth of black Republicans can be traced back to the tax list submitted to Congress by a group of conservatives

35. See plausible discussion of Elliott's probable prewar background in Peggy Lamson, *The Glorious Failure: Black Congressman Robert Brown Elliott and the Reconstruction in South Carolina* (New York: W. W. Norton, 1973), pp. 23-33.

36. Simkins and Woody argue that, given the support of the federal establishment and the overwhelming black electoral majority, the failure of the Reconstruction regime could only have been caused by the venality, ignorance, and corruption of the leadership. *South Carolina During Reconstruction*, p. 112.

37. *Ibid.,* p. 91.

38. 54 percent were slaves, and there are no data on one delegate (Samuel Johnson of Anderson). 46 percent were mulatto, and 39 percent black; data are missing for the other 15 percent. See Appendix A for details on sources.

39. All percentages here and to follow are based on the total Negro delegation of 70. There are no data on literacy for 11 percent of this group.

along with their protest against the convention.[40] First of all, the tax list submitted was for a period immediately after the war, when the state civil service was still affected by postwar instabilities and the collection of taxes was not completed.[41] The inferences intended to be drawn from the tax records were that the black delegates were propertyless and therefore had little stake in the fiscal consequences of their legislative actions. Ignoring for the moment the dubious logic of the latter part of this assertion, one discovers that the facts on which the first part is based were false. Although it is not possible to say precisely how many delegates owned property when they were elected, it is clear that more of them held real estate than has been admitted.[42] Furthermore, statistics from the two years immediately after the convention show that 44 percent of the Negro delegates either owned real estate in 1868 or secured it very soon thereafter. Fourteen of these held land valued between $1,001 and $20,000, while seventeen owned land valued between $50 to $1,000. Only thirteen were listed as having no property. Considering other forms of wealth, one finds that at least 59 percent owned some form of property, real or personal, and twenty-four of these had total assets worth more than $1,000.[43]

Of course, the property held by these men was usually not comparable to that of the former white ruling class, but that does not mean that these blacks can properly be characterized as a penniless proletariat uninterested in the fiscal policies and economic development of the state. Most appear to have been tradesmen, merchants, teachers, ministers, and small farmers. The historical tradition of a proletarian leadership group is almost as much a distortion of their origins as the stereotype of an illiterate rabble. In truth, these men were drawn largely from a "middle class," in some of the subtler meanings of that phrase; they stood some-

40. Simkins and Woody, *South Carolina During Reconstruction*, p. 95.

41. In his message to the extra session of the legislature in the fall of 1866, Governor James L. Orr indicated that he had not pressed the collection of taxes, and in the spring of 1867 he issued an order staying all attempts to collect taxes. *Daily Courier*, September 6, 1866; April 15, 1867.

42. The records show that several of the convention delegates owned real estate in 1868. In Charleston these included Richard H. Cain ($1,825), Francis L. Cardozo ($300), William McKinlay ($20,800), and William J. McKinlay ($1,200). In some cases the wives or families of the delegates owned real property, as with Robert C. De Large, William H. W. Gray, and Thaddeus K. Sasportas. There is evidence that Robert Smalls had made considerable investments around Beaufort by this time, and that Henry Jacobs was a property owner before the war. See *Charleston County Assessments of Real Estate*, 1868, pp. 27, 55, 112; Uya, *Robert Smalls*, p. 37; and U.S. MSS Census, 1860, Population, Fairfield County, p. 1.

43. Data on real property ownership were not available for 36 percent of the 70 delegates, and there were no data on all property, real or personal, for 34 percent. About 6 percent owned no property, real or personal.

where between the former white ruling class and the black masses.

After writing a constitution which would serve as the state's organic law for more than a quarter-century, these delegates returned to their organizational work in the hinterlands. They would prepare the way for scores of other Negroes who would be elected to state and federal offices under subsequent Republican regimes. Their constitutional convention had given some indication not only of the policies and issues of the next nine years, but of the makeup of the Negro leadership cadre as well. Something of the quality of the delegates' political attitudes had been evident two years earlier in their first burst of political activism. It was clear that in 1868, as before, the bourgeoisie would provide the leadership and a far greater proportion of the troops than their share of the population would appear to warrant. Indeed, some members of this class (William J. McKinlay, Thaddeus K. Sasportas, Henry L. Shrewsbury) had left Charleston to settle in the rural counties from which they were elected to the constitutional convention. But while freeborn Negroes and mulattoes constituted about half of the Negro delegates to the convention and of the representatives to the first legislature, their numerical importance declined in later years as more indigenous leaders were elected from the rural districts. Out of a total of 255 Negroes elected to state and federal offices between 1868 and 1876, approximately one in four had been free before the war, and one of every three was mulatto.[44] Almost one in three owned some real estate, and 46 percent possessed some form of wealth, real or personal. One-fifth had combined property holdings in excess of $1,000; 11 percent had over $1,000 in real property alone. Only 15 percent show no property at all. There is no information for 39 percent.

The overwhelming majority (65 percent) were literate, and one-tenth were professionally or college-trained.[45] Of those whose prewar occupations can be identified, both the freedmen and freeborn were drawn heavily from among the artisan class.[46] However, among postwar occupations professionals constituted the largest single category. (See Table 1.) Ministers and teachers predominated among the professionals (76 percent), but ten of these lawmakers were, or became, lawyers during their terms of office. Those engaged in agriculture were the next largest group, and

44. Of the 255 Negroes who served between 1868 and 1876, 65 can be identified as free before the war, 105 as slaves, and 85 cannot be so identified. There were 78 mulattoes, 103 blacks, and 74 unidentified as to color. See Appendix A for details.

45. 10 percent were illiterate; there are no data for 25 percent. 13 percent had a common school and 1 percent a normal school education.

46. The primary prewar occupations of only 25 percent of the ex-slaves can be identified. 15 were artisans, 4 were domestics, 4 were fieldhands. 53 percent of the free Negroes' prewar occupations can be identified. 4 were ministers, 20 artisans, 3 laborers, and 7 in other miscellaneous occupations. See Appendix A for details.

Table 1. Primary Postwar Occupations of Negro Legislators, 1868-76

Occupation	Slave	Free	Missing Data	Totals
Professional				
Lawyers	1	8	1	10
Doctors	0	1	0	1
Teachers	4	17	3	24
Ministers	17	9	6	32
Others	1	3	3	7
Totals	23	38	13	74
Agricultural				
Farm Owners	18	6	11	35
Tenants	12	2	1	15
Others	5	1	1	7
Totals	35	9	13	57
Artisan				
Blacksmiths	3	0	1	4
Carpenters	8	2	2	12
Tailors	0	7	1	8
Masons	2	1	1	4
Others	9	4	1	14
Totals	22	14	6	42
Other				
Merchants	4	2	2	8
Laborers	6	1	2	9
Totals	10	3	4	17

Source: See Appendix A.

more of these appear to have been owners than fieldhands.[47]

These legislators were young men; fully 70 percent of them were not yet forty in 1868. Indeed, almost half were still in their twenties. Most had been born and reared in South Carolina.[48] Thus it was a generation that had matured largely in the late 1850's, when the sectional controversy was greatest and when the slave system was under increasingly militant

47. The category of fieldhand is assumed where a person is listed as "farmer," "farm laborer," or "field hand," and there is no indication of property ownership or management. See Appendix A for methodological discussion.

48. 65 percent were born in South Carolina, and 70 percent were born in the southern or border states. 4 were born in New England, 9 in other northern states, and 4 were foreign-born. 67 were under 30 in 1868, 30 were in their thirties, and 3 in their fifties or sixties.

attack, with southern society growing more repressive and closed. Neither the institution of slavery nor the condition of quasi-freedom had anticipated or prepared these men to legislate and administer the law or to operate the state's civil service. But twenty-four had been tested under fire in the Union Army; sixteen had gained the confidence of command as commissioned or noncommissioned officers. Many of the Northerners had been reared in an atmosphere of agitation and protest over slavery and the racial discrimination of the North. Undoubtedly the fast-paced (some called them revolutionary) events of the postwar years had made a deep impression on all these men, but the large majority had been shaped by the institution of slavery, either directly or indirectly. In large part, what they were and what they would become had already been determined by their prewar experiences.

PART TWO

THE MAKING OF NEGRO POLITICIANS: A BIOGRAPHICAL PROFILE

Chapter Three

Black and Brown:
The Antebellum Origins
of Negro Leadership

A majority of the Negroes who occupied state and federal elective offices under Republican administrations in South Carolina were drawn from the ranks of slaves freed by the Emancipation Proclamation and the invasion of Union armies. But a large number of the Negro leaders had enjoyed freedom long before the war, and many had never known slavery. Coming from a community that constituted slightly more than 2 percent of the state's total Negro population in 1860, they made up more than 26 percent of those elected to office between 1868 and 1876.[1] Consequently, a free Negro in 1860 had better than ten times the chances of his enslaved brother to become one of the leadership group. These leaders of free, and largely mulatto, origins would control a disproportionate share of the key offices in the legislature and party infrastructure. Their aggressiveness alone was enough to arouse the jealousy and resentment of some of their black, ex-slave colleagues; in addition, differences in prewar life experiences, attitudes, and orientations of these two major segments of the Negro leadership would give rise to serious conflicts.

In one sense this phenomenon is unexpected because of the abundant evidence indicating that the free Negro's plight in antebellum society was "comparable" to a slave's and, at best, a "dubious freedom."[2] As South Carolina justice William Harper phrased it in his *Monk* v. *Jenkins* opinion, "the presumption of our law is against a negro's freedom."[3]

---

1. Of 255 persons who served in state offices between 1868 and 1876, 65 (25%) had been free before the war. Excluding the northern and foreign-born leaves 42 native free Negroes, or 26% of the native Negro group. 46 members of the total delegation have been positively identified as slaves, 59 others were "probably" slaves, and 85 are not identified. See discussion in Appendix A.

2. E. Horace Fitchett, "The Traditions of the Free Negro in Charleston, South Carolina," *Journal of Negro History*, XXV (April, 1940), 139; Ivy Marina Wikramanayake, "The Free Negro in Ante-Bellum South Carolina" (Ph.D. dissertation, University of Wisconsin, 1966), p. 246.

3. Wikramanayake, "The Free Negro," p. 70.

Indeed, a free Negro could be sold into slavery for tax default or harboring fugitive slaves. In legal matters he fell under the jurisdiction of the slave courts; like the slave, he could testify neither for nor against a white man. Given the prevailing logic that black men were constitutionally unfit for freedom, every free Negro was considered a ward of the state and was required to solicit an official guardian from among his white neighbors. His freedom of movement was almost as restricted as the slave's, for he ran the risk of seizure and sale while traveling in unfamiliar territories. After the Denmark Vesey trials, free Negroes were prohibited from leaving and subsequently returning to the state, on pain of imprisonment for a first offense and enslavement for a second. In Charleston they were required to register with the intendant twice a year, recording their birthplace, date of entry into the state, and explanations of any absences. While slaves enjoyed protection and physical maintenance of a kind by their masters, freemen were subject not only to all of the taxes levied on whites, but also to a special head tax of two dollars on all between the ages of sixteen and fifty, and "fatigue work" for all between the ages of eighteen and forty-five. A student of the period has characterized their status as a precarious liberty, "hedged about by a multiplicity of qualifications," "enjoyed only on sufferance," and "maintained only by a combination of vigilance, subordination and sheer good luck." [4]

Nevertheless, free status involved many obvious advantages over slavery. Generally, free Negroes were wealthier, better educated, and in many other ways better prepared for political competition than their ex-slave colleagues. Although their own persons were never entirely safe from alienation, free Negroes had been guaranteed the right to private property. They could also avail themselves of certain legal procedures and rights relative to debts and other economic matters, such as bankruptcy. They enjoyed the right of *habeas corpus* and, for a time, the right to sue.[5]

But the advantages of the free Negro population were derived less from the specific rights guaranteed them than from other factors. The laws governing the free Negro community often tell more about the dimensions and ambiguities of white attitudes—especially in times of crisis—than about the actual restraints enforced upon that community. The enforcement of these restrictions appears to have been directed more toward thwarting the "alien" influences of the outside world, at isolating rather than repressing the native free Negro population.[6] The laws were often

4. *Ibid.,* pp. 62-72.
5. *Ibid.,* pp. 2, 75.
6. *Ibid.,* pp. 200-202. For distinction between Upper South and Lower South in this regard, see Ira Berlin, *Slaves Without Masters: The Free Negro in the Antebellum South* (New York: Pantheon, 1974), pp. 215-16.

no more than dead letters, their effects vitiated first by the necessities of an urbanizing economy and the free Negro's importance to that economy, and finally by the peculiar relationship between the freemen and the white ruling elite.

The freemen came to freedom under different circumstances than the freedmen, and as a consequence they sustained a different relationship with their erstwhile white masters. The freedmen were liberated through the exigencies of war against the will of the slaveholding class and under circumstances which often added personal animosities to the general distaste of the ruling class for the "confiscation" of their slave property.[7] Furthermore, general emancipation brought the freedman no compensation for a lifetime of slavery, and none was contemplated by his federal benefactors. Even the limited measures of confiscation and redistribution of rebel land were broached as war measures, not under the principle of just compensation to the ex-slaves. But the antebellum free Negroes had origins primarily among those slaves manumitted between the Revolutionary War and the 1840's, when restrictive legislation was enacted. Most of these manumissions came via a will upon the death of the master. A large number were through self-purchase, and a few in recognition of heroic or meritorious services to the state. The manumitted slave was very often provided with land, capital, or livestock with which to begin his new life and earn a livelihood.[8] Many prospered—some to such extent that they used their prosperity to acquire plantations and slaves of their own.[9]

In some measure this practice of providing for the financial well-being of the manumitted slave was compelled by society's presumption that a freed Negro would otherwise become a pauper and a burden to the state; the legislative petitions for manumission often contained language suggesting this as a motive.[10] But the wills, deeds, and petitions bearing on the subject also indicate that the slaves often had "claims" or obligations upon their masters because of family kinship or sentimental attachments formed from years of faithful service.[11] It is also clear that the

7. For discussion of reactions of freed slaves and their masters to emancipation, see Joel Williamson, *After Slavery: The Negro in South Carolina During Reconstruction, 1861-77* (Chapel Hill: University of North Carolina Press, 1965), pp. 32-40.

8. Fitchett, "The Traditions of the Free Negro," p. 141; Wikramanayake, "The Free Negro," p. 6; Berlin, *Slaves Without Masters,* pp. 150-57, 179-80, 222.

9. Wikramanayake, "The Free Negro," p. 6.

10. This impression is based on the language of numerous wills in the Will Books for Charleston County in the South Carolina Archives. Cf. E. Horace Fitchett, "The Origins and Growth of the Free Negro Population of Charleston, South Carolina," *Journal of Negro History*, XXVI (October, 1941), 425.

11. *Ibid.,* p. 425.

class of slaves likely to be manumitted were house servants (whose proximity to the master allowed these attachments to develop) and artisans (whose expertise enabled them to accumulate the savings required to purchase their freedom). The legions of anonymous fieldhands were not likely to have the opportunity to secure either the master's recognition for "faithful service," or the cash to make themselves free men.

Consequently, manumitted freemen of the prewar period often assumed their new status with financial advantages that the emancipated freedmen did not enjoy. Statistics on this prewar group's resources, which are amazing under the circumstances, suggest how well they had benefited from these advantages. Despite the political and civil inequities with which they were afflicted, by 1859 9 percent of Charleston's free Negro population owned property.[12] In fact, 360 of the freemen were slaveholders, with 130 of them owning an average of three slaves each. Nine members of this group owned property assessed between $10,000 and $40,075, including fifty-four slaves.[13] William McKinlay, who represented Charleston in the constitutional convention and later in the lower house of the legislature, was a member of this elite group, owning $25,320 in real estate in 1860.[14] Many freeborn legislators from other parts of the state were also members of the elite class in their communities. Henry Jacobs, representative from Fairfield County, was a free mulatto carriage-maker who owned $1,200 in real estate and $2,500 in personal properties in 1860.[15] Other freeborn legislators who were perhaps too young to have accumulated much wealth and property were, nevertheless, scions of well-to-do free families. For instance, Thaddeus K. Sasportas, twenty-four-year-old member of the constitutional convention in 1868, was the son of Joseph A. Sasportas, a free mulatto businessman who owned $6,700 worth of real estate and five slaves in 1860.[16] Thaddeus's brother, F. C. Sasportas, owned $2,000 in real estate and two slaves.[17] And State Representative Florian Henry Frost, twenty-two years old in 1868, was the heir apparent to the $2,000 estate of his parents, Henry Maine and Lydia Frost.[18]

Statistics for the postwar period also indicate that freeborn legislators had a median financial worth of $1,100 and freedmen, $300. But when

12. Fitchett, "The Traditions of the Free Negro," p. 143.
13. *Ibid.*
14. "Tax on Property Paid by Persons of Indian Descent and Free Persons of Color," *List of Taxpayers of the City of Charleston for 1860* (Charleston, 1861), p. 328; U.S. MSS Census, 1860, Population, Charleston, Ward 4, p. 69.
15. U.S. MSS Census, 1860, Population, Fairfield County, Winnsboro, p. 1.
16. "Free Persons of Color," *List of Taxpayers of the City of Charleston,* p. 400.
17. *Ibid.*
18. *Ibid.,* p. 390.

all those who were born in or ever resided in the North are excluded, the differential shrinks. The median assets for native-born and -reared freemen was $700.[19]

Yet, despite the freeborn legislators' initial advantages, there was a demonstrable tendency among the former slaves to catch up in the postwar period. In fact, even before the end of the war, observers report a quickening of the acquisitive pulse of the freedmen as they made considerable profits out of garden crops of watermelon, corn, sweet potatoes, poultry, and eggs that the cotton monoculture had long neglected. This sudden metamorphosis from slave to economic man and the resultant preoccupation with money-making both surprised and offended the spiritual sensibilities of one A.M.A. missionary. "In temporal things, the colored people of these islands, are mainly doing well. I do not think it would be for their good, at the present time, to increcis their facilities for getting money. Most of them have ample means for gaining property fast, by their industry & shrewdness: they have become owners of land to a considerable extent, & are raizing cotton, as they say for 'old nigger himself,' & not for 'massa.' " [20]

Hastings Gantt, a plantation slave and later a representative from Beaufort for the better part of the decade, was evidently one of this group of newly freed entrepreneurs. By 1870 he had acquired a farm of eighty-four arable acres worth $900. He owned three milk cows valued at $100, from which he marketed 100 pounds of butter and 200 gallons of milk. Gantt raised 100 bushels of Indian corn, 650 pounds of rice, 75 bushels of sweet potatoes, and ten bushels of beans, in addition to his staple crop of five bales of cotton.[21] In 1871 Gantt's success won him election as president of the St. Helena Planter's Society.

Many other ex-slave legislators could boast of similar achievements in the immediate postwar period, but, unlike Gantt, most of them had origins in the same class of slaves that had produced the earlier free Negro class: that is, artisans and domestics. Some of the leading figures in the General Assembly—William Beverly Nash, Prince Rivers, Robert Smalls, William R. Jervay—had been employed as house servants or artisans while in slavery. When the war broke out, two of them were in the process of buying freedom for themselves or their families, and three used the war to escape from slavery. Nash was a porter in a Columbia

19. The median was calculated by simply arranging the values in ascending order and locating or interpolating the middle position. There were 83 members in the slave group and 41 in the free group.

20. W. T. Richardson to George Whipple, August 25, 1864, American Missionary Association Archives, Amistad Research Center, New Orleans.

21. U.S. MSS Census, 1870, Agriculture, Beaufort County, St. Helena Township, p. 3.

hotel, and Rivers was a coachman "raised in the white folk's house." [22] Early in the war Rivers "expropriated" his master's horse and somehow made his way from far behind Confederate lines in Edgefield to enlist in the first regiment of freedmen to be organized by Union forces in South Carolina.[23]

Robert Smalls was also a favored house servant living in relative comfort during his childhood.[24] When he was twelve years old his master sold his plantation near Beaufort and moved to Charleston, where Smalls was hired out until the Civil War. In Charleston, Smalls worked at a variety of unskilled and semi-skilled jobs—waiter, lamplighter, stevedore, and foreman in Charleston harbor. He was later employed by John Simmons, a rigger, to drive hoisting horses on the wharf for a year, during which time Simmons taught him sail-making and rigging. From 1857 Smalls had an agreement with Henry McKee, his owner, to handle his own employment and earnings and to pay McKee a set income of fifteen dollars per month. Prior to this he had married Hannah Jones, another slave, and arranged to purchase her freedom for seven dollars per month. This arrangement was altered after his first child, Elizabeth Lydia, was born a slave in 1858. He promptly arranged to purchase wife and daughter for $800. At the outbreak of the war he had saved $700 toward that end. The purchase was never completed, because Smalls escaped with his family to Union lines in 1862, delivering a valuable Confederate troop ship, *The Planter,* and its cargo to the Union Navy in the process.[25]

Wilson Cooke, a legislator from Greenville, also attempted to purchase his freedom before the war. Cooke, the son of his owner, was trained as a tanner. Evidently his occupation was lucrative enough to allow him to save $1,500 by working after hours. Although his master's refusal to enter into an agreement temporarily altered Cooke's plans, he was eventually freed by the war and his accumulated capital provided a considerable financial stake with which to begin life as a freedman.[26]

Even those slaves who came to freedom without a stake took advantage of opportunities to accumulate land and small amounts of capital during and immediately after the war. Of course, Smalls received $1,500 for the *Planter* as a prize for its capture, and he promptly invested that amount in land and various business enterprises around Beaufort.[27] Other ser-

22. "Deposition of Patti White," Prince R. Rivers, Pension File, Certificate No. 423234, Civil War, Records of Veterans Administration, Record Group 15, National Archives.

23. *Edgefield Advertiser,* February 22, 1868.

24. Okon Edet Uya, *From Slavery to Public Service: Robert Smalls, 1839-1915* (New York: Oxford University Press, 1971), p. 3.

25. *Ibid.,* pp. 3-14.

26. Reprint from *Chambersburg* [Pa.] *Repository* in *Daily Republican,* February 7, 1870.

27. Uya, *Robert Smalls,* pp. 30, 37.

vicemen were less fortunate, but they generally received enlistment boun-
ties and special privileges at government auctions of confiscated rebel
properties. For instance, soldiers took a lion's share of the $60,000 worth
of land sold to freedmen at an 1864 government auction in Beaufort.
They were extended three years' credit on three-fifths of the purchase
price.[28] The soldiers often returned home with considerable savings as
well. One amazed observer testified that the enlisted men of one regiment
alone deposited $55,000 in the Freedman's Savings Bank at Beaufort
in only a few weeks' time.[29]

Many of the legislators who served in the Union armies must have
taken advantage of these opportunities. William R. Jervay, later a senator
from Charleston, says that he was "a mere boy when the war broke out." [30]
He was a mulatto house slave for Gabriel Manigo [possibly Manigault]
in Clarendon County. As soon as he was big enough, Jervay ran away
to Charleston, where he enlisted in the 128th United States Colored
Troops. He came out of service as an orderly sergeant and with enough
capital to operate a variety store in Charleston for a short time. After
this brief flirtation with the mercantile trade, he turned to carpentry
and farming.[31] By 1870 he had attained success in both areas, being
a major independent contractor for public works in St. John's Parish
and owning a farm of 257 acres valued at $950, plus $350 in livestock
and total production valued at $1,830.[32]

The antebellum experiences of these men are probably indicative of
those of their political colleagues. At least four slave-born legislators had
been primarily house servants, but a much larger number—seventeen—
had been employed as artisans. Given their postwar occupations, one
can identify eighteen as probable fieldhands.[33] One must be careful in
drawing conclusions from such figures, however, for most of the legislators
were employed in diverse occupations during their bondage. William
Henry Heard, a state representative from Abbeville returned in the aborted
1876 election and later an A.M.E. bishop, was employed as a house
servant and an artisan's apprentice for most of his childhood, but was
sent to the fields as a plowboy when he was a young man. Robert Smalls

28. W. T. Richardson to S. S. Jocelyn, March 3, 1864, A.M.A. Papers.

29. F. K. Noble to George Whipple, September 29, 1868, A.M.A. Papers. General Rufus
Saxton stated that black soldiers usually invested $200 of the $300 enlistment bonus they
received into government bonds. *New York Times,* August 6, 1865.

30. "Deposition A," William R. Jervay, Pension File Certificate No. 716457, Civil War,
RG 15, NA.

31. *Ibid.*

32. U.S. MSS Census, 1870, Population, Charleston County, St. Stephen's Parish, p. 5.

33. Those ex-slaves who can be identified as field laborers after the war are assumed
to have been fieldhands before the war also.

began as a house servant and was then hired out as a laborer and finally as a skilled artisan. William R. Jervay was recorded as a porter when he enlisted, but he probably had had some previous training as a carpenter, since this was the employment he undertook a few months after the war. The interrelationship of the various categories of slave employment was probably more fluid than has hitherto been assumed. Consequently, assumptions about the effects of antebellum employment on character and personality formation must be likewise modified.[34]

It is clear, however, that many ex-slaves who later emerged as political leaders, and particularly those who owned some property, had been trained as artisans. Whatever the effects of this training on personality formation, it most certainly gave them advantages in earning a livelihood. Skilled craftsmanship was one sector of the economy on which Negroes in the Lower South had a strong grip. To some extent this resulted from the general distaste with which whites in a slave society regarded manual labor or any occupation associated with "nigger work." One postwar traveler took special note of the abandonment of these employments by

34. In his study of Mississippi, Vernon Wharton identified the occupations of a number of the Negro legislators of that state as mostly "urban slaves, blacksmiths, carpenters, clerks, or waiters in hotels and boarding houses; a few of them had been favored body-servants of affluent whites." Stanley Elkins has seized on this as the final prop for his thesis that the slave system's "authority structure" infantilized the plantation laborers and rendered any leadership from them hopeless. The black leaders of Reconstruction, obvious exceptions to his theory, are accounted for by the fact that they escaped the harshness of the system because they were employed in comparatively privileged occupations. It should be noted, however, that the evidence Elkins chooses to take from Wharton refers specifically to "the minor Negro leaders," and that that particular passage is directly preceded by one describing the leaders at the state level: "In general, it can be said that they were not Negroes who had held positions of leadership under the old regime; . . . Almost none of them came from the small group who had been free before the war. Such men, as barbers, artisans, or small farmers, had depended too long on the favor of the whites for the maintenance of their existence." This writer finds both analyses far too simplistic: first, in assuming that personalities could not change as circumstances and the social and political environment changed; and second, in assuming a bivariate relationship between white actions and black reactions, while ignoring the possible effects of other variables, such as the interactions of blacks with each other and the development of a subculture that could rationalize their inferior position vis-à-vis whites, rather than *internalize* that position. Hence the attainment of positions of leadership or privilege under the old regime, while necessitating a certain amount of "tomming," might also be viewed begrudgingly by other blacks as a kind of success, even while they resented the person who succeeded. In such circumstances the failure of black field laborers to achieve leadership positions does not necessarily prove an absence of motivation or aggressive personalities, but can be explained by the simple absence of the opportunities and the "head start" that artisans, etc., enjoyed. See Vernon Wharton, *The Negro in Mississippi, 1865-90* (Chapel Hill: University of North Carolina Press, 1947), p. 164; and Stanley Elkins, *Slavery: A Problem in American Institutional and Intellectual Life,* 2nd ed. (Chicago: University of Chicago Press, 1968), p. 139.

the whites and declared that "more than half the blacksmiths, most of the brick-masons, and nearly all the hundred or more carpenters that I have seen were colored men." [35]

It was on this sector of the economy that much of the livelihood and all of the wealth of the free Negro group was based. Not only were they drawn mainly from manumitted house servants and artisans, but artisan and day-labor occupations were the only ones open to free Negroes, because planters would not employ them as field laborers.[36] Consequently, they concentrated in the larger towns and cities like Beaufort, Greenville, Georgetown, and especially Charleston, where they constituted 8.8 percent of the total Negro population. Indeed, free Negroes were attracted to Charleston as if by a magnet. Robert C. De Large, born in Aiken, and Joseph H. Rainey, born in Georgetown, exemplify the migration of free Negro artisans to the metropolis.

The concentration of free Negro artisans in the cities led to an even greater expansion of the crafts in which they participated. While the Charleston free Negroes of 1819 were listed in thirty branches of employment, including eleven carpenters, ten tailors, twenty-two seamstresses, six shoemakers, and one hotel proprietor, their descendants in 1859 were listed in fifty different occupations, including fifty carpenters, forty-three tailors, nine shoemakers, and twenty-one butchers.[37] The skills of an artisan were generally passed from father to son to grandson, as with the Holloways (carpenters), the McKinlays (tailors), and the Sasportases (butchers). This tradition solidified not only the grip that free Negroes had on these occupations, but also the evolving class structure of the Negro community.

Inevitably, the white working class rebelled and demanded that their free Negro competitors be restricted. One such petition by white Charlestonians in 1858 led to new city ordinances designed to hamper the free Negro's economic growth. The ordinances required that they obtain a special license to sell produce, and such sales were restricted to the public markets; only licensed fishermen could own boats, and ceilings were imposed on wages ($1 per day or 12½ cents per hour).[38] But the free Negro had become so important to the economy that these ordinances were never vigorously enforced. For instance, when Alonzo J. Ransier, later a congressman from South Carolina, was hired as a shipping clerk in 1850 by a leading merchant, it was in violation of the law restricting

35. Sidney Andrews, *The South Since the War* (Boston: Ticknor and Fields, 1866), p. 225; cf. Berlin, *Slaves Without Masters*, pp. 221.

36. Wikramanayake, "The Free Negro," p. 128.

37. Fitchett, "The Tradition of the Free Negro," p. 143.

38. *Ibid.*, pp. 136-38.

free Negroes to a certain prescribed occupations. Yet the merchant was fined only one penny for the violation.[39]

The free Negro also benefited from the existence of other gaps between the written laws and their enforcement. While slaves were often barred from literacy because of their masters' fears of unfitting them for slavery, freemen of moderate means were generally, though sporadically, able to achieve a fair education. Considering only those legislators born in the South, one finds that only two of the 45 Negroes of free origins were illiterate, as compared with twelve of the 89 slave-born. Furthermore, while nine of the freeborn had some college or professional education, only four of the slave-born had.[40] (See Table 2.)

TABLE 2. MINIMUM EDUCATION LEVEL BY PREWAR ORIGINS OF SOUTHERN-BORN NEGRO LEGISLATORS, 1868-76

Origins	College	Normal School	Common School	Literate	Illiterate	Total
Slave	4(4%)	1(1%)	7(8%)	65(73%)	12(14%)	89(100%)
Free	9(20%)	4(9%)	12(27%)	18(40%)	2(4%)	45(100%)
Total	13	5	19	83	14	134

Source: See Appendix A.

The early efforts to educate South Carolina's Negro population were by-products of religious proselytizing by white missionaries and were directed at slaves and freemen alike. By the early nineteenth century, however, educational activities had come primarily under the direction and sponsorship of the free Negro community with its numerous self-help organizations.[41] One of the more famous schools was that operated between 1803 and 1838 by Thomas S. Bonneau, a wealthy Charleston mulatto who owned a plantation and slaves. Bonneau's school was so large that he required two assistants, F. K. Sasportas and William Mc-Kinney. The school was obviously restricted to those families with some means, as is indicated by an 1827 receipt showing a tuition of $1.50 for two boys for a period of one and one-half months. Bonneau began a tradition in his family, for each generation is reported to have contributed a teacher to serve the free Negro community of Charleston.[42]

Free Negroes of means frequently hired white teachers to educate their children. Joseph A. Sasportas and William McKinlay were on the board

39. Monroe Work, "Some Negro Members of Reconstruction Legislatures," *Journal of Negro History*, V (January, 1920), 96; cf. Berlin, *Slaves Without Masters*, pp. 230, 351, 378.

40. See Appendix A for methods and sources of data.

41. C. W. Birnie, "The Education of the Negro in Charleston," *Journal of Negro History*, XII (January, 1927), 14-15.

42. *Ibid.*, pp. 18, 19.

of trustees of a Coming Street school conducted by a white teacher. The trustees of this school were elected by its patrons, and they paid the teacher a salary.[43] Individual parents also hired white students from Charleston College to tutor their children in college-level subjects.[44] It is not surprising that in 1866 Francis L. Cardozo advised the American Missionary Association of the need to establish a normal (that is, teacher preparatory) school because of the advanced education of many of his freeborn pupils: "Again you are aware that in Charleston, and other similar Southern cities there has always been a large number of colored people who have *always been free,* and who were therefore allowed to educate themselves. One fourth of my school is composed of such, and they are advancing towards the higher branches, and are anxious to be prepared for Teachers." [45]

The success of the free Negro group in attaining some education was not achieved without difficulty, however. One piece of legislation passed in the wake of the Vesey conspiracy and Nat Turner's revolt was a law in 1834, prohibiting the maintenance of schools by and for free Negroes and slaves. The law provided for a hundred-dollar fine and six months' imprisonment for white violators and a fifty-dollar fine and fifty lashes for free Negro violators. For an added measure of control, the act provided that Negro informers be encouraged by rewarding them with half the fine and making them legally acceptable as witnesses.[46] One of the native free Negro teachers employed by the American Missionary Association, a Miss Weston, had been arrested for violating this law by maintaining a secret school during the antebellum period.[47]

Apparently numerous other such schools were maintained secretly in Charleston; they probably existed because the law was not vigorously enforced. In fact, the language of the act had not specifically forbidden the education of free Negroes, but only the maintenance of schools by them. How crucial the distinction was in practice is problematic, but one scholar has concluded that the act was directed at a particular school founded in Charleston by Daniel A. Payne. Payne, a free mulatto carpenter in 1829 and later a bishop of the African Methodist Episcopal Church, operated a school which was considered to be one of the best in the city and was patronized by the leading white families.[48]

Whatever their motivation, similar legislation in the 1850's sparked

43. *Ibid.,* p. 19.
44. *Ibid.,* p. 20.
45. Francis L. Cardozo to M. E. Strieby, June 13, 1866, A.M.A. Papers.
46. Birnie, "The Education of the Negro," pp. 17-18.
47. Jennie Armstrong, "Letter to the Editor," *The National Freedmen,* January 15, 1866, p. 9.
48. Wikramanayake, "The Free Negro," p. 223.

a large migration of free Negroes to Philadelphia and New York. Thaddeus K. Sasportas was one of this number. Sasportas, who had been apprenticed as a shoemaker at one time, was educated in private schools in Philadelphia and completed normal school before returning to South Carolina to teach in a Freedmen's Bureau school at Orangeburg.[49] Possibly because his family had considerably fewer resources, Robert C. De Large went no further than North Carolina, where he attended a normal school.[50] Francis L. Cardozo, who had served five years as a carpenter's apprentice and four as a journeyman, left Charleston to study abroad with $1,000 he had managed to save from his earnings. He studied at Glasgow and then went to London and Edinburgh for three years of theological training.[51]

Other freemen quickly took advantage of the creation of new black colleges in the postwar period to extend their educations. Samuel J. Bampfield, representative from Beaufort, received his A.B. from Pennsylvania's Lincoln University and returned to Charleston to read law under Judge Cage.[52] His colleague in the Beaufort delegation, Thomas E. Miller, followed him to Lincoln, graduating in 1872 and returning home to study law under State Solicitor P. L. Wiggin and Chief Justice Moses. Miller, the son of a free, farm-owning family in Hilton Head, had previously attended schools in Charleston and in Hudson, New York. He was admitted to the South Carolina bar in 1875 and later served in Congress and as president of the Colored Normal, Industrial, Agricultural and Mechanical College of South Carolina (later Orangeburg State College).[53]

Of course, legislators of slave origin had far fewer opportunities to obtain an education; of those whose educational background is known, one in seven was illiterate. Nevertheless, many had been able to attain a basic literacy, and sometimes more, in both the antebellum and early postwar periods. It was often economically advantageous for the slaveowner to give a rudimentary education to his slave. They were often trained to manage their owner's business affairs or were sent out to be

49. Lawrence Bryant, ed., *Negro Senators and Representatives in the South Carolina Legislature, 1868-1902* (Orangeburg: School of Graduate Studies, South Carolina State College, 1968), p. 60.

50. *Biographical Directory of the U.S. Congress* (Washington: Government Printing Office, 1971), p. 796.

51. Francis L. Cardozo to M. E. Strieby, August 13, 1866, A.M.A. Papers.

52. Lawrence Bryant, ed., *Negro Lawmakers in the South Carolina Legislature, 1868-1902* (Orangeburg: School of Graduate Studies, South Carolina State College, 1968), pp. 15-17.

53. *Biographical Directory of the U.S. Congress*, p. 1333; Emily B. Reynolds and Joan R. Faunt, eds., *Biographical Directory of the Senate of South Carolina, 1776-1964* (Columbia: South Carolina Archives Department, 1964), p. 274.

trained for a trade by literate free Negroes.[54] Some of the slave-born legislators obtained their basic literacy training in this manner. Henry Johnson of Fairfield was a bricklayer and plasterer who had obtained his limited education from his master.[55] Bruce H. Williams belonged to Dr. J. D. McGill, who apprenticed him to a plasterer after teaching him to read and write. Evidently this initial literacy training provided him with a good enough foundation to attend high school in Raleigh immediately after the war.[56] House servants were also favored with opportunities for literacy training. Frederick Albert Clinton, member of the constitutional convention and state representative and senator from Lancaster, had probably been a house servant in slavery; he credits his education to his owner Ervin Clinton, a lawyer.[57]

Undoubtedly artisans and other literate slaves often passed along their learning to fellow slaves. Edward J. Cain, a slave carpenter and wheelwright before the war, was elected to the constitutional convention, served in the lower house of the legislature, and was elected sheriff of Orangeburg County. One of his fellow slaves testified that Cain had secretly taught other slaves to read and write during slavery times.[58] Thus the literate slaves constituted a secret educational resource for the slave community, providing a counterpart to the surreptitious educational activities in the free Negro community.

Despite all these efforts, however, most slaves were illiterate at the time of emancipation. As in every other respect, fieldhands had found little opportunity for self-improvement under the slave regime, but they made full use of the period immediately after emancipation to educate themselves. The state representative from Union, Samuel Nuckles, described himself as "a hard-down slave" who had had no opportunity for formal education. But the fifty-seven-year-old legislator managed after freedom to teach himself to write, and to read enough to be able to understand the daily newspapers.[59]

The freedmen's overwhelming thirst for education was legendary and has been attested to by their friends and foes alike. In fact, some postwar travelers contrasted their dramatic efforts to educate themselves with the

54. Birnie, "The Education of the Negro," p. 20.

55. *Testimony Taken by the Joint Select Committee to Inquire into the Condition of Affairs in the Late Insurrectionary States*, Volume I: South Carolina (Washington: Government Printing Office, 1872), p. 322.

56. Reynolds and Faunt, *Biographical Directory*, p. 334.

57. *Ibid.,* p. 197.

58. "Deposition of July Emlily," Edward J. Cain, Pension File Certificate No. 391582, Civil War, RG 15, NA.

59. *Testimony . . . Insurrectionary States,* p. 1161.

apparent apathy of poor whites.[60] Records show numerous efforts of recently freed slaves to establish schools singlehandedly for their people. Even before the end of the war Will Capers, a slave cabinetmaker, operated a secret night school for adult men in Beaufort County. After Union forces arrived, he wanted to continue teaching under their auspices, but Edward Pierce, the Treasury Department agent in charge of confiscated plantations, refused and put him to work in the fields instead.[61] In Greenville, Charles Hopkins enjoyed more success. He solicited building materials and organized the freedmen to build a schoolhouse in which he himself taught.[62] Numerous other freedmen were educated in classes organized for the black troops. This was probably how James Clement Wilson, an ex-slave sergeant major in the 104th USCT and later representative from Sumter County, was educated. According to his enlistment papers, Wilson was illiterate when he joined the army in 1865, but three years after his discharge in 1866 he was able to teach school himself.[63]

Like their constituents, most legislators seized every available means to improve themselves during the immediate postwar period. Given the barriers they had faced, it is amazing that the gap between them and their freeborn colleagues was not greater. The determination and untiring efforts of some of the legislators were indeed awesome. For instance, Robert Smalls spent from five to seven o'clock every morning in independent study, followed by two more hours of tutoring by a Beaufort schoolteacher before going about his daily employments. Smalls also subscribed to the *Washington Star,* to which he faithfully applied himself every day in order to improve his reading skills.[64]

While the gap between the opportunities available to many of the freeborn and the majority of the slave-born was vast, it should be said that not all—indeed, not even a majority—of the free Negroes were literate, or skilled, or wealthy. The burgeoning Charleston population created a large underclass that was only nominally free, mostly black, largely unskilled, and generally poor. There was little social distance between these lower-class free Negroes and the urban slaves; these people often intermarried, they were engaged in the same trades, frequented the same taverns and churches, and often lived side by side in the same

60. Andrews, *The South Since the War,* p. 227.

61. Laura Towne, *Letters and Diary of Laura M. Towne, Written from the Sea Islands of South Carolina, 1862-84,* ed. Rupert Sargent Holland (Cambridge: Riverside Press, 1912), p. 27.

62. John W. De Forest, *A Union Officer in the Reconstruction,* ed. James H. Croushore and David M. Potter (New Haven: Yale University Press, 1948), pp. 118-20.

63. Compiled Military Service Record, James C. Wilson, Hospital Steward, Co. I, 104 USCT, Records of the Adjutant General's Office, Record Group 94; James C. Wilson, Pension File Certificate No. 780295, Civil War, RG 15, NA.

64. Uya, *Robert Smalls,* pp. 25-26.

communities. Indeed, the lower-class free Negroes were often subjected to the scorn of the domestic slaves of upper-class white families, whose well-being and lifestyle might well have been superior.[65] Directly above them was a middle class of propertyless skilled artisans who were employees of white establishments or who struggled along on subsistence incomes in small shops of their own.[66] A few freeborn legislators appear to have been drawn from this group, including Edward Mickey, a Charleston tailor, and William C. Morrison, a Beaufort tinsmith.

But others were drawn from the largely mulatto, free Negro upper and middle classes and had accumulated considerable wealth based on the expansion of their artisan shops into fairly large business establishments. They had used their excess capital to speculate in real estate—the one investment activity in which the laws allowed them to function on a relatively equal basis with whites.[67] William McKinlay, for instance, was the landlord of numerous families, black and white, in the fourth ward of Charleston before the war.[68]

Relationships between the members of this free mulatto upper class and the white upper class based on mutual social respect were not unknown. For instance, Richmond Kinloch, a wealthy millwright, often spent vacation "retreats" with his wealthy white neighbors at Summerville.[69] The unwritten credo of many Latin American slave societies, "Money lightens the skin," affected South Carolina's antebellum race relations as well.[70] William Ellison, a mulatto slave who received manumission at twenty-nine upon the death of his master, is a case in point. Ellison prospered, quickly acquiring a plantation and slaves. He eventually added to this the plantation houses of a former governor, Stephen D. Miller, and a prominent politician, General Sumter. Ellison became a member of the white Episcopal church in Sumter and owned a pew there; his children crossed the color line, marrying white suitors. Ellison himself was buried in the white cemetery.[71] William Ellison's remarkable career is a concrete application of the principle propounded by Justice Harper

65. Wikramanayake, "The Free Negro," p. 99.

66. *Ibid.*, pp. 103-4.

67. *Ibid.*, p. 144.

68. "Table Showing the Number, Construction, Owner, Occupant and Ward Location of Every House in the City," *Census of the City of Charleston, South Carolina for the Year 1861*, comp. Frederick A. Ford (Charleston: Evans and Cogswell, 1861), pp. 50, 71.

69. Wikramanayake, "The Free Negro," p. 102. For a description of the Lower South generally, see Berlin, *Slaves Without Masters*, pp. 263-64.

70. Wikramanayake, "The Free Negro," p. 128. See also the article by "W" on 1875 Civil Rights Bill in which the author, a native, declared the willingness of whites to accept Negroes of the upper class on equal terms. *Beaufort Tribune*, March 21, 1875. Cf. Berlin, *Slaves Without Masters*, pp. 163-64.

71. Wikramanayake, "The Free Negro," p. 128.

in 1835: "The condition [racial] . . . is not to be determined solely by
. . . visible mixture . . . but by reputation . . . and it may be . . . proper,
that a man of worth . . . should have the rank of a white man, while
a vagabond of the same degree of blood should be confined to the inferior
caste." [72]

Little wonder that one student of the antebellum period would refer
to the social distance between the field slave and this Charleston free
mulatto group as a "chasm." [73] One postwar observer reported the existence of a "deep and increasing jealousy between the blacks and mulattoes"
in Greenville.[74]

> To some extent they formed distinct cliques of society and crystallized into
> separate churches. When the mulattoes arranged a series of *tableaux-vivans*
> for the benefit of their religious establishment, the far more numerous blacks
> kept at a distance and made the show a pecuniary failure. When the mulat-
> toes asked that they might hold a fair in the Bureau schoolhouse, for the
> above-mentioned purpose, some of the blacks intrigued against the request
> and were annoyed at my granting it.[75]

The existence of such class divisions and jealousies between the slave-
born blacks and the freeborn mulattoes has been noted frequently in
the historical literature. However, most scholars have dismissed the phenomenon as a short-lived aberration of the slave regime which had little
impact on the course of postwar political developments. "Color variations
within the Negro community were less important than native whites liked
to think," concludes Joel Williamson after studying the period inten-
sively.[76] Another scholar has also concluded that the free mulatto "found
his place" in postwar society and deliberately sought identification with
his own group rather than with the whites.[77]

There is much to support these conclusions. Freeborn mulattoes did
move very dramatically to present themselves as leaders of the black
freedmen and to speak and work for their interest in the political forums
of the day. There was never any perceptible split in the Negro vote on
election day, despite the myriad attempts by white Democrats and mixed
splinter factions of the Republican party itself to bring about such a
division. A reputable contemporary observer also denied the existence
of major divisions in the Negro community.[78] And there can be little

72. *Ibid.,* p. 11.
73. Fitchett, "The Origins and Growth of the Free Negro," p. 429.
74. De Forest, *A Union Officer,* p. 124.
75. *Ibid.*
76. Williamson, *After Slavery,* p. 313.
77. Wikramanayake, "The Free Negro," p. 119.
78. A South Carolinian [Belton O'Neal Townsend], "South Carolina Society," *Atlantic Monthly,* XXXIX (June, 1877), 678.

argument with the conclusion that the major issues in South Carolina, as in the entire American South, were those dividing black and white, not those between black and mulatto. There is little doubt that the white press's numerous reports of division and conflict in the Negro community were often self-serving and not a little self-congratulatory in surmising that Negroes would assume airs of superiority in proportion to their white blood. All this notwithstanding, divisions and conflicts did exist, and they did have political consequences. One black contemporary noted the persistence of these classes, "separate and distinct in manners, habits and customs," well into the last decades of the century.[79]

The legislature reflected the larger society in both its composition and its conflicts. The 1860 census shows that seven out of every ten free Negroes were mulattoes; likewise, one finds that six out of ten native-born free Negro legislators were mulattoes. On the other hand, while only 7 percent of the general Negro population was mulatto, about 43 percent of the legislators were mulattoes. Therefore, mulattoes tended to be disproportionately represented. Of course, there were mulatto ex-slaves as well; but they were more likely to identify with the freeborn mulattoes than with the other ex-slaves.

Even before the first Republican administration was completed, there were complaints about the preference given mulattoes in the distribution of civil service jobs.[80] In the very first campaign of 1868, a mulatto candidate for the constitutional convention reportedly declared: "I never ought to have been a slave, for my father was a gentleman." To this he added: "If ever there is a nigger government—an unmixed nigger government—established in South Carolina, I shall move."[81] This candidate suffered at the polls for his candor, but apparently he won a seat in the convention nevertheless.

These tensions were often exploited for political effect. In one heated political battle between William H. Jones, Jr., a black representative from Georgetown, and Joseph H. Rainey, a very light mulatto congressional aspirant, Jones used the color prejudices of his black audience with devastating effect. He charged that Rainey cared nothing about the poor blacks and looked down on them. He said that Rainey and Lucius Wimbush, another very light mulatto state senator from Chester, had tried to pass for white while visiting the National Negro Laborers Conven-

---

79. D[aniel] Augustus Straker, *The New South Investigated* (Detroit: Ferguson, 1888), p. 81.

80. See "Letter to Major Delany," *The Life and Writings of Frederick Douglass: Reconstruction and After*, ed. Philip S. Foner (New York: International Publishers, 1955), IV, 279. See also Dorothy Sterling, *The Making of an Afro-American: Martin Robinson Delany, 1812-1885* (New York: Doubleday, 1971), pp. 289-90.

81. De Forest does not identify the candidate, but it may have been Wilson Cooke of Greenville. De Forest, *A Union Officer*, pp. 123-24.

tion in Washington, D.C., the previous year. When Rainey tried to reply, he was hooted off the stage by the audience.[82] When some of the mulatto leaders demanded more power and patronage for Negroes in the Republican party, they were sometimes confronted with the suspicions of their darker colleagues. Senator Nash was reported to have sneeringly remarked of the mulatto leaders: "To what race do they belong. . . . I know that my ancestors trod the burning sands of Africa, but why should men in whose veins run a great preponderance of white blood seek to specially ally themselves with the black man, prate of 'our race,' when they are simply mongrels." [83]

Thus, while these intraracial prejudices may not have split the electorate at the polls, they certainly produced tensions among the leadership that could have significant political consequences as far as the unity and behavior of the state's Negro leadership was concerned. Since the free mulattoes became a major element of the leadership that emerged from the Negro community in the postwar period, the sources and nature of these tensions are important.

The issue of intraracial color prejudice emerged in one of the very first political meetings in the spring of 1865, when Reuben Tomlinson advised the assembled Negroes to put aside those old prejudices between browns and blacks. Martin R. Delany, a black, also spoke to this issue in that meeting, attributing the origins of the conflict to the act of a mulatto in betraying Denmark Vesey's rebellion. The slavemaster's only hope, said Delany, was to use the mulattoes as confidantes and spies against the blacks.[84] Other students of the period have subscribed to this theory that whites deliberately exploited free Negroes as a "buffer" between themselves and slaves, and that free Negroes acted as "custodians" of the system.[85]

There were other, more critical historical forces at work, however. Free Negroes, confined by the system to artisan or day-labor livelihoods, were forced to compete with urban slave labor to survive.[86] Because urban slaves were generally supported by their owners, they could afford to work at cheaper rates, thereby undercutting free Negroes who had not only to support themselves and their families, but to purchase licenses and pay taxes as well. This economic competition underscored, if not

82. *Daily Courier*, April 4, 1870.

83. *Beaufort Republican*, January 30, 1873.

84. *Daily Courier*, May 13, 1865.

85. Wikramanayake, "The Free Negro," p. 3; Fitchett, "The Tradition of the Free Negro," p. 147. There is, of course, the contrary tradition developed very persuasively by Ira Berlin that free Negroes both acted and were believed by whites to have undermined the slave system. *Slaves Without Masters*, pp. 343-69.

86. Wikramanayake, "The Free Negro," p. 136.

encouraged, the hostility between freemen and slaves and, as an inevitable corollary, between browns and blacks.

Contrary to the impression that many observers and scholars would convey, conflict between blacks and browns was not simply based on color differences. Rather, color was merely an indicator of a whole complex of interrelated variables of class and acculturation. It was only one of a number of determinants of social rank in the Negro community; others included wealth, occupation, church affiliation, and rural or urban birth.[87] Indeed, many of the observers who indicated that they saw no evidence of division based on color and who declared that blacks and mulattoes associated on "terms of perfect equality" were probably viewing the interaction of mulattoes and blacks of similar social class and status.[88] Being primarily the offspring of the white planter class, the mulattoes were the privileged group of the slave regime. Eye-witnesses give ample testimony to this fact, as do the statistics showing that the overwhelming majority of the free Negroes were mulatto, along with the general prevalence of mulattoes among the domestics and the artisans.[89] They were the ones who interacted most with whites during slavery and who assimilated white mores and lifestyles.

Field slaves, on the other hand, were largely alien to white society even at the end of the war. By the time of emancipation they were definitely a creole population, but postwar missionaries did uncover some individuals who had been born in Africa and had memories of the motherland and the slave trade. One such person was an eighty-year-old grandmother who had been captured and enslaved at the age of ten.[90] Old women like her commanded respect in the slave quarters, and the "Praise House" (the meeting place for religious services) was generally located in their huts.[91] It is inconceivable that the generation from which the legislators came was entirely bereft of an oral tradition, or at least

87. Fitchett concludes: "Basically the difference in skin color was insignificant, in accounting for their patterns of conduct, compared to the impact of these social forces and these social positions" ("Origins and Growth of the Free Negro," p. 429). See also Berlin, *Slaves Without Masters*, p. 277; cf. [Townsend,] "South Carolina Society," p. 677; Allison Davis, Burleigh B. Gardner, and Mary R. Gardner, *Deep South: A Social Anthropological Study of Caste and Class*, abridged ed. (Chicago: University of Chicago Press, 1965), pp. 205, 214.

88. For instance, the observation of T. E. Hilary Skinner on a congregation at a lower-class church service in Charleston in 1865-66: *After the Storm: Or Jonathan and His Neighbors* (London: Bentley, 1866), p. 338.

89. Sir George Campbell found few blacks "among the higher mechanics," except those working as stevedores for lading ships. *White and Black: The Outcome of a Visit to the United States* (New York: R. Worthington, 1879), p. 325.

90. D. B. Nichols to George Whipple, May 6, 1862, A.M.A. Papers. See also Laura Towne, *Letters and Diary*, p. 22.

91. Laura Towne, *Letters and Diary*, p. 20.

an awareness of their African heritage. It is certainly true that, in the areas of greatest black political strength, there was little or no intrusion of white culture. In 1863 one A.M.A. missionary was dismayed that the blacks were so little acculturated to "civilized" society and customs. The reason for this phenomenon was easy to deduce, however: "The proprietors spent very little time on the Island. So that the slaves were nearly isolated from educated people."[92] A South Carolina native confirms those astute observations of the effects of planters' absenteeism. These slaves in "the malarial regions," as he called the sea coast, were the direct descendants of the last Africans imported to South Carolina before the closing of the slave trade in 1808. They had generally worked in large gangs and had little intercourse with whites. As an example, he cited ex-Governor Aiken's plantation of 1,000 slaves on the Island of Jehossee; the blacks were attended by an overseer, a physician, and a Methodist preacher—the only whites they ever came into contact with.[93] Although these conditions were undoubtedly moderated as one moved from the sea coast to the up-country, they surely indicate the opposite poles toward which the socialization of the blacks and mulattoes tended.

Some of the experiences of slave-born legislators also suggest that the men who formed a political alliance in 1868 grew up in radically different social environments. Whatever the other forms of oppression faced by the free Negroes, they were generally able to maintain family patterns which satisfied the accepted norms of their society. Although recent evidence suggests that slaves were better able to maintain a healthy family life than previously thought, the pressures militating against them still appear to have been greater than those against the freeborn; at least this was true for the South Carolina legislators. The situation of Prince Rivers, whose wife lived in a different household on a neighboring plantation, represents one pattern of family ecology.[94] While many of the slave-born legislators reconstituted their slave marriages and families after emancipation, some chose to break entirely with their slave wives, perhaps to symbolize the break with their slave lives.

The desire to put away the memories of slavery was no doubt very strong for some who had watched their siblings and children auctioned away by the planter. Charles Jones was born and raised in Fairfield County and represented Lancaster County in the constitutional conven-

92. Anna A. Carter to S. S. Jocelyn, January 22, 1863, A.M.A. Papers.

93. John A. Leland, *A Voice from South Carolina* (Charleston: Walker, Evans, and Cogswell, 1879), pp. 34-55.

94. "Deposition of Rina Green," Prince R. Rivers Pension File.

tion. He had seen one sister, two daughters, and a son go on the auction block and be sold "down the river" to Florida.[95] It cannot be easy to know, as William Henry Heard did, that your mother is used as a "breeder." [96] Young William watched her, worked to death before he was nine years old, raise three children who were sold away. Yet his family experience also demonstrates the tenacity and resilience of the slave's spirit under such adversity. Heard remembers his father, a blacksmith on a neighboring plantation, as "a strong father figure." The man walked three miles to visit his family twice a week, and as a boy William worked in his blacksmith shop. While there he used his earnings to employ a white youth to teach him to read.[97]

Such experiences must have produced outlooks, expectations, and political orientations different from those of the free mulatto class of Charleston. The latter group—and indeed, some of the families of the Reconstruction legislators—were themselves often the holders of slaves. While some probably were only the nominal owners of relatives whom they could not free because of the restrictive laws of the 1840's and 1850's, it is doubtful that the sizable holdings of others consisted only of relatives.[98] Indeed, some of the free mulatto slaveowners suffered heavy financial losses with the Union victory. A white abolitionist's anecdote about the cold rebuff he received from R. E. Dereef, a wealthy Charleston mulatto, upon expressing his jubilation at the outcome of the war indicates the relationship of many in this class to the old regime.[99]

Of course, most free mulatto legislators were not slaveowners, nor did they have vast financial interests in the old regime. Indeed, most of them were not members of the very top strata of wealthy, free Negro society; they were more likely derived from the upper middle group—well-to-do, but not wealthy. But a cultural distance between them and their slave-born colleagues did exist, and it is reflected in the patterns of religious affiliation among the legislators. Of the twenty affiliated with denominations that one might describe as "liturgical" (that is, Catholic, Presbyterian, Epis-

95. Account No. 2205, Charleston, S.C., Signature Depositor Cards of Freedman's Savings Bank, Records of Comptroller General, Record Group 101, National Archives Microfilm Publication M816, Roll 21.

96. William Henry Heard, *From Slavery to the Bishopric of the A.M.E. Church* (Philadelphia: A.M.E. Book Concern, 1924), p. 21.

97. *Ibid.,* p. 22.

98. The Law of 1841 effectively prohibited any further manumissions. A device resorted to in order to get around the law was trusteeship, whereby a person agreed to hold another in *nominal* ownership. Often the slave himself provided the purchase price with which the "trustee" bought him. See Wikramanayake, "The Free Negro," pp. 47-48.

99. Wikramanayake, "The Free Negro," p. 116.

copal), all but one was freeborn.[100] The slaves, on the other hand, tended overwhelmingly to adhere to the "pietistic" sects—that is, the Baptist, or one of the three Methodist denominations (Northern Methodist, African Methodist, or A.M.E. Zion). Of the fifty-three legislators identified as members of pietistic churches, 70 percent had been slaves.[101]

Some of the prejudices underlying these patterns of religious affiliation can be detected in the complaint of Thomas W. Cardozo, a brother of Francis L. Cardozo, to the A.M.A. headquarters in New York. Thomas Cardozo had been in charge of the A.M.A. school in Charleston for only a few months before he implored the Association to send a missionary to establish a church for himself and his staff. He explained that he could not worship in the Reverend Fulton's church because the congregation was segregated into special pews, but neither could he associate with the lower classes of the Negro churches.

> I cannot worship intelligently with the colored people, and, consequently, am at a loss every sabbath what to do. The more intelligent of the col. people are Episcopalians. They worship intelligently, but they have for the present, a known rebel for their Pastor. Rev. Mr. Adams [a black] is here, but he preaches for the class with whom I cannot worship for want of intelligence. If you would send a Minister to the Teachers, he would have an intelligent congregation of Teachers, their friends, their scholars, and a thriving Sabbath School. I hope you will consider this matter.[102]

Church affiliation was merely indicative of the larger pattern of social intercourse. The small free Negro community of Charleston was extremely inbred. Most free Negroes considered it demeaning to marry a slave, and one scholar has discovered that "rigid caste lines were followed rather closely in the selecting of one's mate. Color, economic and cultural status, and free ancestry played an important part in in-group relations." [103] There is evidence that the choice of marriage partners was often restricted to a small circle of the family's business partners, or fraternal society

100. Liturgical worship is defined as that practiced "according to prescribed ritual, as contrasted with 'free' (i.e., without fixed forms) worship." This is contrasted with pietistic worship, which is a term historically applied to the seventeenth-century German reaction against religion which was regarded as having become too formalized and intellectual. It became associated with John Wesley and Methodism in England and is characterized generally by an emphasis on personal religious experience and conversion. Alan Richardson, ed., *The Dictionary of Christian Theology* (Philadelphia: Westminister Press, 1969), pp. 197, 259.

101. Information on the legislators' religious affiliations is difficult to obtain. This sample constitutes only 28 percent of the 255 legislators but is fairly evenly divided with 38 ex-slaves and 34 freemen. Cf. Berlin, *Slaves Without Masters,* pp. 297-98.

102. Thomas W. Cardozo to S. Hunt, June 23, 1865, A.M.A. Papers.

103. Fitchett, "The Tradition of the Free Negro," pp. 146-48.

associates. The arrangements and betrothals were often extremely formal, with dowries provided for daughters and great care taken to protect the transmission of family property and slaves.

Fraternal organizations were another major institution used to protect class boundaries and to foster class interests. These groups flourished in free Negro communities both before and after the war, and a number of legislators were identified with them. Henry Cardozo, senator from Kershaw, had been a member of the Bonneau Society; Charles Wilder, state representative from Richland, was president of the Friendly Union Society, which was founded in 1852 for "mutual protection, burial, and charitable works." Robert C. DeLarge, William McKinlay, and Dr. Benjamin A. Bosemon were all members of the granddaddy of all such organizations, the Brown Fellowship Society.

The Brown Fellowship Society was founded on November 1, 1790, by a group of Charleston free mulattoes at the suggestion of their pastor, the Reverend Thomas Frost, rector of the St. Philip's Protestant Episcopal Church. Membership was limited to persons twenty-one years old and able to prove mulatto origins. With the motto "Charity and Benevolence," the organization declared that its purpose was to aid the widows and orphans or "our fellow creatures." [104] Its activities soon expanded to include the education of its children and the judicious investment of the dues and fines that it collected. In fact, it served its members as a bank, since they had access to its treasury for loans at 20 percent interest to cover personal expenses and business investments.[105]

But while the "foundation-stone" of the Society was "Charity and Benevolence," the "capstone," according to a twentieth-century descendant, was "Social Purity." The organization was an instrument for maintaining the boundaries of a largely independent and self-conscious class that saw itself threatened from above by "the dominant race" and from below by "the backward race." "The first looked with a scrutinizing eye on our every movement, so as to charge us with being a disturbing element in conditions that existed, and they made stringent legislative enactments, and the public sentiment of the masses was to discourage everything that our Society stood for. . . . " Their response to these threats—the one political and the other social—was to exploit the class divisions within white society to their advantage, for "fortunately there were the Classes in society and as our fathers allided themselves with them, and as a consequence, they had their influence and protection. . . . " Meanwhile, to the threat posed from below, they erected strict institutional barriers

104. G. H. Walker, "The Brown Fellowship Society," WPA transcript, South Carolina Historical Society, Charleston.

105. Wikramanayake, "The Free Negro," pp. 143-44.

and grew more and more socially isolated.[106]

While these responses preserved the integrity and promoted the prosperity of the free mulatto class, they also exacted a price. It was clear that, to enjoy the white ruling class's protection, mulattoes "had to be in accord with them and stand for what they stood for. If they stood for close fellowship, so did our Fathers. If they stood for high incentive, so did our Fathers; if they stood for prosperity, so did our Fathers; if they stood for education, so did our Fathers; if they stood for slavery, so did our Fathers, to a certain degree." The members of the Society helped with the defense of Charleston during the War of 1812. Individuals from the Society helped put out the fires set by Union artillery during the Civil War.[107] Their minutes showed that they had strictly observed a rule against the discussion of any political topic. In 1817 they expelled a member who was implicated in a slave conspiracy. The ruling class was so certain of their loyalty that they were exempted from the ordinance requiring the presence of a white man in any meeting of more than six Negroes.[108]

Their exclusion of blacks fostered destructive enmities and distortions in the Negro community, encouraging the free blacks to form their own society. This black society was short lived, but the Brown Society survived well into the twentieth century and reputedly remained true to its heritage throughout that span. A descendant declared that even postwar events did not alter their outlook, as "they still kept the compact close, feeling that the heritage of the Fathers was only dear to their children, and as we had three generations born since the organization, we could enjoy Social Equality among ourselves [meaning intermarriage with other mulattoes]." [109]

There were, necessarily, ambiguities in their outlook, imposed by their peculiar posture in society. They did sympathize with the oppressed, as indicated by a record of generosity in assisting slaves to purchase themselves or their families. And although the Civil War placed "their material prosperity . . . at stake, their sympathies were with the side that promised more liberties and larger opportunities." Indeed, some members' sons fought with the Union, and at least one died with Colonel Robert Gould Shaw in the famous charge of the 54th Massachusetts in the bloody battle at Fort Wagner.[110]

The development of a free mulatto class that stood as "a custodian of the system" was a phenomenon common to all major slave societies.

106. Walker, "Brown Fellowship Society."
107. *Ibid.*
108. Fitchett, "The Tradition of the Free Negro," p. 144.
109. Walker, "Brown Fellowship Society."
110. *Ibid.*

For instance, the Jamaican slave regime produced a class very similar in origins, occupational and financial status, and attitudes to that in South Carolina. The Jamaican free mulattoes also were descended from the small number of slaves manumitted by white fathers and half-brothers. Their manumissions also were sometimes accompanied by provisions for the economic security of the freedmen. They too developed a relatively wealthy, class-conscious group that was often closely affiliated with or supportive of the white ruling class. Sharp cleavages developed between free blacks and free mulattoes, and these were reflected in separate and distinctive social institutions and attempts to restrict intermarriage. In Jamaica, as in South Carolina, there is evidence that these cleavages continued into the post-emancipation period.[111]

But beyond these shared characteristics as to the origins and development of class consciousness within the two groups, there are striking differences in their political actions after emancipation. The Jamaican free Negroes had gained some political liberties before the slaves were emancipated, but the "browns" did not organize the black ex-slaves politically, as did their South Carolina counterparts. In fact, the ex-slaves remained largely apolitical, making their bid instead for economic independence in peasant villages in the hinterland.[112] Meanwhile, the freeborn mulattoes formed a coalition with urban whites in the coastal cities—the "Town" or "Colored" party—and gained considerable political power. But apparently the political distance between brown and black was greater than that between brown and white. Characterized by a "mild and conservative humanitarianism," their party was in those early years more frequently identified with the status quo than with radical reforms. Indeed, at crucial times they acted to restrict the potential political power of the black settlers. There were, of course, notable exceptions, such as George W. Gordon, the martyr of the Morant Bay Rebellion of 1865; but their exceptional behavior merely highlights the general rule.[113]

At least one Northern observer saw possibilities for a similar political scenario in South Carolina if the blacks and mulattoes had been more evenly divided.[114] After all, urban mulatto elements in and around Kingston and the coastal cities emerged as a major element in post-emancipation politics of Jamaica, and a similar pattern could be observed in South

111. Philip D. Curtin, *Two Jamaicas: The Role of Ideas in a Tropical Colony, 1830-65* (Cambridge: Harvard University Press, 1955), pp. 43-46; M. G. Smith, *The Plural Society in the British West Indies* (Berkeley: University of California Press, 1965), pp. 98-101.

112. See Hugh Paget, "The Free Village System in Jamaica," *Caribbean Quarterly,* X (March, 1964), 38-51.

113. Curtin, *Two Jamaicas,* pp. 182-90; Anton V. Long, *Jamaica and the New Order, 1827-47* (Mona: Institute of Social and Economic Research, University College of the West Indies, Jamaica, B.W.I., Special Series No. 1, November, 1956), p. 16.

114. De Forest, *A Union Officer,* pp. 125-26.

Carolina.[115] But while the state displayed intraracial tensions and stresses similar to those in Jamaica, the political patterns that developed were radically different. The Charleston bourgeoisie took the lead in organizing "country" blacks into an effective political party. And although some of the former did propose measures during the 1868 convention that would have restrained the political power of the masses, comparatively considered, they acted to benefit the black working class, both politically and economically.[116]

The crucial difference may well have been demographic. In Jamaica the brown class was much smaller than the black settler class, but browns still outnumbered whites. In South Carolina they were far outnumbered by both whites and blacks.[117] In Jamaica, therefore, the browns could be a decisive political force in their own right without the aid of the blacks, but in South Carolina a politically mobilized black constituency was essential to the advancement of the brown bourgeoisie. Thus one might speculate that the political conservatism of this element of the South Carolina group was restrained by their dependence on a mainly black, slave-born constituency.

Consequently, the freeborn mulatto, bourgeois legislators by and large reached across the "chasm" to embrace—sometimes belatedly and haltingly, often with vacillation and quibbling at crucial moments—the political and economic agenda of the black peasantry. That agenda called for the acquisition of the land they had tilled and developed and learned to think of as their own. As with peasants everywhere, control of the land was an issue they could understand and mobilize around. For this issue they would fight, with either the ballot or the gun.

"The sole ambition of the freedman," reported a representative of New England capitalists, "appears to be to become the owner of a little piece of land, there to erect an humble home, and to dwell in peace and security at his own free will and pleasure. . . ." [118] Governor Orr be-

115. Curtin, *Two Jamaicas,* pp. 181-84. See also Charles H. Wesley, "The Emancipation of Free Colored Population in the British Empire," *Journal of Negro History,* XIX (January, 1934), 137-70.

116. See the sixth chapter for discussion of moves to restrict suffrage through education and poll tax requirements.

117. Jamaica had about 310,000 slaves and 35,000 free coloreds, approximately 5,000 free blacks and 17,000 whites on the eve of emancipation in 1834. South Carolina had 402,406 slaves, 9,914 free Negroes and 291,300 whites in 1860. Douglass Hall, "Jamaica," in *Neither Slave Nor Free: The Freedman of African Descent in the Slave Societies of the New World,* ed. David W. Cohen and Jack P. Greene (Baltimore: Johns Hopkins University Press, 1972), p. 194; *Population of the United States in 1860* (Washington: Government Printing Office, 1864), pp. 598-605.

118. Letter from "A" to Editor, Orangeburg, S.C., September 8, 1865, *The Nation,* I (September 28, 1865), 393.

sieged the Union authorities with requests to investigate groups of freed-men who organized military units and drilled them "as they say preparing to fight for land." General Canby's agent reported on one such group of three hundred men, organized and commanded by a captain and a lieutenant who were themselves ex-slaves, in Abbeville County. A few of them had in their possession "different kinds of guns—first such as they were able to pick up—some shotguns—old muskets or army guns. . . ." They had organized in September, 1867, and met bi-weekly. The guns had been bought, they said, because of threats by whites. The investigator also found that many of their grievances were justified, and that the magistrates of the area were unwilling to investigate many "well founded complaints" of the blacks against white men. "Unhappily, there are still a great many persons in this State, who are unable or unwilling to learn," Canby lectured the governor, "who still expect from the freed-man the subordination of the slave and resent as Negro insolence what in the white man they would regard as the natural and proper assertion of a right." [119] Evidently many freedmen agreed with Canby, for through-out the Sea Islands they organized and armed themselves to resist the restoration of their land to the white planter, even when resistance put them musket to musket against Union troops.[120]

These were the people that the Charleston bourgeoisie sought to lead. It is very probable that some legislators were shaped and led by their constituents as much as they, in turn, shaped public policy for the people. After all, one must allow for the possibility that men are more than the sum of their experiences. They can possess a broader outlook than that which the circumstances of their birth, class, and religion might indicate. The growth of the human personality is not frozen in puberty, or even young adulthood.[121] To argue otherwise is to impose an incredibly

119. Edward Canby to James L. Orr, November 25, 1867, Governor James Orr Papers, South Carolina Archives, Columbia.

120. Williamson, *After Slavery*, pp. 82, 93.

121. Much of the historical writing that has attempted to make use of psychological concepts has been based on Freudian psychology, which has led inevitably to an overem-phasis on early childhood and adolescent experiences as determinants of the personality. Erik Erikson has attempted to rectify this tendency to view childhood as the beginning and end of personality development. He argues that personality development continues throughout the whole life cycle and has described eight stages during which an individual establishes new and basic orientations between himself and his social world, and in each of these "a new dimension of 'social interaction' becomes possible." Consequently, adult behavioral traits can be treated as products of the adult experience and not as "mere residuals of infantile frustrations and conflicts." David Elkind, "Erik Erikson's Eight Ages of Man," *New York Times Magazine,* April 5, 1970, pp. 25-27, 84ff. See also Erik Erikson, *Identity, Youth and Crisis* (New York: W. W. Norton, 1968), pp. 91-141.

narrow scope on man's maturation and growth, to deny the complexity of human motivation.

These antebellum experiences of the Negro legislators must be taken only as benchmarks for locating the beginning of their development. The Civil War, the early postwar developments in Bureau schoolhouses, and missionary services clearly had an impact on fertile and active minds. There is much truth to the oft-heard contemporary assertion that these men were "newborn" in 1865. Most of the legislators were under forty when the war ended; the freeborn group was even younger, with a median age of only thirty, as compared with thirty-four for the slave-born. Most of them had grown up under slavery's shadow, but not fully matured under it. It was not they, but their fathers, who had tried to earn a living, keep together a family, and protect their manhood under the always uncertain, often oppressive conditions of a slave society.

These children of the old Charleston Negro establishment took leading roles in the efforts to rehabilitate and minister to the freedmen immediately after the war. They filled out the ranks of the teacher corps sent by the northern missionary societies and the Freedmen's Bureau. The list of teachers hired by the A.M.A., for instance, reads like a list of Charleston's leading Negro families: Margaret Sasportas, sister of Thaddeus K. Sasportas; Richard L. Holloway, son of a leading official in the Brown Fellowship Society; Amelia Shrewsbury, sister of State Representative Henry L. Shrewsbury; Mary Weston, daughter of Jacob Weston, a well-to-do mulatto, who taught in one of the secret schools maintained in prewar days; Frances Rollins of the socially prominent Rollins sisters, a women's rights advocate, biographer of Martin R. Delany, and the bride of State Representative William James Whipper.[122] No doubt the motivation of these young men and women was at least partly pecuniary, but they were also inspired by the high ideals and concepts of an age of social reform. Some had been educated abroad or in northern centers of abolitionist thought. Most probably would second the sentiment of Martha Gordon, who said her only desire was "to do good amongst my fellow creatures." [123] They were the backbone of groups like the Ladies Patriotic Society, which sponsored fairs and benefits for the poor throughout the summer and fall of 1865.[124]

The young men generally joined the Freedmen's Bureau or northern missionary societies and spread educational and other social service activi-

122. Thomas W. Cardozo to M. E. Strieby, June 16, 1865, A.M.A. Papers. For a discussion of the socially prominent Rollins sisters, see Lerone Bennett, Jr., *Black Power U.S.A.: The Human Side of Reconstruction, 1867-77* (Baltimore: Penguin Books, 1969), pp. 347-52.

123. Martha Gordon to S. Hunt, October 6, 1865, A.M.A. Papers.

124. *Daily Courier,* July 4, 1865.

ties into the hinterland. Thaddeus K. Sasportas was born into a well-to-do slave-holding Charleston family, but was educated in abolitionist Philadelphia. Returning home with a unit of U.S. colored troops, he convinced William J. McKinlay to accompany him to Orangeburg as a Bureau teacher.[125] Meanwhile, Henry L. Shrewsbury went up to Chesterfield to establish a school. Generally these men settled, at least temporarily, in the communities where they worked and were returned to Charleston in 1868 as representatives to the constitutional convention.

The old regime had imposed upon free brown men a basically distorted relationship with society and their black brothers, but it had also necessitated a kind of discipline and encouraged an aggressiveness which led them to seize a disproportionate share of the leadership positions and the civil service patronage of the Reconstruction government, at least in its initial stage. It had shaped their basic social orientation, their fundamental conservatism. But newborn institutions and forces—indeed, very sinister forces to some—would foster new values and orientations suitable for the times and for the new roles they would play.

125. Bryant, *Negro Senators and Representatives,* pp. 60-62.

Chapter Four

The Sword and the Cross:
Modes of Leadership Recruitment
and Development

Most Reconstruction legislators in South Carolina—white as well as black—were political novices when they first arrived in Columbia. Democrats who had held state office before and during the war shunned any association with the new regime and left the field largely to less experienced men. The northern white Republicans were former army officers, teachers, and missionaries. In one sense or another they were men on the make and, as such, not likely to have left successful political offices in the North for an uncertain competition in the war-torn South. And of course the Negroes had had little opportunity to gain experience in partisan politics, irrespective of status, color, or nativity. In most northern states they had not been able to vote, much less run for office. They more than either of the other two groups would have to be recruited and learn the art of politics, either on the job or under the auspices of non-political institutions.

The opportunity to learn on the job was terribly abbreviated for most Negro legislators, because their tenures were short even by Reconstruction standards. It was possible to serve four full terms in the House during Reconstruction, but 61 percent of the 212 Negroes were one-term members. Only ten men served three terms or more, and of these only two, William M. Thomas of Colleton and Joseph D. Boston of Newberry, served for the entire period. Since but fifteen of these House members moved up to higher positions at the federal or state level, many must simply have failed to gain renomination or reelection. Of course, some may have chosen to take more financially rewarding local appointments. But while the brevity of their service may not be a comment on their capacities, it certainly indicates that for most of the period the House was composed of large numbers of freshmen legislators, unfamiliar with its routines and uncertain of their jobs.

Some House members undoubtedly availed themselves of an introduction to partisan politics through service in county and city offices before their election at the state level. Furthermore, it was not unusual for ordinary employees of the General Assembly—reading clerks, sergeants-at-arms, etc.—to show up later as members of the legislature. For example, Benjamin Byas, Florian Henry Frost, and William A. Hayne were all employees of the state legislature before becoming members. But all of the legislative posts and most of the local offices were appointive, rather than elective; thus, an important aspect of a potential member's political education was neglected.

Such preliminary experiences were not possible at all for Negroes elected to the 1868 Constitutional Convention and the 1868-70 General Assembly. For them the Freedmen's Bureau, the army, and the missionary societies and churches were important factors in their personal and political development. Out of the total group of Negro elected officials serving between 1868 and 1876, at least seventy-three individuals, more than one-fourth, were affiliated with one or more of these institutions. Eighteen of these men served as state senators, congressmen, or executive officers. Furthermore, these organizations had greater impact on the group which served during the early years of Reconstruction than on those serving later in the decade. Of the early convention delegates and legislators, forty-three individuals—more than 37 percent of all Negroes who served in those years—gained their formative experiences through one or more of these institutions.

The churches, missionary societies, army, and Freedmen's Bureau did not set out purposefully to recruit blacks into politics or to prepare them for political leadership. But most northern leaders, white or black, came to South Carolina because of their employment in one or the other of these organizations and gained their earliest experiences and contact with the freedmen through this employment. Although their experiences were diverse, a common factor appears to have been the opportunity such employment allowed for the growth of an ethic of public service and the development of a system of public contacts which could later form a basis for a political constituency. The role of these institutions in the recruitment and development of the Negro leadership was more accidental than deliberate and generally passive rather than active. Indeed, in some cases institutional policies and orientations prevented Negro operatives from fully utilizing the political potential of their clients. Finally, it was in these organizations that the whites and Negroes who would form and lead the Republican party had their first and perhaps their most intimate professional interaction. Significantly, this interaction often resulted in conflicts, mutual hostilities, and suspicions which resemble those that developed in subsequent years.

The Freedmen's Bureau provides one example of the limitations, as well as the potential, of such institutional affiliations. Only fifteen of the Negro legislators were connected with the Bureau, either as agents or as teachers, but several of these men held major offices during Reconstruction. Congressman Robert C. De Large and state senators Stephen A. Swails, Henry E. Hayne, Charles Hayne, Henry J. Maxwell, Samuel E. Gaillard, and Benjamin F. Randolph all gained their initial experience in public service with the Bureau.[1] Employment there was not an unmixed blessing, however, because of the anti-black, pro-planter biases and policies of many Bureau operatives. Always inadequately financed and understaffed, it had to rely on the active and reserve military service for the bulk of its employees.[2] To many of these men this was simply another patronage job to which they were attracted for strictly pecuniary reasons. Not only were many of them not moved by abolitionist sentiments, but some were described as being "more pro-slavery than the rebels themselves. Doing justice seems to mean, to them, seeing that the blacks don't break a contract and compelling them to submit cheerfully if the whites do," complained one northern teacher.[3] And while one scholar has found that most Bureau agents in South Carolina were fair and conscientious, his and other evidence indicates that the Bureau's posture was in most instances clearly nonpolitical.[4]

This nonpolitical posture of the agency did not, of course, deter individual employees from using their positions to curry favor with a potential electorate. Yet only one black agent, Major Martin R. Delany, appears to have had either long enough service or broad enough authority to make effective use of his position. Delany was transferred to the Bureau services from his post as the first black commissioned officer of field grade in the 104th U.S. Colored Troop; though classified as a surgeon, he had worked mainly at recruiting Negro regiments. He served with the South Carolina Freedmen's Bureau from its inception in 1865 to its virtual termination in the summer of 1868. His position as a black abolitionist leader of international reputation probably provided him the security

1. Other legislators who worked for the Bureau at some time were James N. Hayne, W. N. Joiner, Landon S. Langley, Thaddeus K. Sasportas, Calvin T. Stubbs, Florian Henry Frost, William A. Hayne, and Henry L. Shrewsbury.

2. There were "several counties of the state in which, a full year after the Bureau had begun to operate, the freedmen had never seen or felt its presence." Martin Abbott, *The Freedmen's Bureau in South Carolina, 1865-72* (Chapel Hill: University of North Carolina Press, 1967), pp. 20, 21-23.

3. Laura Towne, *Letters and Diary of Laura M. Towne, Written from the Sea Islands of South Carolina, 1862-84*, ed. Rupert Sargent Holland (Cambridge: Riverside Press, 1912), p. 171. Cf. William S. McFeely, *Yankee Stepfather: General O. O. Howard and the Freedmen* (New Haven: Yale University Press, 1968), pp. 157-59.

4. Abbott, *The Freedmen's Bureau*, pp. 32-35.

with which to go beyond the mandate of the bureaucracy and to be pretty much self-directed in his duties and goals. Delany was openly political in his activities, speeches, and advice to the freedmen. He developed labor agreements between freedmen and the planters which were broader in scope than those recommended by the Bureau. For a time he succeeded in establishing an independent cotton press which allowed black tenants an alternative market to the one manipulated by the Charleston cotton factors. All of these activities brought a storm of protests from planters, military authorities, and other Bureau personnel, all of which Delany survived and to some extent overcame. Yet Delany, the most effective black Bureau agent, was one of the few who never held elective office. He ran for lieutenant governor in 1874 on a fusion ticket with a former Confederate but lost badly, and he held a few minor appointive offices in Charleston County. But though he was a ubiquitous figure at Republican rallies and always an effective speaker, he was never an elected delegate to any of these rallies or conventions.[5]

It is very doubtful that any other black Bureau agent could have operated as independently or effectively as Delany. Most were young and inexperienced men with no effective political contacts on either the local or the national level. Their activities were probably restricted by directives like the one received by Benjamin F. Randolph at the beginning of his brief service with the Bureau. He was instructed to visit the plantations in the parishes of St. Thomas, Christ Church, and St. James Santee and "induce the Freed people on the Plantations to labor faithfully, exhort them to be prompt and diligent in the discharge of their duties. . . ."[6] Being instructed to "induce" and "exhort" the freedmen, Randolph may well have felt like the Bureau's overseer—an impression which the following instruction no doubt confirmed: "Whenever you find people who are idle and have not contracted for the present year you will advise them that they must at once enter into contracts and thus become self supporting and say that they will not receive any assistance from Government but must depend entirely upon their own exertions for support."[7]

Randolph was cautioned that his role was "merely advisory." Thus

5. "I shall not be in the Convention, as I never have been in one as a delegate, but I have always had an outside influence among the people, which was effective in many measures of policy before the conventions." Martin R. Delany to Daniel H. Chamberlain, September 1, 1876, Governor Chamberlain Papers, South Carolina Archives, Columbia. See also Victor Ullman, *Martin R. Delany: The Beginnings of Black Nationalism* (Boston: Beacon Press, 1971), p. 369.

6. Edward D. Deane to Benjamin F. Randolph, February 28, 1867, Letters Sent, Bureau of Refugees, Freedmen, and Abandoned Lands, Record Group 105, NA.

7. *Ibid.*

he was given responsibility without authority; he could offer advice, but little else. As further illustration of his role, he was told to *advise* the freedmen to establish schools by subscription among themselves, and that after they had secured the land, the buildings, and the teacher, their bountiful government would give them textbooks.[8] Whatever the political posture of the Bureau, a job like this was not calculated to win friends or influence votes. But it probably did not matter, since Randolph, like most of the civilian agents, was only employed for a few months.[9] Most were not presented with the opportunity of Stephen A. Swails, who was hired to distribute rations in his district during the canvass for the 1868 elections, in which he was a candidate.[10] Indeed, like Randolph, many agents probably worked in areas entirely different from the ones from which they were eventually elected to office.

Most potential black legislators probably found that their brief Bureau employment subserved ends less blatantly political than Swails's timely appointment. At least five black agents came to the Bureau after a stint of military service, and only one of them was a native of South Carolina. Therefore, a latent function of the Bureau was to stabilize the northern settlers by providing transitory employment and, perhaps, to orient these settlers toward the public service sector for a career.[11] In spite of their dubious merit, the wide range of public contacts made by a Bureau agent could provide a basis for political canvassing later on.

Actually, the army may have been a more important contributor to the leadership pool than the Bureau. Twenty-four of the Negro legislators had records of military service, and two-thirds of them were either officers (2) or noncommissioned officers (12).[12] Some of the state's top political leaders in future years—William James Whipper, Benjamin A. Bosemon,

8. *Ibid.*

9. Randolph's appointment as an agent made in February was revoked by September, Edward L. Deane to Benjamin F. Randolph, September 9, 1867, BRFAL.

10. Letter to Stephen A. Swails, July 18, 1868, BRFAL.

11. I observed a similar latent effect as a field representative for the Office of Economic Opportunity in the mid-1960's in Mississippi and Alabama, where, regardless of the effects of the funded programs on poverty, they did stabilize a talented leadership in the rural South which ordinarily would have migrated to the cities, or possibly out of the South.

12. The officers were Stephen A. Swails, a first lieutenant, and Robert Smalls, a pilot in the navy. Benjamin A. Bosemon was an acting assistant surgeon, and Benjamin F. Randolph was a chaplain. The legislators who were noncommissioned officers were Martin Becker, Edward J. Cain, William H. W. Gray, Henry E. Hayne, Richard H. Humbert, William R. Jervay, Landon S. Langley, Henry J. Maxwell, Prince Rivers, William Viney, William James Whipper, and James C. Wilson. Other legislators with military service were Shadrack Morgan, William C. Morrison, Thaddeus K. Sasportas, Aaron Simmons, and Samuel B. Thompson. Lawrence Cain and George Lee have also been identified as veterans, but no military service record was found for either.

Stephen A. Swails—were northern-born Negroes brought to the state by the army. Recognizing that the hopes for the future of black people were more sanguine in the South than in the North, they generally settled in or returned to the state in which they had served shortly after being mustered out. The native ex-soldiers gained other advantages from their military experiences. Some received their first formal education while in the army; others received an education in human relationships that was less formal but perhaps just as important to their personal and political development.

The wartime service of some of these men had been action-filled and heroic. Robert Smalls's exploit in abducting the Confederate steamer *Planter* was clearly the most daring of all, and it became the central part of his repertoire on the stump in later years. His audiences never seemed to tire of hearing how he conspired with his fellow slaves to stow away their families and boldly bluff their way past the Confederate batteries in Charleston harbor and into Union lines in 1862. Nor did Smalls tire of telling it.[13] One cannot determine exactly how much this image of daring and shrewdness contributed to his more than two decades of practically unchallenged political supremacy in Beaufort County, but it surely endeared him to many voters and almost deified him with others. An oft-told anecdote shows that image and charisma were just as important to nineteenth-century black politicians, as they are to contemporary aspirants. According to the anecdote, two of Smalls's Beaufort supporters were debating his merits. "I tell you, Smalls is the greatest man in the world," one of the men insisted. "Yes, he is great, but not the greatest," observed the second. "Pshaw man, who's greater than Smalls?" demanded the first. "Why, Jesus Christ," was the reply. "Oh, Smalls is young yet," the first retorted.[14]

Other ex-soldiers could relate military exploits of daring and courage, too; some, like Stephen A. Swails, W. H. Thomas, and William H. W. Gray, had wounds to prove the stories. Sergeant Stephen A. Swails was cited by his commanding officer, Colonel Norwood P. Hallowell, for "coolness, bravery, and efficiency" under fire, despite a severe wound during the bloody battle at Olustee. In this town fifty miles west of Jacksonville, Florida, three Negro and six white regiments were defeated by a superior Confederate force. The total Union casualties were 1,861; Swails's regiment, the 54th Massachusetts, lost 86 men.[15] Swails was

13. Okon Edet Uya, *From Slavery to Public Service: Robert Smalls, 1839-1915* (New York: Oxford University Press, 1971), pp. 11-14.

14. Carter G. Woodson, "Robert Smalls and His Descendants," *Negro History Bulletin* (November, 1947), quoted in Uya, *Robert Smalls*, p. 23.

15. Dudley Taylor Cornish, *The Sable Arm: Negro Troops in the Union Army, 1861-65* (New York: W. W. Norton, 1966), p. 268.

wounded on February 20, 1864, and less than a month later he was commissioned second lieutenant by Governor John Andrews of Massachusetts. However, the War Department delayed the official mustering of Swails as an officer for ten months; only after a personal appeal by Governor Andrews to Secretary of War Stanton was the commission allowed to take effect. A few months later Swails was promoted to first lieutenant.[16] Other political leaders also carried scars of battle. W. H. Thomas, an Independent Republican candidate from Charleston in the 1874 election, lost an arm in the war.[17] Sergeant William H. W. Gray, a legislator representing Charleston County in 1868-70, served under the martyred Colonel Robert Gould Shaw and was wounded in the left leg in the famous charge on Fort Wagner.[18]

But for most legislators military experience had bestowed benefits other than the glory of battle and the red badge of courage. The army had given many of the ex-slaves their first opportunity to command other men, in addition to bestowing the respect and confidence that might accrue to such positions. Sergeant Richard H. Humbert sought to apply his expertise for direct political advantage during the postwar years. After his election to the lower house in the summer of 1868, Humbert wrote to the newly inaugurated Governor Robert K. Scott to inform him that he had organized two militia companies in Darlington County, and that he planned to form several others in preparation for the presidential elections that fall. He saw his previous military experience as essential to this enterprise and requested a commission from the governor. Humbert did not mince words when he stated that "the organization of the militia will be of great benefit to the Republican Party in this district."[19]

Sergeant Humbert was also one of the several legislators who took advantage of the special literacy classes established for black soldiers and noncommissioned officers. A few others received an education which was less formal, but still more crucial. When Prince Rivers made his way from his owner's refuge in Edgefield to enlist in the First South Carolina Volunteers, for instance, he began a much more significant psychological journey toward the enhancement of his self-regard and the broadening of the narrow, provincial world of his youth. Rivers was made first sergeant of the regiment and taken to New York by General David Hunter in an attempt to gain support for his policy of enlisting black troops. There was considerable antiwar and antiblack feeling in New York City, which

16. *Ibid.*, p. 215. Compiled Military Service Record, Stephen Swails, 1st Sgt., Co. FD, 54 Mass. Inf. (Col'd), RG 94, NA.

17. *News and Courier,* October 8, 1874.

18. Compiled Military Service Record, William H. W. Gray, 1st Sgt., Co. C, 54 Mass. Inf. (Col'd), RG 94, NA.

19. Richard H. Humbert to Robert K. Scott, July 18, 1868, Scott Papers.

would be the scene of the bloody draft riots in 1863. White New Yorkers were incensed at the sergeant's chevrons on the arm of the tall, proud, "jet black" ex-slave; as he walked down Broadway, they attacked him viciously. However, Rivers managed to hold off the mob until police arrived to escort him away.[20]

Robert Smalls had a somewhat similar experience with northern racism when he took his ship to Philadelphia for repairs. During this sojourn Smalls came in contact with veteran black and white abolitionists and was active as a speaker before freedmen's relief societies. He became involved in that city's controversy over segregated public accommodations when he refused to surrender his seat on the streetcar to a white rider and move to the open platform reserved for blacks. Philadelphia abolitionists made very effective use of such insults to Smalls and other black veterans in their struggle to end discrimination in public transportation in Pennsylvania.[21]

It is not likely that black veterans had any illusions about the country's racial climate, or its attitude toward black soldiers. Their experiences in the North and South were quite similar in this regard. For instance, Sergeant William Viney, an Ohioan and member of the constitutional convention in 1868, had been wounded in one of the closing campaigns of the war in the South Carolina low country. He too became embroiled in a public accommodations controversy when he was refused a seat on a first-class car in Charleston in July, 1865.[22]

After such experiences it is doubtful that these future legislators would entertain any naive ideas about racial attitudes in the North, and the subtleties and vagaries of northern political support; nor would they underestimate the obstacles to racial change in the South. Such experiences must have given new insights and a more sophisticated worldview to these ex-bondsmen. In addition to the personal growth that military experience could provide, there were also public contacts developed that might have potential political uses. Many black noncommissioned officers were detached at one time or another and assigned to recruit other black soldiers. Delany, Smalls, Rivers, Bosemon, and Viney all served as recruiters. Of course, there were possible negative results, too, from the authority, responsibility, and contacts of the black officers. For instance,

20. Thomas Wentworth Higginson, *Army Life in a Black Regiment* (Boston: Fields, Osgood, 1870), p. 57.

21. Uya, *Robert Smalls,* pp. 26-27. A law was passed in 1867 outlawing discrimination in every form of public transportation. For a general discussion of the Philadelphia desegregation fight, see James M. McPherson, *The Struggle for Equality: Abolitionists and the Negro in the Civil War and Reconstruction* (Princeton: Princeton University Press, 1964), pp. 233-36.

22. Brunto P. Wilde to Captain L. B. Perry, July 23, 1865, William Viney, Pension File Certificate No. XC 2564446, Civil War, RG 15, NA.

Prince Rivers was allegedly disliked by his men for his overbearing, tin-soldier demeanor. He undoubtedly created a fair number of enemies in the black community when as provost marshal he doggedly and unmercifully hunted down all black deserters. This may have been one reason why he served as the state representative from Edgefield County rather than from Beaufort, where he was born and reared and completed his military service.[23]

The activities of the army and later the Freedmen's Bureau were followed closely by the northern missionary societies and churches, all of which had a significant impact on black legislators. Early in the spring of 1865 the Reverend Mansfield French described the relationship aptly: "The sword has hewn a way for the cross."[24] Parson French was pointing exultantly to the great field for missionary activities opened up by the advancing Union armies. Even as he wrote, every major denomination worth its evangelical salt had workers in the field, to use their favorite metaphor, "harvesting the crop." French's denomination, the Northern Methodists, had been especially favored in securing the special passes and transportation that admitted them into the war zones; they followed, literally, in the track of the Union Army.[25]

The onslaught of workers, funds, and lobbying of northern religious groups did much to shape the national and local politics of the postwar period, and their missionary zeal infused the public conscience with a special kind of urgency. White southern natives reviled these meddling missionaries for corrupting the gospel for their own political and social ends; and indeed, such charges have become axiomatic in the historical literature. Ample evidence of political activism on the part of some religious leaders substantiates many of these charges. On the other hand, it should be noted that many of the alleged connections between political constituencies and religious denominations go largely unsubstantiated, or are grounded on fallacious statistical inferences.[26]

Although the connection between religion and politicization of the black

23. For a description of Rivers's efficiency in recapturing deserters, see Higginson, *Black Regiment*, pp. 56-57. See also Rivers Pension File; and Julian L. Mims, "Radical Reconstruction in Edgefield County, 1868-77" (M.A. thesis, University of South Carolina, 1969), p. 27.

24. M. French to M. E. Strieby, April 24, 1865, American Missionary Association Archives, Amistad Research Center, New Orleans.

25. See Ralph E. Morrow, *Northern Methodism and Reconstruction* (East Lansing: Michigan State University Press, 1956), pp. 34-36.

26. For example, Joel Williamson asserts that the Northern Methodists were the strongest political force among the Negro voters in South Carolina, basing this in part on the fact that areas of high Methodist conversion were also areas of greatest Republican registration. This relationship is not really so obvious, however, for there is no way to establish a causal link between the voting or registration patterns of the black electorate and its religious preferences based solely on the aggregate figures of total black registration and total black Methodist conversion. Indeed, since the aggregate black population and voting percentage

electorate remains problematic, the role of the northern missionary societies in the recruitment of black political leadership is less so. Lawyers make up the bulk of most American deliberative assemblies, but in South Carolina ministers and teachers constituted a significant proportion of the 194 Negro legislators whose postwar occupations can be determined. Of the total black delegation, 42 were ministers and 29 were teachers, most of whom had missionary affiliation and support.[27] Of the ministers, 12 were affiliated with the Methodist Church, North; at least nine, possibly 11, were with the African Methodist Episcopal Church; six with the Baptist; two with the Presbyterian; and one with the Congregational church. Yet their particular institutional affiliation appears to have been less important to the political development of these men than the nature of the experience itself. Missionary and church experience apparently encouraged Negro leaders to commit themselves to public service, provided them with the opportunity to develop their leadership abilities, and opened a wide range of public contacts on which a future political constituency could be built.

The most influential and best financed northern society in South Carolina was the American Missionary Association, which had been established in 1846 as an antislavery organization. Many of the black leaders were either employed by it, supported by it, or in some way affected by it during the early postwar period. Francis L. Cardozo, Benjamin F. Randolph, and Jonathan J. Wright were among the more prominent officeholders initially supported by the A.M.A.[28]

A typical agreement that the A.M.A. made with missionaries was that with Hezekiah H. Hunter, a black Presbyterian minister from Brooklyn who represented Charleston County in the House of Representatives in 1870-72. Hunter had arranged for the Association to send him South and support his teaching and missionary activities for six months, or until he was settled and presumably could sustain himself. Hunter claims to have left a secure pastorship for which he received $1,000 per year

in the lowland areas to which Williamson has reference were overwhelming, the apparent correlation could be specious. In other words, the greater the black population, the greater the voter turnout *and* the greater the Methodist conversion; therefore, conversion and voting are both related to population, but not necessarily to each other. Cf. Joel Williamson, *After Slavery: The Negro in South Carolina During Reconstruction, 1861-77* (Chapel Hill: University of North Carolina Press, 1965), p. 368.

27. These categories are not mutually exclusive since one of the ministers, Francis L. Cardozo, was also a teacher. It should also be noted that teaching was not usually a sole occupation among the legislators.

28. Other legislators who were supported in whole or in part by the A.M.A. were Isaac Brockenton, a delegate to the constitutional convention from Darlington County, and Hezekiah H. Hunter, a state representative from Charleston County.

to take the $40 per month plus rations that the A.M.A. offered for him and his wife.[29] Jonathan J. Wright came less well endowed. He left Pennsylvania in April, 1865, with $94 and "good" clothes, Wright says, but by February he was left with only $10 and his clothes "not so good." Being trained in the law, Wright supported himself by counseling the freedmen, for which he generally received "a chicken, sometimes a peck of potatoes, etc."[30]

Other Negro legislators were members of a large group of ministers affiliated with or supported by various religious denominations; some of them had been sent from the North to work among the freedmen. While most of these missionaries were primarily interested in converting the freedmen to their particular version of Christian faith, their day-to-day labors were as much secular as spiritual. Some of the ministers, like Cardozo and Hunter, were also teachers; other missionaries, like Wright, were not ministers at all but were hired exclusively to teach.

Jonathan J. Wright's experience illustrates the rather catholic approach that some teachers and ministers took to their work. Their conception of a missionary's duties included many decidedly secular activities, and the role of the teacher was also expanded far beyond teaching the three R's. Wright was assigned to teach the 128th U. S. Colored Troop. One group of men was marched to his large tent at 9:00 A.M. and had class until 10:00. They returned at 1:00 P.M. and had class until 3:00. But the teacher's day did not end here.

> My work here is general. I have three hours each day to each in my regiment, the rest of the day is spent among the people teaching them, how to do business, and sustain themselves. Three evenings of the week are spent teaching a class of adults at my room. Thursday evenings I lecture at the AME Church. I am well paid for it all for I feel elevated every day. Yesterday I addressed about five thousand people including two regiments of soldiers. . . .[31]

The material for Wright's regular class consisted of reading, writing, arithmetic, and geography, but the evening classes touched on more topical subject matter, such as "You are no longer slaves, but freemen, show it to be so," "Arise and shine for your light has come," or "Avoid the great *evil*—intemperance."[32] Not resting on the seventh day, Wright taught a Sunday School which had grown tremendously under his tutelage. He kept an office for counseling the freedmen in their legal rights, especially in labor relations, and expected this work to bear fruit. "There has been

29. Hezekiah H. Hunter to A.M.A., August 21, 1865; Hezekiah H. Hunter to George Whipple, November 23, 1865, A.M.A. Papers.
30. Jonathan J. Wright to S. Hunt, February 5, 1866, *ibid.*
31. Jonathan J. Wright to S. Hunt, January 2, 1866, *ibid.*
32. Jonathan J. Wright to M. E. Strieby, July 27, 1865, *ibid.*

great advantage taken of them this year by men who have employed them to work cotton, but I think [in] another year they will know better how to make contracts."[33] Wright's work was not unique. Other missionaries and teachers worked to establish debating societies, lecture forums, and other activities designed, as one put it,"to inspire *goaheaditiveness* and self-reliance" among the freedmen.[34]

To most northern Negroes, missionary work was difficult but inspiring. Some felt that their talents and skills could be better utilized in the South, and that they were needed here more than in the North. Cardozo was convinced that the moral education of southern youth was more important than an exclusively ministerial career. "If I can influence and shape the future life of a great number, if I can cause them to love and serve Christ, I could not aspire to a nobler work," he explained to George Whipple. "There are so many of these boys and girls that are just at that age when their whole future may be determined." [35] This was surely a new and unaccustomed role for these black men, to be movers and shapers of their people's future. Cardozo had come to New Haven from England in 1864 after spending seven years training for the ministry, but his primary ambition was to teach in a normal school. After pastoring a church in New Haven from 1864 to 1865, he offered his services to the A.M.A. in June, 1865. From the outset, he told Whipple, the prospect of eventually founding such a school was his reason for coming South. "It is the object for which I left all the superior advantages and privileges of the North and came South, it is the object for which I am willing to *remain* here and make this place my home." [36]

Other northern Negroes felt like the Reverend Hezekiah H. Hunter, who saw that the future of the southern freedman was his future, too: they would "*rise* or fall" together.[37] Like Wright, northern Negro missionaries were dedicated to working for their fellow blacks because "until we are elevated as a mass let us be ever so worthy and elevated individually we will meet with these oppositions and be crushed down." [38]

There is little evidence that any of the Negro missionaries had chosen this career as a purely political instrumentality. Nevertheless, it is evident that their normal daily activities—widespread contacts with freedmen, counseling them, advocacy in their behalf, the attempt to uplift them

33. *Ibid.*

34. B. F. Whittemore to George Whipple, September 24, 1866, February 25, 1867, *ibid.*

35. Francis L. Cardozo to George Whipple, October 21, 1865, *ibid.*

36. Francis L. Cardozo to M. E. Strieby, August 13, 1866, *ibid.* See also David Macrae, *Americans at Home: Pen-and-Ink Sketches of American Men, Manners, and Institutions* (Glasgow: J. S. Marr & Sons, 1875), p. 211.

37. Hezekiah H. Hunter to A.M.A., August 21, 1865, A.M.A. Papers.

38. Jonathan J. Wright to S. Hunt[er], September 23, 1865, *ibid.*

materially as well as spiritually—bestowed some political advantages. Such activities were clearly adaptable to political canvassing and organizing later on. Indeed, the allegiance that the church commanded might itself prove to be politically powerful on occasion. Negro Methodists in the Summerville area prevailed successfully on Governor Franklin Moses to remove a white county treasurer and appoint in his stead F. C. Sasportas, one of their own ministers and a son of their presiding elder, Joseph A. Sasportas.[39] (He was also a brother of State Representative Thaddeus K. Sasportas.) Churches were also known to have applied religious sanctions against Negro Democrats by ostracizing or even expelling them.[40]

But such overt political initiatives do not appear to have been very prevalent or sustained. The political effectiveness of ministers was probably related more to their personal orientation and the nature of their personal activities than to any denominational allegiance, with its implication of a ready-made constituency. The church provided an arena for leadership development and was likely to attract people who aspired—like the politicians—to be leaders of the flock. The daily activities of a minister were sometimes demanding, but were particularly suited to the development of a personal constituency. For instance, Isaac Brockenton, a Baptist minister and constitutional convention delegate from Darlington, spent the year prior to his election "travelling from place to place—often twenty miles on foot, to preach the gospel . . . or funeral sermons—which . . . [were] important duties with the blacks." [41] A colleague of Brockenton's in the convention was performing similar tasks. Henry Jones, always attired in "a long-tailed, dark-blue Prince Albert coat," frequently walked ninety miles from Wilmington, North Carolina, to Conway, South Carolina, in Horry County, to preach and to help organize an A.M.E. church there.[42]

As with the Bureau and the army, however, there were also limitations to the political usefulness of the church. Conflicts among the various churches and between the missionaries show how competition could restrict the influence of all. It is clear, too, that despite their good intentions the missionaries were sometimes limited in their understanding of the freedmen and grossly manipulative in their dealings with them. Such attitudes may have accounted for some of the hostility that native blacks sometimes displayed toward Northerners, white and black—hostility which might affect their acceptance of these men as political leaders.

39. *News & Courier,* April 3, 1874.

40. A South Carolinian [Belton O'Neal Townsend], "The Political Condition of South Carolina," *Atlantic Monthly,* XXXIX (February, 1877), 193.

41. B. F. Whittemore to George Whipple, October 5, 1866, A.M.A. Papers.

42. George A. Singleton, *The Romance of African Methodism* (New York: Exposition Press, 1952), p. 126.

The northern missionaries saw the southern blacks as an intensely religious people and believed that the latter's religious sentiment was the surest way to their affections. For example, missionary teachers were convinced that tapping this sentiment provided the strongest method for exercising control in the schools.[43] On the other hand, zealots were not above taking advantage of the services and favors they could bestow in order to manipulate the freedmen and splinter their native churches. The Reverend W. T. Richardson deliberately encouraged such a schism in a black Baptist church in Beaufort, using the resources of the A.M.A. to secure a Free Will Baptist minister for the new church.[44] One might also view with suspicion the sudden conversion from the A.M.E. to the Congregational church of a black student from Cardozo's school, when the youth was given the opportunity of receiving an A.M.A. scholarship to Hampton University.[45]

For all their dedication and hard work, the actions and words of many northern white missionaries frequently betrayed a fundamental intolerance, even disrespect, of the freedmen as a people. They were horrified by the "shout," denouncing it as pagan and evidently remaining oblivious to its beneficial function of fellowship and celebration.[46] The freedmen were generally commended for their religious faith and zeal, but condemned for their "defiled" consciences. "They possess *much* that is *good* and commendable, in their religious faith and practice," observed a northern Baptist preacher, "but with *this,* there is much dross and defilement." [47] Their *"gross errors* and superstitions" must be eradicated, declared a Congregationalist. "Their ideas that dreams, visions, voices, spasms &c are necessary to or parts of conversion. Their vague conception of the connection of religh [sic] with morality and the duties of life. All those things must be corrected if this part of the U. S. is ever to advance to a high state of civilization." [48]

The northern black missionaries were often just as culturally distant from the ex-slave as their white colleagues, and, in some cases, just as prone to see their brothers as degraded and themselves as culturally superior. When the Reverend Hezekiah H. Hunter spoke of "the Great

43. Benjamin F. Jackson to George Whipple, February 18, 1868, A.M.A. Papers.
44. W. T. Richardson to S. S. Jocelyn, March 3, 1864, *ibid.*
45. There is no indication of overt coercion of the student, but one can infer that subtle pressures did exist from the context in which this conversion and scholarship were discussed and from Jackson's extreme sectarianism, Benjamin F. Jackson to George Whipple, February 10, 1868, *ibid.*
46. See statement of Laura Towne in *Letters and Diary,* p. 20.
47. W. T. Richardson to George Whipple, August 25, 1864, A.M.A. Papers.
48. Benjamin F. Jackson to George Whipple, February 18, 1868, *ibid.*

Work of Bringing these people to the standard of Man and Woman Hood," he betrayed a not uncommon sentiment. And while his ensuing comments are harsher than most, they indicate the orientation of some northern Negro missionaries: "There are many on the plantations. They are but a step above the *Brute Creation.* Only I know God is able for all States—conditions of mankind [otherwise] I would say none are able for the work."[49]

Such attitudes on the part of northern Negroes could sometimes result in serious consequences for those who had political ambitions. In the A.M.A.-supported school in Charleston which he directed, Francis Cardozo declared his intention to hire native teachers only as a last resort. He vastly preferred "the educated and experienced white Northern Teachers" and insisted on putting them "in the highest and most responsible positions," while relegating "the colored ones in the lower and less responsible ones, where they may improve by the superiority of their *white* fellow-laborers, and whose positions afterwards they may be able to occupy." [50] Evidently Cardozo's sentiments were communicated to some native black Charlestonians who either did not perceive or ignored the subtleties of his policy. "I am sure you are mistaken in saying I ever requested such a thing," he protested to the A.M.A. when accused of having requested that only white teachers be sent to Charleston. "My request was that I should have all *Northern* Teachers. It was and still is perfectly indifferent to me whether they are *white* or *colored,* all I ask is that they be competent for this work, and when I made the request I did so because *Northern* Teachers are more competent than Southern ones." [51] It is probable that such distinctions were lost on the native teachers, since all but one of them were black, and all of the northern teachers in Cardozo's school were white. Furthermore, there was the matter of the considerable salary differential between the white and black teachers.[52] Realizing the seriousness of the incident, Cardozo asked that Hunt send a written explanation of the misunderstanding to the teachers, "for if such a Report were to be circulated in the City it would hurt my influence very much." Cardozo may have been sincere when he disavowed any intention to discriminate racially, avowing such conduct as not only "unchristian, but specially foolish and suicidal" on the part of a Negro. But he was also conscious

49. Hezekiah H. Hunter to M. E. Strieby, May 6, 1865, *ibid.*
50. Francis L. Cardozo to S. Hunt, January 13, 1865, *ibid.*
51. Francis L. Cardozo to S. Hunt, December 2, 1865, *ibid.*
52. The black teachers in Cardozo's school complained at receiving $25 per month while some of the whites got $50. Even when Cardozo moved to remedy this distinction, he only requested a raise for his two best black teachers, Miss Rollins and Miss Weston, from $25 to $35 per month. Francis L. Cardozo to S. Hunt, December 9, 1865, *ibid.*

of the dire political consequences of such attitudes.[53]

Probably the greatest limitation on the influence of these religious organizations was caused less by the missionaries' attitude toward the freedmen and more by the intense, sometimes bitter sectarian rivalries among themselves. Cardozo, for example, feared the competition of the Unitarians in educational affairs; the superintendent of education for the Freedmen's Bureau, Reuben Tomlinson, a Quaker, was believed to be more amenable to the New England agency's influence.[54] Likewise, the Reverend Benjamin F. Jackson strongly resented the Northern Methodists who controlled the only Republican newspaper in Charleston.[55] Indeed, A.M.A. Congregationalists like Cardozo and Jackson were at a considerable disadvantage in the competition for influence among the freedmen. For example, a large majority of the legislators who were ministers were affiliated with either the Methodist (21) or Baptist (6) churches. This pattern of affiliation more or less reflected the religious distribution of the state's black population both before and after the war because most blacks converted to the Baptist or Methodist faiths.[56]

Even within a given denomination there were some very bitter rivalries. For instance, the blacks who had been associated with the Methodist Church before the war were by geography and political necessity members of the Methodist Church, South. Like all of the other black religious denominations, these black Southern Methodists tended to separate and establish their own churches after the war. The Northern Methodists, who had originally expected to compete with their southern rivals for the allegiance of the white natives, soon directed their energies toward these black separatist groups. By 1867 the national conference had made major concessions to admit black ministers for black congregations and had appropriated $25,000 to support missionary work in the state. The new policy bore fruit: the South Carolina membership grew from less than 3,000 served by 16 ministers with no church property in 1865 to almost 12,000 members served by 102 ministers in 43 churches in 1868. The Methodist Church, South, which had had 209,836 black members across the entire region in 1860, was reduced to only 78,742 black members

53. Francis L. Cardozo to S. Hunt, December 2, 1865, *ibid.*

54. Francis L. Cardozo to George Whipple and M. E. Strieby, October 3, 1866, *ibid.*

55. Benjamin F. Jackson to S. S. Jocelyn, March 3, 1868, *ibid.*

56. D. B. Nichols to George Whipple, April 2, 1862; E. J. Adams to George Whipple, September 5, 1865, *ibid. Proceedings of the Meeting in Charleston, S.C., May 13-15, 1845, on the Religious Instruction of the Negroes, Together with the Report of the Committee* (Charleston: B. Jenkins, 1845), p. 48. See also Susan M. Fickling, "The Christianization of the Negro in South Carolina, 1830-60" (M.A. thesis, University of South Carolina, 1923), pp. 21-36; Septima Chappell Smith, "The Development and History of Some Negro Churches in South Carolina" (M.A. thesis, University of South Carolina, 1942), pp. 4-6.

in 1866.[57] Their loss of membership was probably even more drastic in South Carolina, where Northern Methodism was strong.

The Northern Methodists were sharply challenged for these Negro Methodists. The A.M.E. Church had a history in South Carolina dating from 1817, when Morris Brown, a free Negro shoemaker, founded a church in Charleston. The Charleston church quickly grew to 3,000 members and became one of the three major A.M.E. centers, along with Baltimore and Philadelphia. Having emptied the galleries of the white Methodist churches, it soon aroused the jealousy and wrath of the white ministers, who seized the Denmark Vesey conspiracy as an excuse to have it closed. In May, 1865, Bishop Daniel A. Payne returned to Charleston to re-establish the church. To the South Carolina Conference, which included Georgia and North Carolina, the A.M.E. had attracted 22,338 members, 13 ministers, and built 17 churches by 1866.[58]

The church competed with very distinct disadvantages against the Northern Methodists; the statistics on the legislators affiliated with these two denominations may reflect this disadvantage. Twelve of the thirty Negro legislators whose denominations have been identified were Northern Methodists, while only nine were African Methodists. The A.M.E. had very little money to support its missionary activities and, in fact, had to get financial support for its southern ministers from the A.M.A.[59] Since the Northern Methodists were not averse to buying the allegiances of a black church with promises of building funds, Sunday School texts, etc.,[60] the A.M.E. was often clearly outdistanced and could only point out to black deacons and ministers the career advantages in affiliating with an all-black organization, where advancement was open all the way to the top. After all, there was not likely to be a black bishop in the Methodist Church, North, for some time, if ever. But even this color advantage was a two-edged sword, because apparently some congregations hesitated to become identified with an all-black group. As one minister complained, "there was a prejudice born of generations, of the recognized dominion of the whites which we had to meet and overcome in leading the bodies of Negroes to seek a church where they could be free and untrameled [sic] in their religious worship."[61]

57. *Journal of the General Conference of the Methodist Episcopal Church, held in Chicago, Illinois, 1868*, ed. William Harris (New York: Carlton and Lanaham, 1868), p. 511.

58. Nancy V. Ashmore, "The Development of the African Methodist Episcopal Church in South Carolina, 1865-1965" (M.A. thesis, University of South Carolina, 1969), pp. 5-20.

59. Wesley J. Gaines, *African Methodism in the South; or Twenty-five Years of Freedom* (Chicago: Afro-American Press, 1969), p. 6; Daniel A. Payne, *Recollections of Sixty Years*, reprint ed. (New York: Arno Press, 1968), p. 161.

60. Morrow, *Northern Methodism*, p. 131.

61. Gaines, *African Methodism*, p. 13.

The Methodist Church, South, generally encouraged black separatist movements and threw whatever influence it had with its black membership in favor of an A.M.E. affiliation. The Southern Methodists reasoned that it would be better to have blacks go to the A.M.E. than to strengthen their arch-rivals, the Northern Methodists. In Charleston they allowed the A.M.E. to use three of their churches while the new A.M.E. Emanuel Church was being constructed.[62] In contrast, the Reverend T. W. Lewis, representing the northern faction, accused the A.M.E. of being "incendiary and insurrectionary in its instructions and efforts." [63]

The black churches often fought rival white denominations in order to establish their independence, only to splinter again over power conflicts within the congregation. The Reverend E. J. Adams, a black political activist in Charleston, found this sort of situation when he came from New Jersey to reestablish a black Congregational church. It seems that one of the deacons from the prewar days had assumed much of the minister's office during the pastor-less interim and now resented Adams's intrusion. So the group which had just split off from the white parent group now split again into two separate and hostile denominations.[64] Cardozo deplored this situation and saw it as a general tendency, rather than an exceptional case. "The difficulty here among the colored people seems to be a strict tendency to division, when there is such an imperative for union," he declared.[65] Obviously, such divisions and conflicts decreased the possibility that a given church membership or denomination could provide a potent or reliable political constituency in itself. Even A.M.E. minister Richard H. Cain, who was frequently cited as the classic example of a preacher-politician, had his influence among his parishioners shaken by a rebellion led by a faction within the church.[66] As one of its historians described it, the A.M.E. always had at least two factions: one for the minister and one against him.[67]

However, racial friction was more likely to develop between the white missionaries and the freedmen than among rival churchmen. The freedmen in some areas of Beaufort were reported to be indifferent and in some cases outright hostile to the missionaries. The reason adduced by one observer was the freedmen's resentment of the fact that white Northerners had monopolized the land in their area.[68] There were tensions,

62. Ashmore, "The Development of the African Methodist Episcopal Church," pp. 17-19.
63. *Ibid.*, p. 22. See also *Daily Courier*, May 19, June 1, 1865.
64. Francis L. Cardozo to M. E. Strieby, March 17, 1866, A.M.A. Papers.
65. Francis L. Cardozo to M. E. Strieby, April 12, 1866, *ibid.*
66. Ashmore, "The Development of the African Methodist Episcopal Church," pp. 37, 48.
67. *Ibid.*, p. 34.
68. Theresa J. Phillips to M. E. Streiby, April, 1865, A.M.A. Papers.

too, between the black missionaries and their white co-workers. Jonathan J. Wright attributed the "whispers" about him to the jealousies of his white colleagues at his growing influence among the freedmen. In the fall of 1865, he wrote to the Reverend S. Hunt in New York: "It is as evident to yourself as it is to me that there are wolves in sheep's clothing, and a colored man among those, is a pretty good fellow as long as he is under and does not have as much influence among the people as they, but when it comes to that point when the black man is thought the more of by the masses of the people surrounding him; then that class of persons spoken of above they will find a great fault in him." [69] The whispers to which Wright referred were charges that his legal counseling of the freedmen was interfering with his teaching duties. Apparently these charges were made by some of the military personnel with whom he worked. Some months later the issue was raised again by the A.M.A. itself. Evidently Wright had expanded his legal services; when he was accused of giving "a divided service," he retorted, "You say that you hear of me as a lawyer oftener than a teacher. No doubt of that. I was a teacher North [sic] three years, & there was not much said about it; but last spring, when I became a lawyer, I was a perfect show, and heard of a great distance. . . . Had I been contented to settle down, and been what the masses of white persons desired me to be (a boot-blacker, a barber, or a hotel waiter) I would have been heard of less."[70]

Therefore, like the other postwar institutions from which black leaders were recruited, the churches were not available for automatic and unrestricted political uses. Like these others, the church provided a flexible and sustaining employment, an opportunity for developing leadership qualities, and a pattern of public contacts with a potential political constituency. But one feature of the black church was different from all the other institutions: it provided a greater opportunity for recruiting leaders from among native former slaves. It is interesting that most legislators who were ministers were ex-slaves—a pattern completely contrary to that among teachers, for instance, who were mainly of free origins.[71] And although we cannot determine just how many of these ex-slave legislators and ministers were also preachers or exhorters during slavery, it is very probable that some of them were.[72] Such a pattern

69. Jonathan J. Wright to S. Hunt[er], September 23, 1865, *ibid.*

70. Jonathan J. Wright to S. Hunt, February 5, 1866, *ibid.*

71. Of the 32 ministers whose prewar status is known, 21 were ex-slaves. Of the 29 identified as teachers, 20 were freeborn.

72. For example, William Adamson of Kershaw County was identified by his son Frank, also a state representative from Kershaw, as having been brought over from Africa. *Slave Narratives: A Folk History of Slavery in the United States from Interviews with Former Slaves,* Typewritten Records Prepared by the Federal Writers' Project, Library of Congress, Washington, 1941. South Carolina Narratives, XIV, part I, p. 14.

of prewar leadership would suggest the possible existence of leadership identification and recruitment mechanisms within the slave community quite independent of postwar institutions. In other words, the prewar leadership would have actually survived into the postwar period to some extent. Such a phenomenon would also suggest that leadership roles within the slave quarters were less restricted than has been previously assumed.

In the absence of evidence about the antebellum activities of these ex-slave preacher legislators, one can only speculate. It is certain, however, that the northern religious and political leaders—black as well as white— who presumed to lead the blacks, sometimes encountered resistance from ex-slave preachers who resented attempts to supplant them. A white A.M.A. missionary ran into such resistance when he sought to supplant "Brother Barnwell," an ex-slave preacher, as pastor of a Baptist church.[73] Martin R. Delany had similar difficulty when he ignored the political influence of a Reverend Mr. Murchinson in the course of carrying out various Freedmen's Bureau assignments in Beaufort.[74]

In some ways, therefore, the emergence of these slave-born preachers may represent the slave community's mode of asserting its traditional leadership in the face of tremendous political and social change. The political usefulness of the church per se may have been limited, but, like the Bureau and the army, it served an important function in the identification and development of native as well as northern political leaders. Indeed, all of these institutions encouraged new social vistas and presented new opportunities which enabled blacks to assume significant leadership roles among their people. The postwar institutions also provided a setting in which blacks interacted with and grew to know the people who would be their white political allies in the coming decade. Perhaps the fact that misunderstandings between these allies had sometimes limited the potential of black leaders to develop and serve their constituents was a lesson that would grow more significant during the critical years ahead.

73. W. F. Eaton to George Whipple, June 18, 1864, A.M.A. Papers.
74. Ullman, *Martin R. Delany,* pp. 369-71.

PART THREE

THE MAKING OF POLICY:
A POLITICAL PROFILE

Chapter Five

Black Domination or White Control: The Dynamics of Power

The Speaker is black, the Clerk is black, the doorkeepers are black, the little pages are black, the chairman of the Ways and Means is black, and the chaplain is coal black. At some of the desks sit colored men whose types it would be hard to find outside of the Congo; whose costume, visages, attitudes, and expression, only befit the forecastle of a buccaneer.

—James S. Pike, *The Prostrate State*

That they [the Negro leadership] were of the same race as a majority of the voters may have worked to their advantage; but this was not always true, for the race even in this period of innovations, never got over its habit of following white leadership.

—Simkins and Woody, *South Carolina During Reconstruction*

Contemporary observers and recent historians have given us two pervasive yet contradictory images of Negro leaders of the Reconstruction period. James Pike's reaction to his first sight of the Negro-controlled lower house of the South Carolina General Assembly represents one such image. Its negrophobic hysteria is echoed by many other whites of the period. When a black man was nominated for an important judicial post in Charleston, the *News and Courier* ran banner headlines proclaiming its "CIVILIZATION IN PERIL." They saw a plot to create in South Carolina "an African dominion"—indeed, nothing less than "a new Liberia." [1] A new verb was coined to communicate the blood-chilling fears aroused by the threat of black over white: "to Africanize."

On the other hand, tradition has also presented an alter image of black leaders as essentially comic characters and buffoons, a burlesque of legislative dignity. Their legislative addresses are depicted in minstrelsy dialect, "Kingfish-like"; their speech ludicrously pompous and sprinkled with

1. *News and Courier,* December 24, 1875.

malaprops. It was the Sambo tradition presented in a new setting. And while this Sambo was not lovable and genial, he was still docile before white authority and easily led by his northern and southern white colleagues. The tradition gained more credence when a former Republican governor attested to the black leaders' ineptitude by implying that they were really just pawns in the hands of the Republican party, unwitting dupes to the larger designs of the naticnal leadership.[2] By the turn of the century, another Republican governor accounted for the deference of Negroes to their white colleagues as arising from their "natural docility." [3] Nat Turner was really "Step 'n Fetchit" after all.

Obviously, these images are extreme and racist stereotypes. But the chief injury of such stereotypes is not simply that they are uncomplimentary, or even that they perpetuate the "bad nigger–Sambo" Janus-faced images that have always pervaded white America's conception of black personality types. The real injury lies in the fact that these stereotypes have insidiously discouraged other approaches to or conceptualizations of the problem of the political interrelations between white and black Republicans; that is, the true nature and extent of black domination of South Carolina's political life, and the mechanisms of white influence on the black leadership.

There is ample evidence of both black domination *and* the exercise of controls over black leadership by the white minority. South Carolina was unique among the reconstructed states in that blacks constituted about 60 percent of the population. This population advantage was converted into a substantial numerical advantage in the legislature, where Negroes held a two-to-one majority in the lower house and a clear majority on joint ballot of House and Senate throughout the nine-year period of Reconstruction. (See Table 3.) During this same period they held the office of secretary of state (from 1868 to 1877), lieutenant governor and adjutant general (after 1870), secretary of treasury, Speaker of the House, and president pro tem of the Senate (after 1872). Only nine of the twenty congressional terms were filled by Negroes during this nine-year period, but this included nine out of the last fifteen, and four of the five available during the years 1870-74.

On the other hand, Negroes never held the governorship, the office of U.S. senator, any of the eight circuit judgeships, the offices of comptroller general, attorney general, superintendent of education, or more than one of the three positions on the state supreme court. As late as the spring

2. Robert K. Scott to Richard H. Gleaves, June 12, 1875, newspaper clipping in "Reconstruction Scrapbook," South Caroliniana Library, University of South Carolina, Columbia.

3. Daniel H. Chamberlain, "Reconstruction in South Carolina," *Atlantic Monthly*, LXXXVII (April, 1901), 477.

TABLE 3. MEMBERSHIP OF HOUSE OF REPRESENTATIVES AND SENATE, 1868-76

House

Session	68 Spec.	68-69	69-70	70-71	71-72	72-73	73 Spec.	73-74	74-75	75-76
Democrats	15	14	15	14	10	21	20	21	34	34
White Republicans	34	33	32	35	35	23	25	25	20	18
Negro Republicans	75	74	76	77	75	81	80	80	70	71
Total	124	121	123	126	120	125	125	126	124	123

Senate

Session	68 Spec.	68-69	69-70	70-71	71-72	72-73	73 Spec.	73-74	74-75	75-76
Democrats	6	6	6	5	5	8	8	8	8	8
White Republicans	15	15	14	15	15	9	9	10	8	8
Negro Republicans	10	10	11	12	12	16	16	15	17	17
Total	31	31	31	32	32	33	33	33	33	33

NOTE: These figures represent persons who actually served; consequently, vacancies and contested elections caused variations in the total membership from session to session. There were 124 seats in the House throughout the period; the increases in Senate membership reflect the admission of new counties in 1870 and 1872.

of 1872 there were no Negroes among the thirty-one county sheriffs, none among the thirty-one clerks of court, just one among the thirty-one county treasurers, another among the thirty-two county auditors, eleven among the thirty-one school commissioners, and only about one in every five trial justices.

Furthermore, there *were* recorded instances of black officeholders serving as mere pawns of shrewder white colleagues. The northern-born county treasurer of Colleton County boasted to Governor Scott that he could "controll every colored man's vote in St. Paul's Parish and St. Bartholomew Parish." [4] The Negro treasurer of Orangeburg County found himself in jail charged with malfeasance in office, while the white mentor who had gotten him the appointment and directed his peculations went free. [5] On another occasion it was alleged that the white political boss of Colleton County engineered the removal from the county auditor's position of a well-educated Negro political enemy, replacing him with another Negro who was illiterate. The latter was expected to be auditor in name only, while another white crony performed the duties of his office. [6]

Evidence can be found to lend credence to either proposition of black-white power relationships, but a proper evaluation of this evidence depends upon the context in which it is considered. Much of the discussion of these power relationships consists merely of reactions to, or variations on, the two pervasive and racist images of black officeholders: bad nigger and Sambo. These images are based in turn on racist presumptions about the nature of black-white relationships in general. They equate the mere presence of blacks in positions of power with black domination in the first case; they assume a natural subservience of blacks to a white presence regardless of the specific context in the other. Indeed, the reactions of historians to these traditional images has often been in kind, betraying more emotion than analysis and, more important, often accepting the context of the original discussion. Du Bois, for example, accepted the idea of the essential powerlessness of blacks in South Carolina's Recon-

4. James Grace to Robert K. Scott, February 24, 1871, Robert K. Scott Papers, South Carolina Archives, Columbia.

5. A black man, John Humbert, was jailed for malfeasance in office while treasurer of Orangeburg County. He claimed that his appointment had been arranged by Thad C. Andrews, the white state senator, so that the latter could use Humbert. *News and Courier,* December 28, 1874. The *Courier*'s version of the story is apparently confirmed by Robert B. Elliott in his plea to the governor for clemency for Humbert. Humbert, said Elliott, was merely "the dupe of others more experienced and designing." Robert B. Elliott to Daniel H. Chamberlain, October 23, 1875, Governor Daniel H. Chamberlain Papers, South Carolina Archives, Columbia.

6. In an anonymous letter to the editor it was charged that Governor Moses removed William F. Myers and replaced him with George Washington. It should be noted, however, that editor A. C. Shaffer was a partisan of Moses. *Walterboro News,* April 4, 1874.

struction government in order to minimize the culpability of blacks for the corruption of that government, even though the acceptance of the former idea actually contradicts his thesis of black labor's control of the government. Faced with a choice between venality and gullibility—the choice fostered by Pike and Simkins and Woody—Du Bois, like many others to follow, chose the latter.[7]

The problem can be resolved only by seeking a new context in which to evaluate the evidence. A problem of determining political power relationships can be most appropriately dealt with in an institutional context—that is, in terms of the party machinery, the legislative process, the state and federal bureaucracy, and the roles that Negro leaders played vis-à-vis whites in each of these settings. The attainment of a numerical majority in various offices represents only the *potential* power of the Negro leadership. Power is not simply a static phenomenon of majorities and minorities, but a dynamic interaction within the context of institutions.

Carl Friedrich, a political theorist who attempts to distinguish between power as possession and power as a relationship, defines some concepts which might be helpful here. Power as a possession involves the ability to command by virtue of overt control of given administrative machinery; it is essentially coercive. In contrast, power as a relationship involves the ability to persuade and is essentially consensual. Friedrich goes on to distinguish between power and authority: "Authority is not a kind of power, but something that accompanies power. It is a quality in men and things which enhances their power, something which creates power but is not itself power."[8] Thus, one's ability to gain and to fully exercise the powers of an office may well depend on the authority one can demonstrate. One source of authority is the general success of one's policies and actions—in short, the ability to deliver.[9]

Although one cannot measure directly the power or influence which one man has over another, much can be inferred from the context in which the two function. In the legislative setting, the only meaningful objective toward which influence might be applied is the successful attainment of one's legislative goals. This legislative success can be measured directly; from its presence or absence, the relative extent of the members' legislative influence can be inferred. If one subtracts the number of times

7. "The responsibility of Negroes for the government of South Carolina in Reconstruction was necessarily limited," writes Du Bois. *Black Reconstruction . . . in America, 1860-80* (New York: Harcourt Brace, 1935), p. 411.

8. Carl J. Friedrich, *An Introduction to Political Theory: Twelve Lectures at Harvard* (New York: Harper & Row, 1967), p. 126.

9. Friedrich uses as examples of this tendency the increment in President Lyndon Johnson's power as a *result* of the success of his legislative program and the decline of Premier Khrushchev's because his foreign policy initiatives were failures. *Ibid.*, pp. 130-31.

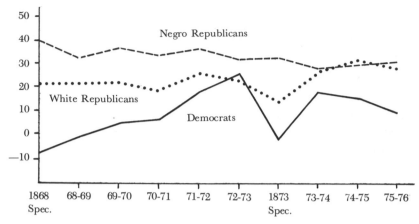

FIGURE 1. AVERAGE SUCCESS SCORES FOR LEGISLATIVE SUBGROUPS, 1868-76

a legislator voted with the losing side from the number of times he voted
with the winning side and divides by the total number of his chances
to vote, the result is a simple index of his legislative success which can
be compared with the scores of his colleagues.[10]

In almost every legislative session Negro Republicans were much more
successful on legislative roll calls than their white counterparts. During
the ten sessions of the South Carolina House of Representatives held
between 1868 and 1876, Negro legislators had an average collective success
ratio of 33, while white Republicans scored only 22. Not until the final
two sessions did white Republicans achieve average success scores comparable to those of blacks. (See Figure 1.) Furthermore, in most sessions
no whites ranked higher than twelfth, and the scores of the most prominent
white Republican leaders were consistently low.[11]

Of course, one cannot conclude from the fact that one legislator manages
to pick the winning side more frequently than another that the former
is more influential or powerful than the latter. However, the obverse

10. I am indebted to Charles Dollar and Richard Jensen, who developed this index
of legislative success. It should be noted that the denominator used to calculate this index
is the total roll calls in a given session; consequently, a member with numerous absences
will have a low index of success. But since we are trying to measure influence, the fact
that a legislator was absent or abstained should be reflected in his score. After all, the
degree of influence a legislator exercises is likely to be reduced if he is not present and
voting. A computer program for calculating individual and aggregate success scores was
written by the author in Fortran and is available upon request. See Charles Dollar and
Richard Jensen, *Historian's Guide to Statistics: Quantitative Analysis and Historical Research* (New
York: Holt, Rinehart and Winston, 1971), pp. 111-16.

11. The average collective success ratio of each group is calculated by totaling its average
for each session multiplied by the number of roll calls in that session and dividing by
the total roll calls recorded for the period.

is true: one *can* infer from the fact that one legislator is on the losing side more often than another that the former is *not* controlling the latter's vote. Clearly, South Carolina's white Republicans were on the losing side of legislative contests too often to be credible masters, and the blacks had the upper hand too frequently to be mere tools.[12]

Although legislative voting is an important indicator of political relationships, it still represents only one dimension of the political environment. The interactions between people and among institutions can be complex, and the patterns of power and influence can involve numerous subtleties. Certainly this is true of the relationship within the Republican party between the black majority and its less numerous white colleagues, particularly the Northerners. Both coercive and consensual factors governed their relationship. Whites clearly had more training and political experience than blacks as a group, though not more than many individual blacks. Most northern whites came to the South and into politics by a process of self-selection, which probably made them more highly motivated politically and more aggressive in the competition for offices.

Because of various political considerations Negroes did not always push other Negroes for offices that became vacant. For instance, State Representative Junius S. Mobley, generally considered an ultraradical, attempted to secure the removal of a black conservative and to replace him with a white radical whose political opinions were closer to his own.[13] In another instance, Negro Republicans in the hill country of Anderson County recommended a white Democrat for a vacancy on the board of county commissioners in order to demonstrate that they were "not mere blind partisans" but favored an honest and capable man of whatever party. They urged this policy, they said, in spite of the fact that' the nominee was known to favor white immigration to displace black laborers, and that he refused to employ blacks on his plantation.[14]

However, the key advantage of the white Republicans probably lay in their presumed or real contacts in the North which enabled them to promise and sometimes to deliver funds, patronage, or protection. White Northerners often passed themselves off as representing "the powers at Washington" in order to secure the political obedience of the Negroes, according to ex-Governor Chamberlain.[15] Indeed, it would not be unreasonable for black voters to think that, in a white-controlled society, white representatives would have more access to the levers of power and could

12. Cf. Francis B. Simkins and Robert H. Woody, *South Carolina During Reconstruction* (Chapel Hill: University of North Carolina Press, 1932), pp. 91, 124.

13. Junius S. Mobley to Daniel H. Chamberlain, December 18, 1874, Chamberlain Papers.

14. "Resolution of Republicans of Anderson," May 8, 1876, *ibid.*

15. Chamberlain, "Reconstruction in South Carolina," p. 477.

more successfully obtain funds and influence from that society. Blacks had ample evidence of this fact even before the Reconstruction Acts ushered them into political society. For example, B. F. Whittemore was the only white representative in the Darlington County delegation, yet he remained the undisputed leader of that delegation for the entire period. Whittemore probably gained some of his authority by virtue of his contacts with the American Missionary Association, which enabled him to obtain funds, school books, churches, and (for at least two men who would later be members of his delegation) jobs.[16]

This necessity of dealing with and influencing powers outside the state appears to have been one reason why black leaders never even considered pushing one of their own for governor, a position which required constant and sensitive contacts with power centers in Washington, Wall Street, and even Europe. "We don't want a colored Governor," declared Delany after listing the other offices that the Negro leadership *did* demand, "our good sense tells us differently. . . ." [17]

Negro leaders recognized the importance of these outside forces very early in their political careers. Just after the passage of the Fourteenth Amendment, a committee of South Carolina's Negro leaders made a secret trip to Washington to confer with Thaddeus Stevens and Charles Sumner about the formation of a political organization. Both Sumner and Stevens were said to have advised them "to tender the leadership to native whites of the former master class of conservative views." However, it appears that "the plan was frustrated because they were not able to secure the consent of desired representatives of the former master class to assume the proffered leadership." [18]

Reports of leading white Republicans' fears that the election of blacks to southern offices in too great and conspicuous numbers might cause a racial backlash in the North lend credence to this scene.[19] During the initial stages of Reconstruction, Republicans did offer nominations for various offices to white Democrats. In many instances they were refused,[20] but evidently in others they were accepted. In the fall of 1868 B. F.

16. Whittemore got support for Isaac Brockenton from the A.M.A. in 1866. B. F. Whittemore to George Whipple, October 6, 1866, American Missionary Association Archives, Amistad Research Center, New Orleans.

17. *Daily Republican,* June 25, 1870.

18. Cardozo gave this report to two Washington associates several years later: *Journal of Negro History,* V (January, 1920), 110-11. There is possibly confirmation of this trip, if not its outcome, in a letter Cardozo wrote directly afterward to E. P. Smith, March 9, 1868, A.M.A. Papers.

19. *Daily Courier,* November 11, 1867.

20. See testimony of State Representative Henry Johnson of Fairfield County in *Testimony Taken by the Joint Select Committee to Inquire into the Condition of Affairs in the Late Insurrectionary States,* Volume I: South Carolina (Washington: Government Printing Office, 1872), p. 323.

Whittemore took a step aimed at "harmonising the elements among" his constituents by calling a meeting with the prominent men in his county and working out a combined list of Democrats and Republicans which he recommended to the governor for appointment to county offices. In a county that was 63 percent black, white Democrats were recommended for the key position of county treasurer, all four county assessor openings, and two of the four magistracies. A white Republican was recommended for county auditor and two black Republicans for the remaining magistrates' positions.[21]

Apparently Republicans were so anxious to attract white Democrats that, in at least one case, they elected a Colleton County man to a position he had formerly declined.[22] And the fact that all of the circuit judges were white, and many of them Democrats besides, appears to have been the result of a policy decision by the administration. Soon after the inauguration of the new government in the summer of 1868, Franklin J. Moses, Jr., then speaker of the House and later governor of the state, wrote a confidential note to Scott; he urged that the election of circuit judges be apolitical, because these offices were crucial and it was here that the confidence of the white people could be won.[23] B. O. Duncan, another prominent native Republican, urged a similar policy.[24]

Evidently this policy was short-lived, possibly because it made no real headway in converting any sizeable number of white Democrats to Republicanism or softening the vitriolic attacks of the Democratic press, and possibly because the growth of Ku Klux Klan violence made rapprochement untenable. In any case, some of Scott's local advisors soon began urging that Democrats be removed and only radical Republicans be appointed.[25] Thomas J. Mackey, one of Scott's chief political confidantes, asserted that the "only true policy is to rigidly refuse to give any patronage to a democrat or to a democratic journal." [26]

But many white Republicans continued to advocate efforts to attract native whites into the Republican party and the appointment of northern whites to sensitive positions. This policy often reflected their lack of confidence in black officeholders and was clearly discriminatory. "My policy is to get as many of the native whites of the state to unite with us as we can and try and induce Northern men to come and settle among

21. B. F. Whittemore to Robert K. Scott, November 3, 1868, Scott Papers.

22. John Burbridge to Robert K. Scott, July 7, 1868, *ibid.* Also see letters from a group of officers-elect seeking removal of their political disabilities so that they could take their offices. William A. McDaniel *et al.* to Robert K. Scott, July 8, 1868, *ibid.*

23. Franklin J. Moses to Robert K. Scott, August 17, 1868, *ibid.*

24. B. O. Duncan to Robert K. Scott, November 27, 1868, *ibid.*

25. R. W. Cousart to Robert K. Scott, February 13, 1870, *ibid.*

26. Thomas J. Mackey to Robert K. Scott, October 2, 1871, *ibid.*

us," one Republican wrote the governor. "There is not enough virtue and intelligence among the Blacks to conduct the government in such a way as will promote peace and prosperity." [27] In other instances, white Republican officeholders urged the governor to replace with whites those black colleagues whom they considered "unbusinesslike" or incompetent.[28]

Apparently the uncertainties of the national temper in the 1868 presidential election and an awareness of their own inexperience led black leaders to accept the policy of maintaining a low profile initially. But before the end of the first legislative term, they abandoned this policy and began to demand in very strong terms a more equitable division of offices. Of course, some of them—mainly Northerners—had never fully acquiesced in the low-profile policy. At the Republican nominating convention in the spring of 1868, three northern blacks had been candidates for the office of lieutenant governor: Jonathan J. Wright, William James Whipper, and Robert Elliott. On the first ballot Lemuel Boozer, a white native, led with 40 votes; Wright was second with 35; Elliott had 19; Whipper, 10; R. J. Donaldson, a white Northerner, 8; and 2 votes went to two other candidates. Before the second ballot Elliott withdrew in favor of Wright, but Whipper, who later developed a vitriolic feud with Wright, withdrew in favor of Boozer. Apparently these withdrawals had little effect on Wright's fortunes, since the second ballot ended with Boozer at 73 votes and Wright still at 35, with 4 scattered. It is very probable that the "policy" had been invoked again.[29]

When the special session of the state legislature convened, Whipper launched another attack on "the policy." When the nominations for Speaker of the House were opened, Whipper offered Robert B. Elliott as a candidate, declaring defiantly that it was "hightime" a black man was placed in a key position, "the offices have heretofore been invariably given to white men, on the pretext of policy," and that many of these whites were ignorant and incompetent at that. In a fierce challenge, he insisted that "if the Republican party could not venture to put black men in office, but must content itself with inferior white men, it was time it should fall to the ground." [30] But after an "animated debate," the policy was reaffirmed with the election of Franklin J. Moses, Jr., as Speaker.

There were two other challenges to the policy of limiting black officeholding before the first year of Republican rule ended; one was successful,

27. T. N. Talbert to Robert K. Scott, January 12, 1871, *ibid.*

28. John Terry to Robert K. Scott, September 7, 1868; Frank Arnim to Robert K. Scott, October 10, 1868, *ibid.*

29. *Daily Courier,* March 11, 1868.

30. *Ibid.,* July 8, 1868.

the other was not. In the first, Negroes elected Benjamin F. Randolph over Daniel H. Chamberlain as chairman of the Republican state central committee just before the presidential campaign of 1868. This action was taken despite the strong objections of national, as well as local, Republican leaders. When Randolph was elected, several conservative Republicans were reported to have staged a walkout, and plans were laid to undo his authority.[31] (Later Randolph was assassinated while canvassing the up-country districts, but he was succeeded as party chairman by another Negro, Alonzo J. Ransier.) In the second challenge, William James Whipper announced his intention to run for Congress from the Third District, even if he had to bolt the party and run against the Republican nominee. Evidently he cooled down or failed to get enough support, because he did not carry out his threat.[32]

A little more than a year later the demands for a greater share of the major offices grew more vocal, more insistent, and developed a stronger and more solid base of support among not only the Negro leadership, but their constituents as well.[33] By spring of 1870—just prior to the nominating conventions for the fall elections—Negro leaders resolved to make a major policy statement on the issue. The occasion was one of the many celebrations and parades that blacks staged in Charleston during this period; as usual, everyone ended up at the Battery with a round of political speeches. De Large began.

Why is it that we colored men have become identified with the Republican party? Is it because there is loadstone which attracts and holds us there, or is it because we are deluded and follow blindly certain men? No! We joined this party because it professed equal right and privileges to all, and as long as they do as they profess I stay with them. We joined the party, and we are thankful because they gave us our freedom. We thought, on the ground of expediency we must do nothing to offend them, but some impudent scoundrels in the party now say: "You want too much; you want everything!" We placed them in position; we elected them and by our votes we made them our masters. We now propose to change this thing a little, and let them vote for us. It is no more than reasonable they should do so.[34]

Hereafter he would insist on colored men being placed in any offices they were qualified to fill, and he proposed to fight for this principle over the entire state. This policy was not being embarked upon without

31. *Ibid.,* September 11, 1868. John Morris to William Claflin, September 14, 1868, William E. Chandler Papers, Library of Congress.
32. John Morris to William Claflin, September 14, 1868, Chandler Papers.
33. See *Daily Courier,* January 27, 1870.
34. *Daily Republican,* June 24, 1870.

consultation with other Negro leaders, he informed the audience, and their plans had been matured over a long period. He confidently declared that the doctrine he was proposing would be supported by the major Negro leaders in the state.[35]

It appeared that this was no idle boast, for De Large was followed by several prominent representatives of the Negro leadership group who supported his position. First came Ransier, who was generally very cautious (indeed, outright timid on occasion) when it came to taking a forthright position on any controversial issue. Characteristically, he urged blacks not to discriminate against whites as they themselves had been discriminated against. Yet it was clear that blacks had not been treated fairly, he ventured, especially with respect to federal patronage jobs. These jobs were controlled by the conservative Republican Senator Frederick A. Sawyer, but Ransier avoided a direct personal attack. Warming to his subject, however, he did declare somewhat uncharacteristically: "Though we dread the issue, it must come. It may drive colored men in South Carolina to take a stand which may ruin the ship." [36]

Ransier was followed by Delany, who had urged a more equitable distribution of patronage and elective offices as early as 1867 during a lecture tour through the South.[37] "I take the ground that no people have become a great people who had not their own leaders. Take the world over and all nations are represented by their own people, and let it be known that neither Major Willoughby, Mr. Fox [owner and editor of the Daily Republican, respectively], Governor Scott, or any one else, can lead black men." This movement was not an attempt to form a third, all-black party, he insisted, for in a predominantly white nation with a white population perpetually swelled by millions of immigrants, such a policy would be "folly." Nevertheless, it must be clearly understood that blacks were the majority in South Carolina and held the balance of power. "We are the strongest and propose to elect no candidate whom the colored man does not approve of." Delany then outlined a specific formula for the equitable distribution of offices based roughly on population ratios; it entailed demands for the lieutenant governorship, two congressmen, one senator, and the appropriate quota of state and county offices.[38]

Delany was followed by the generally conservative Joseph H. Rainey. Perhaps taken aback somewhat by the militancy of his colleagues, Rainey avoided speaking directly to the issue of obtaining an equitable distribu-

35. *Ibid.*
36. *Ibid.*
37. See discussion in Victor Ullman, *Martin R. Delany: The Beginnings of Black Nationalism* (Boston: Beacon Press, 1971), p. 414.
38. *Daily Republican,* June 24, 1870.

tion of offices, emphasizing instead the dangers of factional disputes.[39]

The Battery speeches were followed up quickly with mass meetings and rallies in various Charleston wards in an attempt to organize grassroots support and to build a delegation committed to this policy for the county and state nominating conventions of the fall campaign. At one such mass meeting De Large declared: "Are not in all States, and in all parties, the classes who have the largest majorities first considered? But some white men want us to act according to their dictation without consulting us." [40] De Large, Delany, Ransier, and other leaders took a similar message to the other wards in the city.[41]

The reaction of white Republicans was verbally fierce and physically violent. The editors of the *Daily Republican* tried to discredit the movement's leaders by insisting that the demands were self-serving: their goal was "not simply to put forward colored men, but to put forward these individual colored men." [42] Ignoring all denials by the Negro leaders, the editors insisted that this was a plot to found a black man's party in the state. If so, they sneered, such advocates as De Large would lose out since they were mulattoes, and it was frequently noted that the prejudice between blacks and browns was even greater than that between whites and blacks.[43] Delany's plan to impose a racial quota on the allocation of offices would backfire, they insisted, and fewer Negroes would be elected.[44]

Meanwhile, the De Large group had allied itself with the Mackey forces against the Sawyer-Bowen group for control of Charleston County. The Mackeys had once controlled the Customs House in Charleston, only to be deposed after senatorial candidate Frederick A. Sawyer defeated Dr. A. G. Mackey, the senior member of the family and collector of the Port of Charleston from 1866 to 1869. C. C. Bowen was elected to Congress from the Charleston district and quickly formed an alliance with Sawyer to control federal patronage in the county. There were several violent altercations between these factions, with the Bowenites disrupting several of the ward meetings organized by the De Large-Mackey supporters.[45] The control of the Customs House appears to have generally determined the outcome of elections in Charleston during the Reconstruction era, but on this occasion De Large succeeded in defeating Bowen for the regular party nomination and again in the general election,

39. *Ibid.*
40. *Ibid.*
41. *Ibid.,* June 25, 27, July 8, 1870.
42. *Ibid.,* June 27, 1870.
43. *Ibid.,* June 24, 1870.
44. *Ibid.,* June 27, 1870.
45. *Ibid.,* June 30, July 1, 12, 1870.

although the result was close enough to be contested and both men were eventually refused seats.

Indeed, the entire 1870 campaign was highly successful and represented a turning point in black-white relations within the Republican party. Alonzo J. Ransier was nominated and elected lieutenant governor. Not the quota of two demanded by Delany in his Battery speech, but three congressmen were elected—Robert C. De Large in the second district, Robert B. Elliott in the third, and Joseph H. Rainey in the first.[46] Jonathan J. Wright was elected to the state supreme court by the General Assembly. In the 1872 elections Richard H. Cain was elected to the at-large seat, giving Negroes four of the five congressional posts. Samuel J. Lee became speaker of the House; Francis L. Cardozo, secretary of treasury; Henry E. Hayne, secretary of state; and Henry W. Purvis, adjutant general, giving Negroes four of the eight executive offices.

In a sense, the real turning point came in a less publicized move long before the elections or the Battery speeches. Indeed, it probably laid the groundwork for the latter movement. Late in 1869 the office of land commissioner was in deep trouble. It was controlled by the irascible and erratic Charles P. Leslie, a white New Yorker. The commission had never been properly organized under Leslie and had overspent its appropriation by $250,000. When the Scott administration sought a new appropriation to bail it out, a committee of prominent Negro leaders—De Large, Elliott, Whipper, Nash, Ransier, and Rainey—paid a confidential call on the governor to demand Leslie's resignation and the appointment of a Negro in his place.[47] The governor acquiesced, for not only were these men the most prominent Negro members of the General Assembly; they also controlled some of its key committees. De Large was chairman of the ways and means committee, through which any appropriations bill had to pass; Whipper chaired the judiciary committee; Ransier, committee on privileges and elections; and Elliott, railroads. Nash and Rainey headed the Senate committees on claims and finance, respectively. The administration was so compromised by the speculations and kickbacks of the land commission that Leslie was able to exact $45,000 as the price of a quiet resignation. It took another illegal transaction to raise the money for this extortion, but Leslie resigned on March 1, 1870, and De Large was appointed to take his place.[48] Three months later, De Large announced the new demands of the Negro leadership at the Charleston Battery; in eight more months, the complexion of South Carolina's government had grown significantly darker.

46. Although De Large was eventually unseated, he was seated until the contest was decided.

47. See Carol K. Bleser, *The Promised Land: The History of the South Carolina Land Commission, 1869-90* (Columbia: University of South Carolina Press, 1969), pp. 59-65.

48. *Ibid.,* p. 58.

A key factor in the success of the Negro leaders in taking over the land commission was their control of some key committees in the General Assembly. In fact, this incident is an excellent illustration of the fact that power depended more on legislators' particular roles in a structure than on the mere possession of a numerical majority. Indeed, by this standard the extent of black control of the South Carolina legislature is far more impressive than a mere nose count of the membership would indicate.

After 1872 the chief Senate and House officers were Negro. Samuel J. Lee was Speaker of the House from 1872 to 1874, and Robert B. Elliott resigned his seat in Congress to take the speakership from 1874 to 1876. From 1872 to 1876 Stephen A. Swails was president pro tem of the Senate. Aside from the power that these men exercised in controlling the flow and shaping the content of the administration's legislative program, they also dispensed the many patronage jobs connected with the operations of the legislature. These attachés were of course a major part of the party's campaign force, and this gave the Speaker some influence on the fortunes of Republican candidates.

The House Speaker also controlled the appointment of committee chairmen.[49] Ironically, the election of a Negro Speaker seems to have done very little to increase the number of black committee chairmen; indeed, their share of the most important committee posts actually declined while the Speaker was Negro. In the first legislative session ten of the twenty-two committee chairmen were Negro. The deaths of two white Republican members gave Negroes slightly more than half the chairmanships by the end of 1869, but the major change in the House leadership structure coincided with the pressure by De Large and his group for more key offices. After 1870 Negroes held a two-to-one advantage in chairmanships, with about 70 percent in the 1870-72 legislature, 65 percent in 1872-74, and 70 percent in 1874-76.[50]

Among the eight committees generally considered the most powerful and influential (ways and means, judiciary, privileges and elections, education, claims, contingent accounts, railroads, and public printing), the situation was somewhat reversed.[51] In the five sessions between 1868 and 1872, Negroes headed five of these key committees, but they only controlled two in 1872-74 and three in 1874-76. This decline in their power

49. The speaker may have sought advice on these selections in party caucus, but the evidence indicates that the choices were his prerogative. Chairmen were elected in the Senate.

50. All of these statistics were compiled from the journals of the House and Senate.

51. These offices are considered critical in most legislatures because they control either the flow of legislation or the flow of money. In this case, however, the committees were also specifically identified in the South Carolina press as the most powerful: *Daily Courier*, November 27, 1872.

may have been more apparent than real, however. They still controlled the speakership and always controlled ways and means. With the passage of time, some of these committees which Negroes surrendered to whites had become less important than formerly. The judiciary committee was traditionally given to a Democrat after 1870, apparently as a gesture of non-partisanship. No important railroad legislation was considered after the 1870-71 session, and printing contracts were routinely let to a Republican syndicate after 1872. So it may well be that, after 1872, control of the speakership and the committee on ways and means was sufficient for effective control of the House.

Many observers felt that the fact that Negroes never had a majority in the Senate made it impossible for them to dominate the legislative process. But while the Negro senators never possessed power comparable to that of their House colleagues, they did exercise a significant degree of control. During the first five years of Republican rule, Negroes held only about a third of the chairmanships in the Senate. After the 1872 elections, however, they took sixteen of the twenty-four chairmanships and maintained that control until the end of Republican rule in 1877. The distribution of key committee posts followed a similar pattern, with Negroes holding fewer than half of the seven most important committees during the first five sessions, but a majority after 1872.[52]

Another aspect of a senator's power was his influence over the patronage decisions affecting his county. Not only did senators tend to be acknowledged leaders of the legislative delegations from their respective counties; their concurrence was also required for all gubernatorial appointments. The Senate could and occasionally did reject the governor's attempt to appoint or remove a county officer.[53] Under appropriate political circumstances, they could dictate the governor's nominations and removals outright. This could occur either if they were political allies (or at least not enemies) of the governor, or if they had sufficient control or influence in their counties to unify the major local political elements for or against

52. In the 1872-74 and 1875-76 sessions Negroes held four of the key committee chairmanships; in 1874-75 they held five. During nine Republican-controlled legislative sessions Negro senators held the chairmanship of the committee on printing during six sessions, the committee on finance and the committee on claims during five, the committee on contingent accounts during four, and the committee on elections during three. However, no Negro senator ever chaired the judiciary committee. Nevertheless, during the last two years of Republican rule they controlled the three critical committees through which any and all money measures had to pass—the committee on finance (William Beverly Nash), the committee on claims (Nash), and the committee on contingent accounts (Nash and then Samuel E. Gaillard).

53. For example, see letter advising Chamberlain that the Senate would not consent to the removal of George Holmes as county treasurer of Beaufort. Joseph Woodruff to Daniel H. Chamberlain, December 10, 1875, Chamberlain Papers.

a given aspirant. In either case their power was shared with the governor, whose political needs or designs could severely affect their own.[54]

Therefore the power of a legislator derived not simply from his office, but from a subtle mix of political circumstances and interrelationships that gave him authority over a given situation. "Do nothing in the matter of Co. Treasurer until you see me Monday," James L. Jamison, the Negro senator from Orangeburg, wired Governor Scott. "Rumor says that some one newly elected can control the delegation. Do not be deceived, the majority will stand by me through hot or cold." [55] Senator Stephen A. Swails represented the county of Williamsburg, where he commanded overwhelming election margins. When Scott's private secretary referred a white office-seeker to Swails for concurrence, the man fired off an irate letter demanding to know if Swails were "Governor" of Williamsburg County that his O.K. had to be sought for any appointments.[56]

On the other hand, one's power and influence might depend on one's personal affinity and contact with the governor. Such power was exercised through informal meetings and conversations—through consensus, not coercion. Such was the relationship which Robert C. De Large appears to have sustained with Governor Scott. Far from controlling his delegation, De Large was usually at odds with it. He was, however, ways and means committee chairman, and his letters to Scott betray the tone of a close personal friend and political confidant. He was the governor's agent in Charleston, a city he knew well and where he had influence. He worked out compromises on patronage problems there, suggesting where the most benefit could be derived from appointments and how the axe could be applied to enemies and lukewarm friends without liability.[57]

The governor was potentially the single most powerful politician in South Carolina. Since all of the members of the executive branch were popularly elected (and, indeed, all except the lieutenant governor were elected for a term two years longer than the governor's), his power base lay primarily in his appointive powers over local offices. Most key local offices were appointive, including county treasurer, auditor, jury commissioner, and trial justices; various other elective offices were subject to gubernatorial appointment when vacancies occurred. For example, in a

54. For example, see Junius S. Mobley to Daniel H. Chamberlain, December 18, 1874, ibid.

55. Telegram, James L. Jamison to Robert K. Scott, November 4, 1872, ibid.

56. Samuel W. Maurice to Robert K. Scott, January 3, 1872, Scott Papers.

57. "I will play to employ on the streets our friends, and control or divide that influence [of their opponents]. If any applications come to you for appointments of any kind from this County do communicate with me before you make them." Robert C. De Large to Robert K. Scott, July 13, 1869, ibid.

two-year term Governor Daniel H. Chamberlain made almost 1,000 appointments.[58]

The peculiar private circumstances of Republican politicians in South Carolina during Reconstruction increased the power of the governor. Many whites not only faced social ostracism, but were also forced out of business because of their alliance with the Republican party.[59] Even lawyers, doctors, and other professional men whose occupations allowed them to serve as essentially part-time political officers were subject to insecurity. Because of economic ostracism by native whites, these men were often forced to combine their elective offices (which paid small per diem incomes) with some other local office in order to survive.[60] Such pecuniary considerations led Dr. John W. Lunney, the senator-elect from Darlington County, to seek the office of county auditor as well.[61] Likewise, E. B. Seabrook, Chamberlain's law partner, declared that he was impoverished and his family practically reduced to begging.[62] One senator went so far as to resign his Senate seat for the less prestigious but more remunerative office of county treasurer.[63]

Many Negro politicians found themselves in similarly depressed situations. Directly after the inauguration of the reconstructed government in South Carolina, the Reverend Hezekiah H. Hunter wrote the governor to ask for any position, so long as it paid "a living salary." [64] In the final days of Reconstruction, former Congressman Alonzo J. Ransier found himself similarly situated.[65] Even Richard H. Cain, a successful newspaper editor, minister, and landowner who had prided himself on never asking for political patronage, soon found that he "must look after something or . . . be left out in the cold." [66] Martin R. Delany was beginning a real estate venture in 1871 and wanted the position of jury commissioner simply to "help bear expenses till I begin to make money by my business." [67]

Of course, other Negroes were fortunate enough to be financially independent of politics. Some, like the McKinlays, had inherited wealth and long-term investments in real estate and other capital enterprises. Others

58. Tabulated from "Appointments by Gov. Chamberlain," a typescript in the South Carolina Archives, Columbia.

59. James Bynum to Robert K. Scott, n.d. [1869], Scott Papers.

60. J. H. Jenks to Robert K. Scott, December 10, 1870, ibid.

61. B. F. Whittemore to Robert K. Scott, January 12, 1869, ibid.

62. E. B. Seabrook to Robert K. Scott, May 31, 1872, ibid.

63. T. J. Coghlan to Robert K. Scott, January 7, 1869; cf. Coghlan to Scott, October 12, 1868, ibid.

64. Hezekiah H. Hunter to Robert K. Scott, July 11, 1868, ibid.

65. Alonzo J. Ransier to Daniel H. Chamberlain, September 8, 1876, Chamberlain Papers.

66. Richard H. Cain to Robert K. Scott, November 1, 1870; cf. Cain to Scott, July 15, 1871, Scott Papers.

67. Martin R. Delany to Robert K. Scott, March 25, 1871, ibid.

had built up successful businesses after the war. William R. Jervay actually resigned his position as trial justice because it was taking too much time from his plantation and construction businesses.[68]

The governor might also exercise power by virtue of his own wealth and resources. Francis L. Cardozo approached Scott for a $2,000 loan to build a house in 1868. Although apparently he later decided not to build and did not need the loan, he was a strong booster of Scott for the gubernatorial nomination in 1868.[69] When he needed to meet a payment on some land he had purchased in Hamburg, Prince Rivers asked Scott for a $225 short-term loan.[70] A local Negro politician in Charleston made a similar request just two months later.[71]

No officeholder could ignore the governor's ability to manipulate local constituencies through his appointive powers. For example, in a heated dispute between Senator George F. McIntyre and Governor Moses in 1872, the governor was staunchly defended by a local newspaper. Moses appointed the newspaper editor, A. C. Shaffer, as county treasurer and began building a rival political organization directed toward unseating McIntyre.[72] In fact, practically all local Republican newspapers were owned by officeholders who used them as their personal political instruments. These papers were sustained almost entirely by the patronage of the central administration, which gave them contracts to publish the laws and various public announcements.[73] So again the local politicians were to some degree dependent upon the governor for their survival, just as he was dependent upon legions of political appointees to carry the election for him.[74]

More directly concerned with the business of carrying elections was the party apparatus itself. The state central committee, the party conventions, the county chairmen, and to a lesser extent the Union Leagues controlled the process by which aspirants were nominated, campaigned, and were elected to office. All of these institutions were to a large degree controlled by Negroes. For example, in 1869 most officers of the Union League organizations in Charleston and Edgefield counties were Negro, and Cardozo was president of the state organization.[75] Generally a Negro

68. William R. Jervay to Robert K. Scott, May 26, 1871, *ibid.*

69. Francis L. Cardozo to E. P. Smith, May 1, 1868, A.M.A. Papers.

70. Prince Rivers to Robert K. Scott, December 29, 1871, Scott Papers.

71. L. Bunch to Robert K. Scott, February 25, 1872, *ibid.*

72. *News and Courier,* April 3, 1874.

73. Robert Smalls's paper, the *Beaufort Standard,* was accused by a rival, the *Port Royal Commercial,* of receiving $6,000 a year from the county to publish the laws. *Port Royal Commercial,* February 12, 1874.

74. See E. P. Wall to Robert K. Scott, March 7, 1872, Scott Papers.

75. *Daily Republican,* October 31, November 22, 1869.

presided at state party conventions—indeed, Robert B. Elliott presided at most of them—and Negroes held practically all of the key offices in these conventions.[76]

A nominating convention's results often depended on the county chairmen who called and presided over the local precinct meetings where delegates to the state convention were selected. The chairmen exercised a great deal of discretion in determining when and where a meeting would be held and who could participate. Some, like Robert Smalls, were not above calling "rump" sessions at their homes and dictating a slate of hand-picked delegates in order to out-maneuver their political opponents. It was by such a maneuver that Smalls beat Whipper out of the nomination for the state Senate seat in 1872.[77] Not only did the county chairmen exercise considerable influence on the nominations; they also determined the commitment of the county's party machinery to the campaign of a particular candidate. Negroes appear to have had a decisive edge in this powerful position throughout the Reconstruction period, holding more than half the chairmanships between 1870 and 1876. When the six solidly Democratic up-country counties are excluded, the predominance of Negro chairmen is even more impressive. Of the remaining twenty-five Republican counties in 1870, for example, fully 72 percent of the chairmen were Negro.[78]

The other important element in the Republican party machinery was the state central committee, which normally planned and administered statewide campaigns and raised and distributed the campaign funds. The central committee chairman was white for the first few months after the Republican party was organized, with C. C. Bowen, J. H. Jenks, and B. F. Whittemore all serving for brief periods, but Negroes took over its leadership very early in the 1868 presidential campaign and never relinquished it thereafter. They held the chairmanship and a majority of the seats on the committee for most of the Reconstruction period.[79]

As with other institutions, however, effective control was dependent on more than a simple numerical domination. The key function of the committee was to manage the election campaign; in order to do that, it had to raise and distribute money. The funds for the first election campaigns appear to have come largely from individual party members

76. *Charleston Advocate,* May 11, 1867; *Union-Herald* (Columbia), September 8, 1874.

77. Okon Edet Uya, *From Slavery to Public Service: Robert Smalls, 1839-1915* (New York: Oxford University Press, 1971), p. 74.

78. These statistics were compiled from lists of county chairmen reported in various newspapers of the period.

79. Alonzo J. Ransier (1868-72) and Robert B. Elliott (1872-76) were party chairmen after Benjamin F. Randolph was assassinated in October, 1868. See *Charleston Advocate,* November 5, 1867, August 15, 1868; *Daily Republican,* February 26, 1870; *Daily Courier,* September 10, 11, 1868.

who could draw on private resources.[80] For example, De Large claimed to have donated most of his earnings from the Confederate Navy to the Republican campaign.[81] Whittemore put $2,000 of his own money into his 1868 congressional campaign.[82] Evidence indicates that some white Northerners were able to tap private sources in the North in order to assist some of the Negro politicians who had none to draw on. It is possible that William Viney, a delegate to the constitutional convention, was assisted in this manner by a Massachusetts agency after Viney's crop had failed because of his arduous campaign efforts.[83]

Later, when the party had held office and controlled a respectable amount of federal and state patronage, it could tap internal sources with more authority and assurance. Funds were regularly solicited from state employees, including even the professors at the state university. The job security of the vast army of federal officeholders, especially at the Customs House, depended upon their meeting these periodic assessments.[84] But in the earlier phase some assistance was expected and received from the national party. South Carolina was given $5,000 for the presidential and congressional campaigns of 1868. The state's internal resources had reportedly been exhausted in the gubernatorial and legislative campaigns of the previous spring; without aid from the national organization, the party could not conduct the campaign.[85]

In situations like this, where assistance had to be solicited from outside the state, funding controls threatened policy controls as well. When Negro leaders ignored the policy of not electing blacks to conspicuously high offices and elected Benjamin F. Randolph as chairman of the state central committee—the first black in a key party post— John Morris, an agent for the national committee, was in South Carolina. He deplored the apparent disposition of blacks to push their own people into key positions, and he found it unfortunate that the black Republicans so greatly out-

80. J. H. Jenks to William E. Chandler, June 17, 1868, Chandler Papers; Richard H. Cain to Robert K. Scott, December 12, 1870, Scott Papers.

81. *Daily Republican,* June 24, 1870.

82. B. F. Whittemore to William E. Chandler, September 16, 1868, Chandler Papers.

83. E. G. Dudley to John A. Andrews, July 31, 1867, John Albion Andrews Collection, Massachusetts Historical Society. I am grateful to Larry Powell for bringing this evidence to my attention.

84. See circular requesting political contributions to Professor Fisk Brewer of the University of South Carolina, and his reply: Fisk Brewer Papers, South Caroliniana Library, University of South Carolina, Columbia. A Customs House employee was alleged to have been dismissed because he failed to contribute. *News and Courier,* October 2, 1874. These methods were of course common to nineteenth-century politics and have survived into the twentieth century in some states.

85. J. H. Jenks to William E. Chandler, July 17, 1868; T. L. Tullock to Chandler, August 8, 1868; Jenks to William Clafin, August 10, 1868; Jenks to Tullock, August 10, 1868; Tullock to Chandler, September 4, 1868, Chandler Papers.

numbered the whites. He found the black leaders to be very "shrewd, but not yet educated politically." Their election of Randolph as party chairman over Daniel H. Chamberlain demonstrated this fact, for while Randolph was "quite a speaker and a good man," he was "totally unfit for that position." Since it would be too irregular and disruptive to form an alternative state organization, Morris recommended that the national committee simply bypass Randolph's committee in distributing funds. The money which the state party so desperately needed could be sent directly to the four congressional district campaign committees. Morris had already advised some of the state's prominent white Republicans to use this expedient, and the national office could expect a letter requesting the same within a few weeks. Sensitive to the explosive import of this policy recommendation, Morris hastened to add: "Do not let any Southern man see my letter." [86]

Such direct grants of campaign funds were much less important than the distribution of federal patronage in influencing local politics, however. In addition to the usual federal offices connected with the district courts, internal revenue service, and post office, there were three ports in South Carolina—Charleston, Beaufort, and Georgetown—which all required inspectors and laborers to man them. A small port like Beaufort could employ about twenty workers in some periods, while a larger facility like Charleston's would have more than twice as many. Indeed, some years later a knowledgeable South Carolina politician called the office of collector of customs the most important and influential in the state.[87]

The patronage of the Customs House was controlled by the senior U.S. senator, in cooperation with the congressman representing the Charleston district. For much of the Reconstruction period this prerogative was exercised by Senator Frederick A. Sawyer and Congressman C. C. Bowen. Sawyer had been born in Massachusetts, but he came to South Carolina before the war to take a position as superintendent of the Charleston public schools. After the war he was appointed collector of internal revenue. He was elected as a delegate to the constitutional convention of 1868 but resigned, begging that the pressing duties of his office made it impossible for him to serve.[88] He later defeated the native-born Dr. A. G. Mackey for the vacant Senate seat; his election was generally credited to a coalition of white conservative Republicans and Democrats.[89]

86. John Morris to William Claflin, September 14, 1868, *ibid.*

87. W. N. Taft to John A. Logan, November 18, 1881, Collector of Customs Applications, Box 210, Records of the Bureau of Customs, RG 56, NA.

88. *Proceedings of the Constitutional Convention of South Carolina* (Charleston: Denny and Perry, 1868), p. 22.

89. *Daily Courier*, July 17, 1868.

Congressman Bowen was a Georgia native whose aborted service with the Confederate Army ended in his court-martial for murder. He was a delegate from Charleston in the constitutional convention and was later elected to Congress from the Charleston district.[90] Unlike Sawyer, Bowen never evidenced any particularly conservative ideological tendencies, leaning instead toward the radical wing of the party.

It appears that no detail of the appointments policy in the Customs House and no position, however small, escaped the attention of these or subsequent congressional representatives.[91] Here, as elsewhere, the Customs House jobs were largely sinecures used to reward the party faithful, who sometimes carried on with their other occupations while holding a customs appointment.[92] Officers were also chosen for their political proficiency, as well as their political loyalties, and were used extensively for electioneering purposes.[93] Black leaders realized the potency of these lures when they saw many of their erstwhile supporters working against De Large and for Bowen in the 1870 congressional election.[94] A Customs House job was extremely precarious, however; an employee was subject to dismissal whenever the political winds or alignments changed, or if he betrayed any signs of disloyalty.[95]

The first postwar collector of the Charleston Customs House was Dr. A. G. Mackey, a South Carolina native of Unionist sentiments who later served as president of the constitutional convention of 1868. Mackey received his appointment from President Johnson because of his wartime loyalty and Johnson's policy of building a personal constituency among the prominent and influential native white Southerners. The fact that Mackey was a nationally prominent Mason appears to have benefited him also.[96] As collector, Mackey faithfully executed the Johnson policy of appointing white natives even when many of them were tainted with

90. Simkins and Woody, *South Carolina During Reconstruction*, p. 118.

91. See George S. Boutwell to George W. Clark, March 24, 1870, Letters Received, 1869-70, Collector of Customs, Charleston; A. Kalstrom to H. G. Worthington, August 28, 1874, Letters Sent, 1873-76, Superintending Architect, Charleston Customs House, RG 56, NA.

92. See Cecil Neil to Hugh McCulloch, January 29, 1867, Collector of Customs Applications, RG 56, NA.

93. Cecil Neil to Hugh McCulloch, July 31, 1868; Neil to James B. Campbell, September 5, 1868, *ibid.*

94. "Ciroco" to George S. Boutwell, September 10, 1870, *ibid.*

95. See for example the wholesale house-cleaning by Collector H. G. Worthington: Worthington to B. H. Bristow, February 27, 1875; Daniel A. Straker to Bristow, December 27, 1875, *ibid.*

96. A. J. Pierson to Andrew Johnson, May 1, 1866, Naval Officers Applications, Box 19; Charles Northrup to Andrew Johnson, June 3, 1865, Collectors of Customs Applications, Box 210, RG 56, NA.

the rebellion. Applicants who could take the loyalty oath were extremely hard to find; this resulted in some appointments of officers who refused to take the oath, and of others who perjured themselves.[97]

With the defeat of President Johnson and the beginning of the congressional phase of Reconstruction, Mackey changed his allegiances (verbally, at least) to the radical wing of the Republican party. He identified himself very closely with most of the Negro leaders, whom he coopted into supporting his 1868 senatorial bid. Mackey lost to Sawyer after eight ballots, mainly because Sawyer gained the support of the Democrats and a few Negro legislators like Robert Smalls who did not trust Mackey's conversion, seeing that he still had not hired any blacks at the Customs House.[98]

One of Sawyer's first acts as senator was to organize a campaign to replace Mackey. The fact that Mackey still employed former Confederate soldiers and men who had held government positions in the Confederacy was sufficient to obtain his removal and the appointment of George W. Clark, a Northerner who had served as mayor of Charleston under the military government and was himself very much identified with the Democrats.[99] Sawyer succeeded in securing the support of such key state Republicans as Senator T. J. Robertson, Congressmen C. C. Bowen and B. F. Whittemore, and Attorney General Daniel H. Chamberlain in his bid to remove Mackey. Governor Scott, on the other hand, supported the retention of his political friend and was left red-faced and perplexed by President Grant's decision to remove Mackey.[100]

The Mackey-Bowen political feud continued for most of the decade. Although the alignments shifted and the issues or offices at stake varied, the common factor was control of the Customs House and its effect on electoral politics in Charleston. A year after Mackey's removal as collector, his family and partisans allied themselves temporarily with De Large

97. A. G. Mackey to Hugh McCulloch, August 16, 1866; B. F. Perry to McCulloch, May 27, 1866; E. G. Hoffman to McCulloch, July 20, 1866; Mackey to McCulloch, September 8, 1865, Nominations File, RG 56, NA.

98. *Daily Courier,* July 16, 1868.

99. *Daily Courier,* August 5, 7, 1869.

100. The following items of correspondence reveal the basic alignments in this fight. Wellington Starr to John Heart, October 1, 1868, Scott Papers; Henry Beecher to U. S. Grant, July 7, 1869, Collector of Customs Applications; "Cover sheet to Collector of Customs Applications," Box 210; Frederick A. Sawyer *et al.* to George S. Boutwell, May 27, 1869; Daniel H. Chamberlain to C. C. Bowen, June 19, 1869; Stanley Trott to Bowen, July 7, 1869; Robert K. Scott to Grant, June 29, 1869, Nominations File, RG 56, NA. S. L. Bennett wrote Scott warning that Mackey was no friend when he learned of Scott's letter to Grant: Bennett to Scott, July 7, 1869, Scott Papers. After his removal Mackey refused to surrender the Customs House to Clark: A. G. Mackey to Boutwell, July 5, 22, 1869, Nominations File, RG 56, NA.

and other Negro leaders who were then making a bid for a greater share of the key political offices for blacks. The De Large group only narrowly won Charleston that year, despite a black majority in the county. Collector Clark's use of black Customs House employees to campaign for the Bowen-Sawyer group appears to have undercut De Large's appeal for black solidarity somewhat.[101] And although his ticket did win, De Large eventually lost his congressional seat when Bowen contested the narrow election margin.

The Negro leaders were not alone when they found their drive for power was hampered by their lack of control of federal patronage generally and the Customs House in particular. No Reconstruction governor ever controlled the Customs House patronage, and that patronage was used against all of them. Robert K. Scott wrote with greatest bitterness about this aspect of his tenure as governor; he had been forced by the national administration to fight the Democrats with one hand and the Customs House gang with the other, he complained.[102] In each of the gubernatorial elections of 1870, 1872, and 1874, a segment of the Republican party had bolted the state convention and supported a rival slate of state officers and legislators. The Customs House group composed a major segment of these bolters, who were to a greater or lesser extent allied with the Democrats in a fusion movement.[103] And in some of these elections the national administration either partly or wholly, directly or indirectly, supported the bolters against the regular party. Although the bolting or fusionist ticket lost the state by a wide margin in each election, it is significant that they carried Charleston County, where the Customs House had its greatest influence, in every election except the one in 1870. (That was the election in which there was a coalition between the Mackey family and the Negro leaders.) In the subsequent campaign in 1872 the bolters carried only nine up-country counties and Charleston County, where their entire legislative ticket was elected. Bowen defeated E. W. M. Mackey in the race for sheriff of Charleston County.[104]

Some observers insisted that the Customs House had little influence outside Charleston.[105] But Charleston was the single most important county in the state, because of its population and the sheer size of its

101. See "Ciroco" to George S. Boutwell, September 10, 1870, Collector of Customs Applications, RG 56, NA.

102. Robert K. Scott to Richard H. Gleaves, June 12, 1875, newspaper clipping in "Reconstruction Scrapbook."

103. For example, see Henry C. Carter to U. S. Grant, October 3, 1872, Collector of Customs Applications, RG 56, NA.

104. The *Union-Herald* claimed that the Grant administration forced the party to dump Moses in 1874; *Union-Herald,* July 11, 1874; *Beaufort Republican,* July 11, February 8, 1872; *Daily Courier,* July 22, 1870, July 21, 1872.

105. *Union-Herald,* June 11, 1874.

legislative delegation: two senators (all other counties had one) and eighteen members of the House of Representatives (about one-sixth of the total). Certainly, Scott acknowledged the importance of the Customs' patronage to his political fortunes; so did Chamberlain, who sought to purge Collector Worthington in preparation for his 1876 reelection campaign.[106]

Worthington had been appointed collector at the insistence of Senator John J. Patterson. (Patterson had replaced Sawyer in the Senate—evidently against the wishes of the president, since Grant had publicly endorsed Sawyer prior to the election.[107]) With Patterson as the senator controlling the Customs nominations, Negro leaders appear to have gained a larger measure of influence over this patronage. It is likely that their support of Patterson in the senatorial contest gave them leverage, just as their general opposition to Sawyer and Bowen had denied them any significant influence before. For instance, De Large found that even after he had replaced Bowen in Congress, he had virtually no voice in the distribution of patronage, even in the less significant post at the Port of Beaufort. After promising J. P. M. Epping a position after the congressional election, De Large found that he could not deliver because of Sawyer's opposition.[108]

The ability to reward friends and punish enemies is axiomatic to the development of a political machine: unity based on race and color is simply not enough. Their failure to control the Customs House had weakened the Negro leadership in its drive for other more powerful positions, and, consequently, for a larger voice in the development of policies in the state. During the 1876 campaign there were rumors rife in the Republican camp that Smalls and other Negro leaders planned a coup with respect to federal patronage in the state, if the Republicans won. If this rumor was true, the disastrous results of the campaign of 1876 foreclosed that possibility.[109] Yet such intentions on the part of the Negro leadership further illustrate their growing political sophistication and the determined and steady extension of their domination of the major instruments of political power in the state.

The nuances of the power relationship between black and white Republicans were diverse and multifaceted. For most of the Reconstruction period, the patterns that emerge depict a situation of neither complete

106. Daniel H. Chamberlain to U. S. Grant, January 12, 1876, Collector of Customs Applications, RG 56, NA.

107. *Union Herald,* September 30, 1872. John J. Patterson to General Babcock, June 13, 1873, Collector of Customs Applications, RG 56, NA.

108. J. P. M. Epping to Robert K. Scott, April 28, 1871, Scott Papers.

109. *Beaufort Tribune,* July 12, 1876.

black domination nor unchallenged white control. The success of black legislative initiatives (as reflected in their success scores in Figure 1) declined relative to those of white Republicans, but this reflects a general decline in overall Republican effectiveness as their majority in the General Assembly shrunk. In fact, if any pattern emerges it is that as Negro politicians grew more experienced politically, they discerned the key levers of power in the state and moved to take them over. That they did not move more quickly and precipitously to control these institutions probably reflects the extent to which they were themselves divided by suspicions of each other that sometimes rivaled those which they harbored about their white colleagues. The occasional failures of black legislators to support other blacks for key offices such as U.S. senator may reflect a deeper problem than a mere lack of aggressiveness. The obstacle to establishing black dominion may have been less a matter of countervailing white control than a problem of the new leadership's definition of itself. Who, after all, was black?

Chapter Six

Radicals and Conservatives: The Voting Behavior of Negro Legislators

On March 21, 1867, when delegates met at Military Hall to organize the Republican party and agree upon the principles and policies for which that party would stand, they were keenly aware of the many dangers that imperiled their success in the coming campaign. Speaker after speaker alerted them to be wary of attempts by their former masters to beguile them and control their votes. But one speaker, Francis L. Cardozo, warned of another more subtle threat to their political success. It was a danger, he said, "peculiar to ourselves."

> From the unhappy state of things which has existed here in the enjoyment of this new privilege the colored find themselves divided and disunited by a variety of sentiments and feelings. Whatever may be a man's social status, whatever may be his religious views, whatever may be the state of his knowledge, if he will come with you and vote for this platform, unite with him, if it be Satan himself. (Cheers) Let no cause of dissension, no feeling of animosity, no objection to social condition, prevent you from securing to yourselves and your children the liberty that has been committed to you.[1]

Subsequent events disproved the fears that freedmen would vote for their former masters. The masses of black voters remained staunchly Republican during that decade and for several more to come. As one black politician in South Carolina reminisced in the 1880's, "The condition of the South made it as natural for the Negro to be Republican as for the young of animals to follow their parents."[2] With the Negro voters, as with Frederick Douglass, the Republican party was the deck; all else, the sea.

1. *Daily Courier,* March 22, 1867.
2. D[aniel] Augustus Straker, *The New South Investigated* (Detroit: Ferguson, 1888), p. 57.

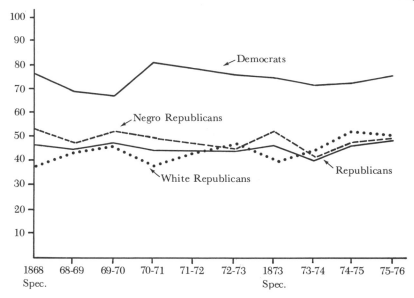

FIGURE 2. AVERAGE RELATIVE COHESION FOR LEGISLATIVE SUBGROUPS, 1868-76

But the danger of factionalism and dissension among the Negro leadership soon proved all too real. Indeed, the Republicans' overwhelming electoral majorities have contributed to the traditional image of Negro leaders as a political monolith, undifferentiated in their political opinions, but there was significant disagreement among these politicians on some of the major issues of the period. While it is true that much of this conflict derived from narrowly personal or factional interests, there were also divisions that appear to have been ideological in content and related partly to the differences in social status and condition to which Cardozo had alluded in 1867.

Of course, the cleavages among Negro leaders were never as sharp as those between Republicans and Democrats, or even those between Negro and white Republicans. However, the differences were significant enough to contribute to the failure of some of the party's legislative initiatives, and to restrain some of the more radical or experimental policies that were put forth.

One measure of the internal conflicts of these legislative subgroups—Democrats, white Republicans, and Negro Republicans—is the index of relative cohesion developed by sociologist Stuart Rice in the 1920's. If the members of a particular group all vote the same way on a roll call, they are perfectly cohesive and score 100 on this index. If they vote half for and half against a given proposition, the group's cohesion score is zero. All other voting patterns for the group other than these two extremes will lie between o and 100 on the Rice index.[3]

Although the conservative press continuously bemoaned the alleged tyranny of the Republican party caucus over individual Republican legislators, it would appear that the Democrats applied the party whip more decisively. In all ten legislative sessions between 1868 and 1876, Democrats were consistently and (in comparison with Republicans) almost perfectly united. (See Figure 2.) Their average index of relative cohesion on roll call votes never fell below 68, while the Republican index never rose above 50. Negro Republicans were fairly consistent in the degree of cohesion they maintained for much of the period, and during most sessions they were more united than their white Republican colleagues. However, the cohesion among white Republicans did increase toward the end of the decade, and in fact exceeded that of Negro legislators in the final two sessions.

Underlying the Republican legislators' lack of unity was a fairly continuous conflict between white and black members. When the most critical issues came to a roll-call vote, a majority of the white Republicans opposed a majority of the blacks on at least one out of three. In fact, during the administration of Franklin J. Moses, Jr., the black and white Republican majorities voted against each other on six out of every ten critical votes.[4]

3. To calculate the relative cohesion index for any legislative subgroup, one must first determine the proportion voting yea and the proportion voting nay as percentages of that group present and voting on a given issue. The absolute difference between these two percentages yields the index of relative cohesion. The indexes for individual roll calls can be cumulated and then averaged to get a single index for the entire legislative session. These averages can be calculated for subsets of issues as well. In this analysis no significant differences were found between the indexes for various issue types, so only the overall averages are reported here. For a more detailed discussion of the Rice index, see Lee F. Anderson, Meredith W. Watts, and Allen Wilcox, *Legislative Roll-Call Analysis* (Evanston: Northwestern University Press, 1966), pp. 32-39.

4. The "critical" roll calls are selected using a mathematical formula, William Riker's coefficient of significance, which applies the criteria of degree of participation and closeness of the outcome on a vote as measures of significance. It is assumed that the more sharply a vote is contested, the more critical it is in the eyes of the legislators. The word "critical" is used here—implying the significance of the vote outcome—rather than the word "important," which implies the substantive effect the decision will have outside the legislature. A roll call can be important, but not critical. In this analysis all roll calls with a coefficient of 0.40 or more have been selected as critical. This figure corresponds roughly to a situation where the absentee rate is 25% or less and a division among Republicans of less than two to one. Using this criterion, the percentage of critical votes in which the majority of white Republicans opposed the majority of Negroes was as follows: 37% in 1868 special session, 29% in 1868-69, 38% in 1869-70, 40% in 1870-71, 38% in 1871-72, 59% in 1872-73, 54% in 1873 special session, 60% in 1873-74, 16% in 1874-75, and 20% in 1875-76. For more detail on the coefficient of significance, see Anderson *et al.*, *Legislative Roll-Call Analysis*, pp. 81-86.

While the conflicts between white and black Republicans were often clear, these were not the only sources of disunity and perhaps not even the most significant ones. The fact is that Negro Republicans could outvote the whites—Republicans and Democrats combined—in a purely racial test of strength, since the Negro majority in the House never fell below 57 percent.[5] But the Negro members came from disparate backgrounds and sometimes betrayed severe intragroup strains along color and, ultimately, class lines. The debates among the delegates to the Colored People's Convention of 1865 indicated that the interests and political orientations of the relatively affluent, freeborn mulattoes of Charleston might develop along lines divergent from those of the generally poor, slave-born black masses.

The debates of the 1868 constitutional convention showed similar differences in interests and political orientations. Negro delegates differed on the major issues before the convention, which included disfranchisement of former Confederates, land reform measures, suffrage for freedmen, and integration of public schools. It should be noted, however, that the ultimate resolution of some of these issues often seems to have been dictated or influenced by political forces emanating from outside the state, more than from the personal convictions or social backgrounds of the legislators. However, some of the patterns vaguely discernible in the earlier meetings became overt here.

For instance, there were frequent and almost universal professions of moderation on the question of the disfranchisement of the planter class. A. G. Mackey, the shrewd native white who presided over the convention, declared his opposition to "any general disfranchisement" practically at the opening gavel. And Landon S. Langley, a Vermont-born mulatto delegate representing Beaufort, moved almost immediately after the organization of the convention to offer a resolution calling for a permanent halt to the confiscation of land and disfranchisement for political offenses. In response William A. Driffle, a mulatto South Carolinian, offered a counterresolution to leave the entire matter in the hands of the federal authorities. The latter motion was referred to and apparently died in committee.[6]

However, on the fourth day Robert C. De Large moved to take up Langley's resolution, forcing the first test vote on this issue and the first roll call of the Reconstruction period. The motion was defeated on a racially split vote, 46-61, with more than 60 percent of the whites voting

5. Of course, blacks did not have a racial majority in the Senate, but after 1870 they constituted at least 47% of the Senate's membership, and the president was a Negro.

6. *Proceedings of the Constitutional Convention of South Carolina* (Charleston: Denny and Perry, 1868), pp. 17, 40.

in favor of considering the measure and almost 70 percent of the Negro delegates opposing it. This first major roll call of the new leadership also displayed some other divisions among the delegates. Most white leaders were on the losing side of this vote, including two future governors, Daniel Chamberlain and Franklin J. Moses; two future congressmen, C. C. Bowen and E. W. M. Mackey, and the convention's president, Dr. A. G. Mackey, who cast one of his infrequent votes on this critical issue. Many prominent Negro leaders also voted in favor of the motion, including Robert B. Elliott, William James Whipper, Joseph H. Rainey, Henry E. Hayne, William Beverly Nash, and Benjamin F. Randolph, all of whom would soon hold powerful offices in the party, state, and federal administrations. However, among the opponents were some Negro leaders of equal prominence, such as Robert Smalls, Jonathan J. Wright, Francis L. Cardozo, Richard H. Cain, William McKinlay, and Alonzo J. Ransier.[7]

There also appear to have been subtle divisions in the way the various segments of the Negro delegation voted. Of the sixty Negroes voting on this issue, twenty-six were freeborn and thirty-two were slave-born, twenty-six mulatto and twenty-nine black. Although a majority of all these groups voted against the resolution, the freeborn and mulatto delegates were more likely to support it than were their slave-born and black colleagues. Over 40 percent of the freeborn group favored the motion, while less than a quarter of the slave-born did; a similar proportion of mulattoes voted affirmatively (42%), in contrast with a smaller proportion of blacks (24%). Apparently the slave-born and black delegates took a somewhat harder line against acting precipitously to relieve the planter class of the disfranchisement and confiscation measures that had been imposed upon them.[8]

Of course, some delegates voting against De Large's motion were evidently not opposed to the idea of relief for the planters per se; they merely felt that the resolution was premature. William McKinlay, one of the eleven free mulattoes who opposed the motion to consider relief measures, declared his support of the resolution's intent, but felt it should be delayed until later in the session.[9] This kind of sentiment, combined with the fact that most of the convention's key leaders—Negro and white—favored some measure of relief, probably caused this early vote

7. *Ibid.,* p. 43.

8. A measure of correlation shows a moderate relationship. Yule's Q for these distributions are 0.36 for that based on prewar origins and 0.39 for that based on color. These statistics are interpretable as a proportional reduction in error; that is, the knowledge of a delegate's origins and color would enable one to reduce by 12% and 15% the errors made in predicting how he voted.

9. *Constitutional Convention,* p. 43.

Date   Motion Maker   Motion.   Polarity*

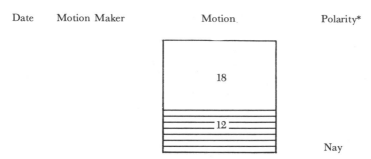

Nay

1/27/68   De Large   Take up resolution to stop disfranchisement and confiscation for
                     political offenses

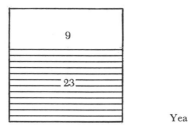

Yea

3/14/68   Bell   Indefinitely postpone resolution to petition Congress to remove political
                 disabilities

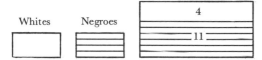

*Polarity indicates how radical group voted.

FIGURE 3. VOTING ALIGNMENT IN CONSTITUTIONAL CONVENTION ON REMOVAL OF POLITICAL
DISABILITIES, 1868

to be reversed toward the end of the session, when the delegates overwhelmingly supported a second resolution introduced by De Large peti-
tioning Congress to remove all political disabilities.[10]

The new proposal was shorn of the confiscation issue, and it actually
postponed any final decision on disfranchisement by leaving it to Congress.
But beyond these factors the motivations of the delegates, though not
entirely clear, probably involved the growing conviction that they must
project a more moderate image during the closing days of the convention.
On several occasions speakers warned the delegates of the need to be
politic if the constitution was to have any hope of success. This was

10. *Ibid.*, p. 877.

especially true after the Alabama constitution was defeated at the polls.[11] For instance, Cardozo, who had voted against the earlier disfranchisement proposal and against other relief measures, urged the delegates to favor De Large's resolution so as to demonstrate the absence of any desires for revenge on their part.[12] Furthermore, given the opposition of many of these same delegates to propositions for general amnesty in later years, it is very possible that their support of this amnesty resolution was based more on political strategy than on political principles.

The key votes in this turnabout by the convention were cast by thirty-two delegates who had voted against the De Large motion, but in favor of the later petition. Negro delegates contributed twenty-three of these swing votes. Figure 3 shows the relative proportion of white and Negro delegates in each of the three major groups: first, the bloc of conservative voters who favored the earlier De Large motion to take up the disfranchisement issue and opposed the Bell motion to kill De Large's second resolution to petition Congress; the second bloc made up of swing voters who opposed the first motion but supported De Large's second proposal; and the third bloc of radical voters who did not waver in their opposition to the removal of political disabilities at the beginning or at the end of the session. On this issue Negro delegates had a considerably more radical record than whites, casting more than twice as many radical votes in proportion to their numbers.

A cautious approach was also urged upon the delegates when they considered the confiscation issue in another context. No one in this convention of delegates elected by an overwhelmingly black, land-hungry constituency ever proposed outright, uncompensated confiscation of the kind that Thaddeus Stevens had already urged on an unwilling Congress. Indeed, outright confiscation was no longer a tenable alternative for a new regime unsure of its tenure, beginning its reconstruction of southern society when popular and congressional support for radical social measures—as opposed to strictly political measures designed to ensure continued Republican hegemony—had definitely waned. By 1868, summary confiscation was an idea whose time had passed.[13]

Nevertheless, the generally desperate economic plight of the planter class did present another alternative. The debt-ridden planters could be

11. *Ibid.*, pp. 473, 703.

12. *Ibid.*, p. 878.

13. For discussion of the briefness of the radical phase and quick resurgence of conservatism, see C. Vann Woodward, *American Counterpoint: Slavery and Racism in the North-South Dialogue* (Boston; Little, Brown, 1971), pp. 163-83; William S. McFeely, *Yankee Stepfather: General O. O. Howard and the Freedmen* (New Haven: Yale University Press, 1968); John McCarthy, "Reconstruction Legislation and Voting Alignments in the House of Representatives, 1863-69" (Ph.D. dissertation, Yale University, 1970), pp. 317-20.

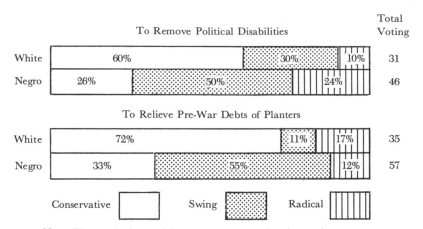

Note: The graphed quantities are proportions of each constituent group.

FIGURE 4. VOTING ALIGNMENT IN CONSTITUTIONAL CONVENTION ON DISABILITIES AND DEBTS, 1868

turned off their lands through aggressive taxation policies, if at the same time all measures designed to relieve those debts were resisted. Theoretically, these actions would force the devalued lands of the planters onto the market, where their former slaves could buy them. The issue of land reform was generally broached in these terms when several propositions for temporary and permanent debt relief were introduced into the convention.[14] A major argument of the proponents of debt relief, aside from humanitarian appeals to save the poor widows and orphans, was the necessity of saving the state from economic collapse. This argument was underscored with an insistence that these relief measures were necessary to mitigate the political opposition of the planter class, and the hope that some of this class could be attracted into a new Republican coalition by such displays of magnanimity. Franklin J. Moses, himself an apostate Confederate, must have been moved by such considerations when he introduced a resolution to petition the military governor to suspend for three months the collection of debts contracted prior to June 30, 1865.[15] Francis L. Cardozo strongly opposed this resolution, basing his argument primarily on the contention that such laws unconstitutionally violated the rights of creditors.[16] But Richard H. Cain struck at the heart of

14. This issue of relief for planters who were burdened with slave debts was debated very heatedly in the 1866 provisional legislature. Delegates from rural districts generally opposed urban representatives; in fact, General M. C. Butler, prominent in the overthrow of the Republicans in 1876, introduced the relief bill in 1866. *Daily Courier,* September 4, 17, 1866.

15. *Constitutional Convention,* pp. 62-64, 105-7.

16. *Ibid.,* pp. 116-18.

the matter when he pointed out: "If we pass this resolution, the large landowners will keep the lands in their hands. If they are obliged to sell their lands, the poor man will have a chance to buy." [17]

But Negro leaders were sharply split on this issue, one which they appear to have approached from very divergent perspectives. On the day following Cain's impassioned plea, De Large countered with the charge that the opponents of debt relief were all speculators out for private gain, alleging that it was obvious that the freedmen would not be able to buy the land at auction, because it would be sold in large tracts.[18] On the contrary, insisted Cardozo, it was possible for blacks to get land, as proven by the example of the Charleston Land Company, a corporation of 100 poor blacks which had recently bought a 6,000-acre plantation, worth $25,000 in better times, for a greatly deflated postwar price of $6,600. Pressing the political necessity of passing some measure to relieve the planters, De Large warned the delegates: "The defeat of this measure [the Moses resolution for planter relief] may lead to the defeat of the ratification of the Constitution framed by this Convention." Yet, Cardozo reasoned, the convention's very raison d'être was involved in this question: "We will never have true freedom until we abolish the system of agriculture which existed in the Southern States. It is useless to have any schools," insisted this devoted educator, "while we maintain the stronghold of slavery as the agricultural system of the country." [19]

Nevertheless, Moses's resolution eventually passed by a close vote of 57-52.[20] Nine whites and eleven Negroes who had voted on the radical side of the disfranchisement issue switched to the conservative side on debt relief. Thus the Negro delegates provided the larger proportion of the swing votes on both measures. Those who switched from a radical position on De Large's original motion to the conservative side of Moses's resolution a few days later provided the slim margin of victory for the latter. At the same time, it is clear that the Negro delegates approached these measures with caution, and that a much smaller proportion of them were consistently conservative on these issues than the whites. (See Figure 4.) Of the delegates voting on both roll calls, 55 percent of the Negroes took a radical to centrist position, as compared with a like proportion of whites who took a staunchly conservative position. Therefore, in a sense, a key element in the moderate-to-conservative actions of the convention with respect to the political rights and financial survival of the planter class was the rather solidly conservative voting behavior of the white

17. *Ibid.*, p. 110.
18. *Ibid.*, p. 113.
19. *Ibid.*, pp. 115, 117.
20. *Ibid.*, p. 148.

delegates. While some prominent Negro leaders spoke forcefully in favor of a conciliatory policy, many Negro delegates either opposed such policies outright or acquiesced only begrudgingly. Since in doing so they also resisted the bulk of the Republican party leadership, black as well as white, they must be credited with more independence of thought and action than has been generally accorded them.

Other measures related to land reform were more successful, though also subject to fierce debate. Given the increasing demands of their constituents for some kind of land reform, the strong opposition to these measures by some Negro leaders is surprising. On the sixteenth day of the convention Joseph H. Rainey pushed through a resolution disavowing any prospect of the freedmen getting land other than through their own private initiatives.[21] William James Whipper dismissed the whole notion of government grants to the poor, declaring at one point: "There has already been too much holding out this idea whereby a poor man shall be a land owner without any help of his own." [22] Richard H. Cain proposed to petition Congress for a million-dollar loan fund to purchase and subdivide land for resale to blacks at low prices. Whipper ridiculed this idea as well, insisting that it would be better to have no farms at all than farms of five to ten acres, which would be "just about enough to starve to death decently that one-fourth of the people [who received them]." [23] Opposition to Cain's resolution evaporated during the debate, however, and the measure was passed by a unanimous vote. Without serious opposition the convention also passed a constitutional provision instructing the legislature to create a state land commission, funded by an issue of interest-bearing bonds, to buy and subdivide plantations and resell the plots on five-year installment contracts.[24]

Considerable disagreement also developed among Negro delegates on the question of universal, unrestricted suffrage for the freedmen. Benjamin F. Randolph, a northern Presbyterian minister, Landon S. Langley, and such freeborn natives as Henry E. Hayne and William McKinlay argued strenuously that illiterates and those failing to pay the poll tax should not be allowed to vote.[25] Randolph and Langley insisted that their motive was to foster education among Negroes by tying the privilege of suffrage to literacy on the one hand and the poll tax, which was to be set aside exclusively for educational purposes, on the other. However, Joseph H. Rainey, a well-to-do barber, declared that "if a man could not raise one dollar a year poll tax for the educational fund of the state, they

21. *Ibid.*, p. 213.
22. *Ibid.*, p. 129.
23. *Ibid.*, p. 401.
24. *Ibid.*, pp. 438-39.
25. *Ibid.*, pp. 735-38.

should look upon him as a pauper that has no right to vote." [26] Fortunately for the paupers, Cardozo and Elliott argued against these restrictions, pointing out that, in the hands of a conservative regime, they could be used to disfranchise blacks. After some debate the political suicide of instituting literacy and poll tax requirements for suffrage was made clear, and these measures were overwhelmingly defeated.[27]

But generally the extension of ordinary civil and legal rights and privileges to the freedmen was not debatable in the convention, except where those measures might be construed as encouraging interracial contacts. These latter were gingerly handled. Such caution is understandable, given the rejection of black suffrage in many northern states just months before the convention. Even those black delegates who argued most aggressively for equal access to public accommodations and institutions demurred on an issue which they saw as involving strictly "social" equality. Indeed, only Cardozo suggested that integration might be a positive good. He put forth a somewhat advanced social-psychological concept that the integration of schools might deter the growth of prejudice in future generations by encouraging children to associate before adult prejudices had been established.[28] But even Cardozo took pains to point out that the proposed section of the constitution on education merely made integrated schools a legal possibility; it did not outlaw segregated schools. Indeed, he fully expected the matter to be regulated solely by racial pride and demographic considerations, wherein integrated schools would be established in the "sparsely settled country districts" and segregated ones in the cities.[29] Therefore his proposition was still something of a compromise between segregated and integrated schools, a compromise confirming a vague freedom-of-choice concept. The demands of William Beverly Nash and Benjamin F. Randolph for some positive constitutional mandate for integrated schools were resisted by Robert B. Elliott and Richard H. Cain, who insisted that integration should not be the issue here.[30]

Alonzo J. Ransier saw the education issue from a slightly different perspective, arguing that the proper goal was to create a constitution in which the very words "race and color" would not appear.[31] However, to other delegates a colorblind policy was no policy at all; positive legal safeguards were necessary to protect blacks from discrimination. "I want to fix the Constitution in such a way that no lawyer, however cunning

26. *Ibid.*, p. 737.
27. *Ibid.*, pp. 825-35.
28. *Ibid.*, p. 901.
29. *Ibid.*
30. *Ibid.*, p. 694.
31. *Ibid.*, p. 354.

Figure 5. Summary of Voting Alignment on Financial Policy, South Carolina House of Representatives, 1868 Special Session

Synopsis of Roll calls	Voting Bloc	Schematic of Members
For authorizing state loans..	1	☆ ☆ ☆ ☆ ☆ ☆ ☆ ☆ ☆ ☆ ☆ ☆ ★
For closing S.C. Bank	2	○ ○ ○ ○ ○ ○ ○ ○ ○ ○ ○ ○ ○ ○ ● ● ● ● ● ● ● ●
For closing S.C. Bank	3	● ● ● ● ● ●
For closing S.C. Bank	4	● ● ●
For closing S.C. Bank	5	● ●
Against financial inquiry........................	6	○ ○ ○ ○ ● ● ● ● ● ● ● ● ● ● ● ● ● ● ● ● ●
	7	○ ○ ○ ○ ○ ○ ○ ●

Note: Exhibits 5 through 10 are schematic representations of the distribution of individual members of certain legislative subgroups along a conservative to radical continuum. Each bloc is numbered in ascending order from least radical to most radical. A general synopsis of the roll calls which divided the legislators is also provided. (See Appendix B for fuller listing.) The voting bloc above a given cutting line opposed all those below the line on the roll call or roll calls indicated. Each symbol represents one person. The key is as follows: (☆) white Democrat, (★) Negro Democrat, (○) white Republican, and (●) Negro Republican. A member of the House leadership is indicated by underlining the respective symbol.

or astute, can possibly misinterpret the meaning," declared Cardozo. "If we do not do so, we deserve to be and will be cheated again." [32] He urged an amendment to the bill of rights that would have unequivocally prohibited racial discrimination in all public accommodations. Benjamin F. Randolph cosponsored Cardozo's resolution and argued throughout the session that provisions should be included that would create an integrated society. "The day is coming when we must decide whether the two races shall live together or not," he warned.[33] After advocating the conservative position on major issues like disfranchisement, unrestricted suffrage, and economic matters, Randolph sought to make the integration issue a test of radicalism. "Some of you accused me of being too conservative," he observed, "but you will see who are the conservatives in this house." [34] Evidently, using his criteria, the majority of the conven-

32. *Ibid.*
33. *Ibid.,* p. 747.
34. *Ibid.,* p. 750.

Figure 6. Summary of Voting Alignment on Financial Policy, South Carolina House of Representatives, 1869-70

Synopsis of Roll calls	Voting bloc	Schematic of Members
	1	☆ ☆ ☆ ☆ ☆ ○ ○ ● ● ●
For Sinking Fund and Wilmington RR	2	●
For Wilmington RR	3	☆ ☆ ☆ ○
For Phosphates Bill and Wilmington RR	4	●
For Wilmington RR	5	☆ ☆ ○ ○ ○ ○ ○ ● ● ● ● ● ● ●
For Gold Bill	6	●
For Gold Bill	7	● ●
For Gold Bill	8	● ● ● ● ● ●
For Gold Bill	9	☆ ☆ ○ ○ ○ ○ ○ ○ ○ ○ ○ ○ ○ ○ ○ ○ ●

tion delegates were conservative: Randolph's constitutional ban on racial discrimination failed, and the "freedom of choice" version of the section on schools passed with dissents from only four white up-country delegates who had insisted instead on a specific prohibition of integration.[35] On these matters the final draft of the state's constitution was silent, therefore, explicitly favoring neither segregation nor integration measures.

However, Randolph's challenge—"to see who are the conservatives in this house"—points up the rather difficult problem of gauging the relative ideological postures of individual delegates. How does one measure conservatism or radicalism? Traditional sources, such as memoirs and letters, are relatively scarce for the Negro legislators of this period. Indeed, such sources may be of limited use anyway in determining the political behavior of a group of politicians on several issues over an extended period of time.[36] A different approach is required—one which involves some objec-

35. *Ibid.*, p. 902.

36. Aside from the possible biases of observers who comment on a legislator and the

FIGURE 7. SUMMARY OF VOTING ALIGNMENT ON FINANCIAL POLICY, SOUTH CAROLINA HOUSE OF REPRESENTATIVES, 1870-71

Synopsis of Roll calls	Voting bloc	Schematic of Members
	1	☆ ☆ ☆ ☆ ☆ ☆ ☆ ☆ ☆ ☆ ○ ○ ○ ○ ○ ○ ○ ○ ○ ● ● ●
For Greenville RR		
For Sterling Fund	2	☆ ● ●
For Greenville RR	3	○ ○ ○ ● ● ● ● ● ● ●
For Greenville RR	4	●
For Greenville RR	5	●
For Sterling Fund	6	○ ○ ○ ○ ○ ● ● ● ● ● ● ● ● ● ● ● ● ● ● ●
Against furnishing State House	7	○ ○ ○ ○ ○ ○ ○ ○ ●
Against furnishing State House	8	○ ●
Against furnishing State House	9	●
	10	○ ○ ○ ○ ● ● ● ●

tive criteria for characterizing the political posture of a legislator, and which can be applied to all members for equivalent results.

A computer-assisted form of Guttman scaling provides one approach to this problem, for it is possible to determine simultaneously the interrelationships among roll calls and the pattern of members' responses to them. The responses can be summarized as scores, and these scores can be correlated with other information on the legislator, such as his constituency, his special political role, and his social and economic background. The scale analysis procedure involves a search of a given set of roll calls for subsets of votes that are statistically related, in that a member's vote on one roll call can be predicted from a knowledge of how he voted on the other roll calls in that subset. The individual roll calls are then

fact that his own interpretations will generally be self-serving, the major weakness of these methods, particularly for a study of the more obscure and forgotten Negro legislators, is that they focus almost invariably on the most prominent and vocal members of the group.

FIGURE 8. SUMMARY OF VOTING ALIGNMENT ON REPUBLICAN HEGEMONY, SOUTH CAROLINA HOUSE
OF REPRESENTATIVES, 1868 SPECIAL SESSION

Synopsis of Roll calls	Voting bloc	Schematic of Members
For ratifying 14th Amendment	1	☆ ☆ ☆ ☆ ☆ ☆ ☆ ☆ ☆
For Elections Bill	2	☆ ☆ ★ 〇 〇 〇
For Militia Bill	3	〇
For Dill's widow	4	〇 ●
For Elections Bill	5	〇 〇 〇 〇 ● ●
For qualifying county officers-elect	6	〇 〇 〇 〇 〇 〇 〇 〇 ●
For county prosecutor	7	〇 〇 ●
For altering Charleston Charter	8	● ● ● ● ● ●
	9	〇 〇 〇 〇 〇 〇 〇 〇 〇 ●

arranged in a cumulative order or scale. This scale is an arrangement
of the issues so that the first proposition was the easiest one for the members
to take a position on, since most could either support or oppose it, and
each succeeding proposition becomes increasingly difficult. This scale of
roll calls can be used like a yardstick to rank the members according
to their responses on the items within it. Ideally, the voting pattern of
legislators at one end of this yardstick is directly opposite that of the
members at the opposite end.[37]

The voting behavior of members of the early sessions of South Carolina's
reconstructed House of Representatives can be summarized through scale
analysis into three broad policy issues. The 511 roll calls in these sessions

37. See Appendix B for a more detailed discussion of the specific techniques applied
here for generating and selecting these scales. For fuller discussion of theoretical aspects
of Guttman scaling in general and its application to roll call analysis, see Anderson *et
al., Legislative Roll-Call Analysis,* pp. 90-119; Duncan MacRae, *Issues and Parties in Legislative
Voting* (New York: Harper and Row, 1970). Some of the specific methods, computer programs,
and techniques adopted here are discussed in McCarthy, "Reconstruction Legislation and
Voting Alignments," ch. 1 and appendices.

FIGURE 9. SUMMARY OF VOTING ALIGNMENT ON REPUBLICAN HEGEMONY, SOUTH CAROLINA
HOUSE OF REPRESENTATIVES, 1870-71

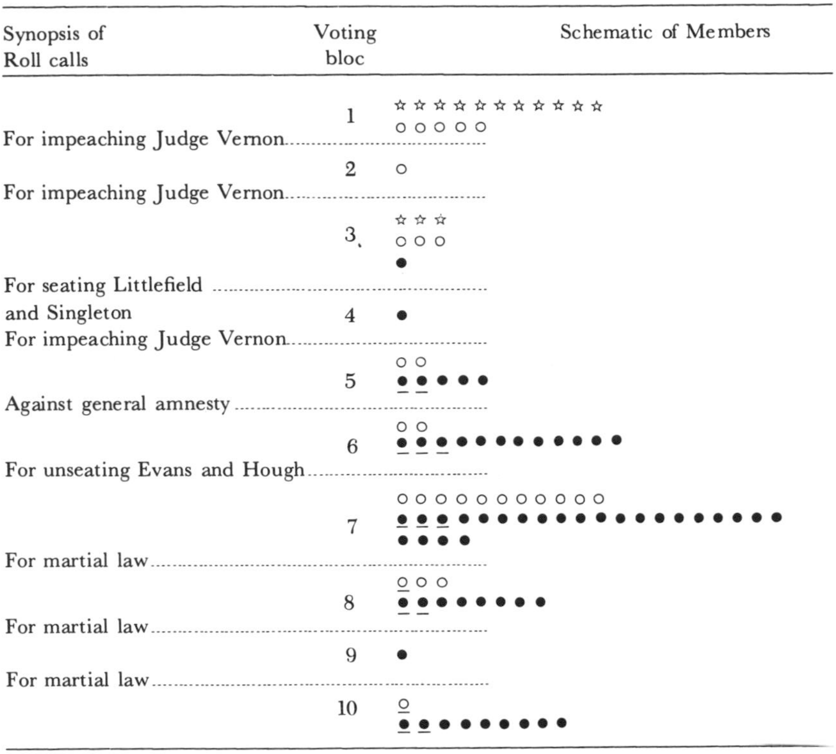

Synopsis of Roll calls	Voting bloc	Schematic of Members
For impeaching Judge Vernon	1	☆☆☆☆☆☆☆☆☆☆☆ ○ ○ ○ ○ ○
For impeaching Judge Vernon	2	○
For seating Littlefield and Singleton	3.	☆☆☆ ○ ○ ○ ●
For impeaching Judge Vernon	4	●
Against general amnesty	5	○ ○ ● ● ● ● ●
For unseating Evans and Hough	6	○ ○ ● ● ● ● ● ● ● ● ● ● ●
For martial law	7	○ ○ ○ ○ ○ ○ ○ ○ ○ ○ ○ ●
For martial law	8	○ ○ ○ ● ● ● ● ● ● ● ●
For martial law	9	●
	10	○ ● ● ● ● ● ● ● ● ●

yield six scales with similar voting alignments. Two of these scales can be most succinctly described as involving the issue of political hegemony; three, financial policy; and one, civil rights policy. Figures 5-10 show how the legislators were arrayed on these issues.

The two political policy scales include proposals designed primarily to maintain Republican hegemony and protect Republican legislators. In 1868 the specific roll calls involved were concerned with securing and holding local offices for the Republican party, disfranchising ex-Confederates, and protecting Republican lawmakers from terrorism. The political policy measures in 1870-71 involved essentially the same issues. General amnesty, the unseating of two Democratic legislators, and the declaration of martial law in the up-country were key political proposals raised during that session. At issue in the financial policy measures was the method of financing governmental operations, and the commitment of the state's public credit to support railroads and other internal development projects. Meanwhile, the scale in Figure 10 displays one of the

FIGURE 10. SUMMARY OF VOTING ALIGNMENT ON CIVIL RIGHTS, SOUTH CAROLINA HOUSE OF REPRESENTATIVES, 1869-70

Synopsis of Roll calls	Voting bloc	Schematic of Members
For U.S. Civil Rights Bill...............................	1	☆ ☆ ☆ ☆ ☆ ☆ ○
Against repeal, Airline RR charter	2	☆ ☆ ☆ ☆ ○ ○ ○ ○ ○ ○ ○ ● ● ● ● ●
For repeal, Airline RR charter	3	●
For repeal, Airline RR charter	4	☆ ☆ ○ ○ ○ ○ ○ ○ ○ ○ ●
	5	○ ○ ○ ○ ○ ●

major civil rights issues which surfaced in these early sessions, namely, the integration of public transportation.

The overall voting alignments on these three issues were very similar. In each instance the Democratic legislators tended to be the most cohesive group and to form a bloc at one end of each scale. The voting pattern of Negro Republicans was directly opposite that of the Democrats, but much less cohesive. However, the Negroes showed greater unity than their white colleagues; the latter tended to scatter into more centrist positions between the other two major blocs, a few voting with the Democrats and often a similar number with the Negro majority at the opposite end of the scale.

These voting patterns present one way of defining and measuring a conservative-to-radical continuum, although the definition implied here is behavioral rather than ideological. A legislator's position on a scale is not absolute, but relative to other members voting on the same subset of roll calls. If the Democrats voted as a cohesive bloc and occupied one end of each scale, then the opposite end represents the obverse of the conservatives' stand on those issues. In short, a legislator's conservatism can be measured by determining how closely he approximates the voting behavior of the conservative-Democratic bloc, and his radicalism by how unlike theirs his voting is.

Naturally, this approach has disadvantages. It embodies a very limiting operational definition of radicalism-conservatism which cannot necessarily be interpreted in strictly ideological or attitudinal terms, and therefore the contextual significance of a member's position on one scale is not necessarily comparable to a similar position on another. For example, a vote with the most radical bloc on economic policies in 1868 will not necessarily be equivalent to a vote with the most radical bloc in 1869, because the specific issues may be quite different. But clearly these difficulties are not unique to the quantitative approach. Even in the letters and diaries of members one cannot separate purely ideological concerns and motivations from more pragmatic ones. Beyond the traditional notion that the "radical" advocates change to an uncertain future and the "conservative" the preservation of the status quo or a return to a secure past, the meaning of these terms is never absolute and must vary with the time and circumstances.[38] It is clear, too, that whatever one's approach, there is inevitably some reference group which willy-nilly, explicitly or implicitly defines the standard against which the beliefs or activities of others are judged. In effect, those beliefs or activities are measured against some scale, but unfortunately the scale and its criteria are usually undefined and vary widely with the interpreter.

Therefore, the advantage of this analysis is that the scale *is* defined, easily replicated, and has its limitations explicitly stated. Furthermore, this quantitative scale is more sensitive to nuances of behavior than most non-quantitative ones because it *ranks* the legislators along a continuum, rather than *categorizing* them into discreet groups. With the support of contemporary sources one can partially reconstruct the political atmosphere in which the roll calls were debated and thereby develop a policy framework against which a member's position can be interpreted.

The three broad issues represented by these six scales—maintaining Republican hegemony, financial and internal development, and civil rights—involve many of the major policy questions raised under the Republican regime.[39] When the legislature convened for the first time during the hot summer of 1868, the newly inaugurated Governor Robert Scott declared policies that would be standard Republican positions during the decade. Railroads were "the main arteries of commerce" and should be subsidized in order to make South Carolina an entrepot for the agricultural riches of the west. The state's internal resources, such as the phosphate deposits along the Ashley River, should be developed. Agriculture should be encouraged to diversify and apply more scientific methods. Public systems should be instituted for universal education and relief of the destitute. And since there were still groups violently opposed

38. For a discussion of a contemporary Republican's understanding of the terms "Radical" and "Conservative," see editorial in *Daily Republican,* December 4, 1869.

39. One issue not included here is the labor question, because there were not enough roll calls on this issue to constitute a meaningful scale. However, the legislators' responses to the labor question will be discussed in the next chapter.

to the Republican regime, the governor should be granted emergency powers to suppress resistance to lawful government.[40]

Like most keynote speeches, this one embodied goals that were general enough to gain the consent of most Republicans. Conflicts would develop largely over matters of detail and the specific application of these policies. This was especially true of financial and internal development issues, where often the dispute concerned simply whose ox was gored. This may have been the case, for example, with the proposal presented during the special session in 1868 to close the South Carolina Bank. This bill threatened a direct devaluation or repudiation of the stocks and bonds held by merchants and capitalists before and during the war. The closing of the bank was a foregone conclusion; the only issue was which of its creditors and investors would take precedence in the division of the assets.[41]

However, the competing interests involved in financial policy decisions were generally much more complex. There were often heavy overtones of corruption surrounding these decisions, and no doubt some of the legislation for bond issues and railroad subsidies did involve sharp, if not shady, dealings.[42] But a more consistent theme of those opposed to financial legislation during this period was retrenchment of government expenditures and a reduction of the state's indebtedness. The support of railroads and other development projects generally involved state subsidization of the bond issues of a private company. To be profitable, the new bonds required measures to establish and maintain the state's credit with northern and foreign financiers. Following the example of the national Republican administration, South Carolina sought to inflate the value of its securities by establishing sinking funds reserved especially to redeem its debts and requiring that the interest and principles of these bonds be paid in gold coin instead of deflated paper currency.[43] Of course,

40. *Journal of the House of Representatives of the State of South Carolina, Being the Special Session of 1868* (Columbia: John W. Denny, 1868), pp. 61-71.

41. Daniel H. Chamberlain to the Speaker of the House, "Attorney General's Opinion on a Bill to Close the South Carolina Bank," August 24, 1868. MSS, Legal System, "Green File," South Carolina Archives, Columbia.

42. Of course, it is difficult to get a positive statement or confession of corrupt practices, but some letters in the papers of A. B. Andrews, a lobbyist for the Chatham Railroad, appear to implicate Robert B. Elliott, chairman of the House committee on railroads, and Lucius Wimbush, chairman of the Senate committee on incorporations, in questionable relationships with railroad titans. Elliott to Andrews, August 31, 1868; W. B. Gulick to Andrews, September 13, 1868; C. D. Melton to Andrews, June 16, 1872, Alexander Boyd Andrews I Papers, Southern Historical Collection, University of North Carolina, Chapel Hill. Also see letter implicating Governor Scott in shady bond deals made with some Democratic financiers in Charleston: Joseph A. Green to Joseph Woodruff, Legislative Papers, "Green File," South Carolina Archives.

43. For coverage of part of the public debate, see *Daily Courier*, December 13, 1869.

the net result of these policies was to raise taxes—which naturally increased the animus of large taxpayers toward the administration. Indeed, the only creditable form of political organization that Democrats could manage during the early years of Republican rule consisted of a series of taxpayer conventions organized primarily to protest the government's fiscal policies.[44]

A majority of the Negro members generally favored the policy of subsidizing railroads and internal development projects, as well as the bond issues and tax policies necessary to support these subsidies. (See Figures 5, 6, 7.) Interestingly, much of the opposition to these policies came from men like the McKinlays, *père* and *fils*, Benjamin A. Bosemon, Florian Henry Frost, Thaddeus K. Sasportas, and Henry L. Shrewsbury, who were products of or closely associated with Charleston's colored bourgeoisie. Since Negroes of this class had been known for their extensive investments in real estate and city securities before the Civil War, it is not inconceivable that their financial interests (or at least those of many members of their social class) were at stake in much the same way, though not to the same extent, as were the interests of the wealthy native whites who also opposed these financial policies.[45]

It is unlikely that a legislator's position on these financial policies involved simply a question of immediate profit and loss, however. Perhaps some members were simply predisposed to conservative or radical approaches to the policy questions of the day, because their relative positions on financial issues closely paralleled their voting records on political issues, especially in the 1870-71 session, when Republican differences had crystallized. From their opening campaign in the spring of 1867, Republican legislators had worked under the threat of violent death. Solomon Dill of Kershaw County had served in the constitutional convention of 1868 and had been elected representative to the first legislature. He was murdered before the legislature was convened. A few months later two other members, Benjamin F. Randolph and James Martin, were killed during the recess between the special and regular sessions. Most of these atrocities occurred in predominantly white hill counties, where the arrest and conviction of the persons charged with the crimes proved practically

44. Francis B. Simkins and Robert H. Woody, *South Carolina During Reconstruction* (Chapel Hill: University of North Carolina Press, 1932), pp. 156-59, 181-84.

45. There is evidence to suggest that some legislators continued to have a financial stake in the fiscal institutions of the old regime which might be injured by taxation and other policies of the new government. For instance, William McKinlay and Florian Henry Frost died intestate on June 12, 1873, and October 2, 1872, respectively. McKinlay had $500 in City of Charleston stock maturing in 1896 and $6,200 in "Old State of South Carolina stock" among his effects. Frost had interests in City of Charleston stock ($750) and a sloop, *Martha Raven.* Estate Papers, Office of the Probate Judge, Charleston.

impossible. Partly in reaction to this situation, many Republicans hardened their opposition to general amnesty for ex-Confederate leaders, often favored expedient measures to protect their party's hegemony in the state legislature and local governments, and demanded strong, militant action to suppress the violence.

The incidents and legislative responses during the 1870-71 session illustrate some of the major political conflicts of the period. A fusion movement of Democrats and dissident Republicans known as the Reform party had challenged the Republicans in the 1870 elections. The contest had been accompanied by considerable violence in the up-country and border counties aimed primarily at the black militia that had been organized the previous spring. In some cases all-white militia companies had been organized to oppose the blacks.[46] Reacting to this situation, the Laurens County grand jury recommended that the all-black state militia in that county be disarmed. Acting on this request, Seventh Circuit Judge T. O. P. Vernon, a Conservative elected by Republican legislators during the previous session, gave orders for the confiscation of the militia's arms, which were stored in the home of State Representative Joseph Crews. Crews responded by introducing a resolution in the House to impeach Judge Vernon.[47]

Meanwhile, the Negro radicals moved to strengthen the militia. Junius S. Mobley, himself threatened and forced out of Union County by the Klan, introduced a bill repealing the State Police Act and giving expanded martial law powers to the militia. Moreover, the bill also instructed the governor to call out the militia immediately in the troubled counties of Union, Laurens, Spartanburg, Newberry, and York. But having used the militia effectively to ensure his own reelection in 1870, Governor Scott now advocated disarmament.[48] To this end Attorney General Chamberlain advanced a counterproposal embodied in a bill to detect and punish crime. Evidently Chamberlain's more moderate approach "received the approval of members of both parties"—except, of course, those blacks who were being shot at in the up-country—and the martial law bill was

---

46. Richard B. Carpenter, a Kentuckian, and M. C. Butler, a South Carolina Democrat, headed a Union Reform party ticket which challenged the regulars in 1870. These Reformers did not attract too much support from either Democrats or Republicans and lost badly, 85,071 to 51,537. Nevertheless, there was a great deal of violence both before and after the election. See Sheriff Wilson to "Goss," August 28, 1870, Anderson C.H., Letters from Pickens County, Comptroller General Hagood Johnson, 1877, "Green File," South Carolina Archives.

47. *Daily Courier,* December 3, 17, 1870.

48. *Ibid.,* December 15, 1870; testimony of Henry Johnson, in *Testimony Taken by the Joint Select Committee to Inquire into the Condition of Affairs in the Late Insurrectionary States,* Volume I: South Carolina (Washington: Government Printing Office, 1872), p. 325.

killed.[49] In explaining their votes on the motion to strike out the enacting clause of the martial law bill, five mulatto delegates—Benjamin A. Bosemon, Thomas Davis, Florian Henry Frost, Thomas McDowell, and William R. Jervay—issued a statement declaring that a declaration of martial law would first of all "depress the credit of the State," as well as expend large sums of money. Besides, it might be construed as a confession of weakness or an act of revenge, they argued, since these counties were now quiet. Benjamin Byas and Junius S. Mobley retorted that if anything were to be done to save the up-country for Republicanism, it had better be done immediately. Subsequent events appeared to substantiate this argument: the martial law bill was defeated, and many of the up-country counties were lost by the Republicans in the next election.[50]

There was much greater unity among Negro Republicans on civil rights issues than on political or financial policies. White Republicans, especially native whites representing up-country constituencies, were generally opposed to civil rights legislation. When a bill prohibiting discrimination in all public accommodations was introduced in the House during the 1868 special session, most white Republicans either abstained or voted against it. The bill introduced by Bosemon was a strong one, providing for the repeal of a business's charter or license as a penalty for racial discrimination in public services or facilities, in addition to a $500 fine and twelve months' imprisonment. One section of the measure prohibited the issuance of acts of incorporation to any company with rules that were "incompatible" with this proposal. The bill languished in committee for several months until an incident spurred the Negro legislators into action. In an attempt to gain legislative support for its aid bill, the Blue Ridge Railroad treated members of the legislature to a railroad excursion to Greenville. Upon arrival, the whites obtained overnight accommodations at the local hotel, but the Negro legislators were refused. When George Lee depicted for the House how black members were forced out into the rain by this up-country innkeeper, they were infuriated.[51]

The issue produced the first open black-white split on policy in the new government. Perhaps fearful of the reaction of their black constituents, white Republican opponents generally confined their opposition to the cloakrooms. William James Whipper caustically berated them for their cowardice in "lurking in committee rooms and around the outside of this hall for the purpose of avoiding the vote on this question." [52] As on former occasions when faced with radical demands by the black leadership, white Republicans argued the necessity of expediency. A civil

49. *Daily Courier,* January 26, 1871.
50. *House Journal,* 1870-71, pp. 288-89.
51. *Daily Courier,* July 25, August 17, 1868.
52. *Ibid.,* August 17, 1868.

rights bill at this time, they said, would imperil the Republican party in the fall elections in the North.

However, some native white Republicans joined the Democrats in a more forthright denunciation of any scheme for social equality. "A man's house is his castle," declared Patrick O'Connell. And to the plaudits of the Conservative press, John Feriter, a white native from Sumter, warned ominously: "I have always maintained that whenever this question becomes a matter of color I would be obliged to take sides with my own color." [53] Evidently the Negro legislators were similarly committed, and as a bloc they pushed the bill through the House. The proposal was tabled in the Senate, however, and no action was taken during that session.

During the fall of 1869 the black legislators were angered once again by an insult to one of their own. While traveling through Virginia to Washington on official business, Jonathan J. Wright was thrown out of the first-class car on the Richmond-Danville Railroad. This line had just recently secured a South Carolina charter for one of its subsidiaries, the Airline Railroad, to operate in the state. As a penalty for their racial discrimination policy, a bill was introduced to rescind the railroad's right to do business in the state. Evidently this proposal was too radical or inexpedient for a majority of the House members, for while the bill to repeal the incorporation was passed to a third reading by a vote of 48-23, some of those who had abstained or had been absent for that vote returned to defeat the measure 42-53 on the final roll call.[54] But this series of votes provided the first instance of any disunity of the Negro legislators on civil rights policy. They divided into roughly three blocs: the conservatives who opposed any action against the Airline's charter, the centrists who switched from pro to con on the final vote, and the radicals who consistently favored repeal of the charter.

With the exception of the civil rights issue, for which several staunch conservatives became the foremost advocates, the general voting alignments of Negro legislators were fairly consistent throughout these two almost entirely different legislative bodies.[55]

A statistical analysis of their voting behavior indicates that information about their social origins, color, and wealth gives one a better chance of predicting the political stances of individual members than other data. A mulatto of free origins, especially one with above-average income, was more likely to be conservative, while a black legislator—of either slave or free origins—would be at the opposite end of the political spectrum. Mulatto ex-slaves were less predictable, swinging from conservative to

53. *Ibid.*
54. *House Journal,* 1869-70, pp. 289, 299, 305, 314-15.
55. Of the 124 members elected to the 1870-72 House, 83 were new.

radical and back in no apparent pattern, except for their generally more conservative position on civil rights legislation.

Of course, there were enough exceptions to warn us that information on the social group membership of a legislator will not give an entirely clear indication of how that legislator might vote. Legislative behavior is more complex than that, because any given decision might involve either a conscious weighing of or simply an unconscious response to a number of factors. The socioeconomic origins or status of a legislator would be just one of these factors. The other major factors which would influence voting behavior under normal circumstances are partisan pressure, constituency pressure, and possibly aberrant or erratic phenomena that cannot be predicted.

It is possible, however, to test the relative impact of most of these factors on the legislature. Obviously, the position of his party on an issue has some influence on a member's decisions. In a broad sense, all voting was a measure of party loyalty, since Democrats were usually arrayed against Republicans on any action. The ultimate question is how strongly partisan concerns overpower other influences on voting behavior. When a legislator casts his vote, it is in a structured political environment; so in that sense a partisan response can be taken as the norm, while the other influences or factors cause deviations from that normative behavior. Therefore, an observer must look for some indicator of extraordinary partisan influence exerted in a particular instance to overcome competing pressures from other sources.

One might look to the behavior of the party leadership as one index of overt exertion of partisan pressure on a given issue. Thus, if the Republican party were exerting abnormal pressure and invoking party loyalty on a series of votes, the effectiveness of that pressure should be reflected in the voting behavior of the House Republican leadership, namely, the committee chairmen and officers. If the House leadership is substantially split on a vote, then that vote can be treated as something other than a straight test of party loyalty.

Using this indicator, one finds that partisan pressure does not appear to have had much influence on the issues involved in the six scales described above. A visual check of the positions of the party leaders, represented pictorially in Figures 5-10, indicates that they were scattered throughout the various voting blocs. On three scales—1868 hegemony, 1869 financial policy, and 1869 civil rights policy—half or more of the House leadership voted with the most radical bloc, while other leaders took less radical positions. On the other three scales—1868 and 1870 financial policy and 1870 hegemony—far fewer than a third of the House leaders voted with the most radical blocs. Furthermore, on most of these issues a number of House Republican leaders, especially whites, voted with the most conservative coalitions.[56]

South Carolina was a volatile state during the Reconstruction decade, and the political situation in his home district might also influence a member's vote. The radical votes of the generally conservative Benjamin A. Bosemon, William McKinlay, and several other Charleston representatives on political issues during the 1868 special session suggest that this could be a telling factor. The numerous mass meetings and public agitation against Governor Scott's veto of a bill designed to amend the Charleston election law so as to strengthen Republicans in their struggle to control city hall put the city's delegation on notice that it must vote solidly to overturn that veto. Indeed, the only representative from Charleston who supported the Governor in this fight was Robert De Large.[57]

Of course, the influence of constituents on legislative voting might derive from any number of sources, but one would expect its effectiveness to depend on its potential impact at the polls. In a politically volatile district where a party's margin of victory was close, a member would be more likely to respond to constituency pressures than in a "safe" district. Therefore, if the voting behavior of members from districts with close electoral margins does not deviate materially from that of members representing safe districts, it is doubtful that constituents played a significant role in determining their votes. For the first two Reconstruction legislatures, 1870 represents a pivotal election year, since it reflects the political uncertainty of members in the 1868-70 legislature (those in danger of losing their seats in the coming election) and the margin of victory for the members in 1870-72.[58] Using the electoral margin of this pivotal year as an index of effective constituency pressures, one discovers that this information alone would give no help in predicting a member's vote. The cross-tabulation of voting behavior with margin of victory in the 1870 election shows little difference in the voting behavior of Negro legislators from safe lowland districts and those from closely contested and violent up-country districts.[59]

56. The statistical evidence presented in Table 4 will illustrate this conservative tendency of the Negro leadership; a pattern often quite opposite that of the membership as a whole. The large number of freeborn mulattoes among the House leadership probably caused this pattern.

57. *Daily Courier*, July 27, 31, 1868.

58. The election of 1870 was more sharply contested than either the 1868 or the 1872 elections. The Republican percentages of the vote in 1868 and 1872 were 75 and 66, respectively, as compared to 62 in 1870.

59. The inferences here as to the usefulness of one variable in predicting the values of another are based on the proportional reduction in error statistic, lambda-b. See Table 7 in Appendix B for statistical evidence and a fuller discussion of the analysis on which all the inferences in the following pages are based.

TABLE 4. CORRELATION OF VOTING BEHAVIOR WITH SOCIOECONOMIC STATUS CONTROLLING FOR ROLE ATTRIBUTES (Kendall's Tau-b)

Scales	Socioeconomic status	Status by leadership		Status by election margin	
		Members	Leaders	Close election	Safe election
Republican Hegemony 1868	—0.01	+0.03	—0.14	+0.28	—0.08
Republican Hegemony 1870-71	—0.18	+0.07	—0.47	......	—0.19
Financial Policy 1868	—0.19	—0.15	—0.22	0	—0.20
Financial Policy 1869-70	—0.25	—0.27	—0.29	—0.21	—0.26
Financial Policy 1870-71	—0.01	+0.36	—0.48	—0.50	—0.03
Civil Rights 1869-70	+0.17	—0.03	+0.42	+0.34	+0.13

Given the prevailing political morality of the post–Civil War period, corruption was a factor that could not be ignored. But by its very nature corruption is an erratic phenomenon, difficult to detect or predict. The concern here is not with political morality as such, but with the effect of political corruption on legislative behavior. Specifically, the question is, did bribery cause legislators to deviate significantly from their normal voting behavior—that is, from the determination of political decisions according to partisan, constituency, and attitudinal factors?

Of course, one cannot even pretend to answer such a question completely. But the evidence suggests the intriguing possibility that bribery, although widespread, did not ' have a dominant influence on political decisions in South Carolina. The testimony of some of these legislators before the Cochran fraud committee in 1877 provides support for such a view. For example, several members testified that they had accepted bribes from "Honest" John Patterson to support him for U.S. senator, but that they had actually intended to vote for him anyway. Many of them, like James C. Wilson of Sumter, had actually refused the proffered bribes at first, but had changed their votes when it was obvious that Patterson would win anyway. Others, like Frank Adamson, had already decided to vote for Patterson *before* the bribes were offered because of pressures from their constituencies. On the other hand, the entire Edgefield delegation resisted inducements from Honest John ranging from $500 to $1,500 and supported their favorite son candidate Robert B. Elliott instead.[60] The members of this Edgefield delegation were, by their own testimony, no less approachable than any other members; therefore, their decision was apparently based on political, not moral grounds. Clearly, corrupt inducements were simply one of several factors that must be weighed by a lawmaker in arriving at a political decision. Though obviously self-serving to some extent, the testimony of these legislators cannot be entirely discounted, and it certainly indicates the necessity for determining the "weight" of corruption in relation to other political variables.

In any event, corruption was relevant primarily in disputes on financial policy. There a legislative vote often meant the difference between red ink and black for some entrepreneurs, and they were willing to invest a bribe to ensure victory. There was no hint of corrupt influence in connection with any of the roll calls considered here except the financial policy issues of 1869 and 1870, which were dominated by legislation on railroads and bonds. It is significant that the voting alignments of legislators on those issues that were subject to corrupt influences did not deviate materially from their alignments on issues unaffected by corruption.

Therefore, of all the factors that normally affect or influence legislative voting, the social and economic status of the Negro legislators shows the strongest correlation with their scale scores and offers the most help in predicting their votes. The statistical evidence suggests that neither color, prewar origins, wealth, constituency pressure, nor party leadership, taken independently, had discernible associations with voting patterns. (See Table 7 and Appendix B for discussion of preliminary steps in this analysis.) However, a consistent pattern does emerge when the attributes of color, origins, and wealth are combined and ordered in a hierarchical construct, with freeborn well-to-do mulattoes at the top and poor black ex-slaves at the bottom. Table 4 presents a statistical summary of this pattern; the negative values indicate that the higher-status legislators voted conservatively on most issues, while the lower-status members voted with

60. "The Election of Hon. John J. Patterson," *Report of the Joint Investigating Committee on Public Frauds and the Election of Hon. John J. Patterson to the United States Senate* (Columbia, S.C.: Calvo & Patterson, 1878), pp. 29-59.

the radicals.[61] The correlations vary widely, being weakly manifested in some cases (Republican Hegemony 1868 and Financial Policy 1870-71) and moderately so in others. But they are fairly strong among the party leadership, suggesting that the contrast was greatest among the most critical and articulate, if not most influential group. In contrast, the nature of a member's constituency, safe or contested, appears to have had an appreciable effect only on those representatives from contested areas, which were usually in the midlands and up-country districts. The conservative tendency among higher-status members from safe districts was only slightly greater than for the whole Negro membership. The contrast with members from closely contested areas is more dramatic, but less reliable because the number of representatives from such areas was so small. But even among these less secure members the basic pattern was strengthened more often than it was reversed. One can infer, therefore, that a member's specific ideological orientation or political attitude was shaped to some extent by his social status and background—or, at least, that status was a more important influence than normative political factors.

Certainly one finds support for this inference in the political patterns evident in early Negro conventions and in the collective biographies of these legislators. Each distinctive segment of the Negro leadership had a different life experience which must have shaped its political outlook. We are reminded once again that freeborn mulattoes tended to be natives of South Carolina and to have specific ties to a well-developed and class-conscious community. Blacks of free origins tended to be either Northerners who had served with the Freedmen's Bureau and the Union Army, or poorer artisans who were natives of commercial centers in the state. Mulatto former slaves were generally derived from the retainer class of plantation society, having assumed such occupations as house servants and artisans under the slave regime. The black ex-slaves were more likely to have been drawn from the ranks of fieldhands. It is clear that, for Negro South Carolinians, prewar origins, color, and wealth were attributes closely associated with and indicative of social status. Among the freeborn mulatto group a rather well articulated class consciousness had developed in connection with these status indicators; and even if the other groups did not see themselves as a separate class with distinct class interests to protect, they were no doubt aware of this status hierarchy.

Consequently, the well-to-do native freeborn mulattoes, like the Mc-Kinlays, Thaddeus K. Sasportas, Henry L. Shrewsbury, Florian Henry Frost, and Nathaniel B. Myers, tended to vote rather consistently with

61. See Appendix B for fuller discussion of methodology in general and the construction and interpretation of the status index in particular.

the white conservative members on financial issues and with the radical coalition on civil rights policy. Their positions on the political issues were less clear, but still leaned toward the conservative blocs. The major exception was the fact that most of these men voted with the most radical bloc on political issues during the 1868 special session. (Of course, it should be recalled that one of the issues in this scale involved the Charleston city election, a matter which created a great deal of specific constituency pressure on Charleston legislators and may have caused them to make pragmatic political choices rather than ideological ones.) These members of the Charleston bourgeoisie were joined by northern representatives of like minds and complexions. Henry W. Purvis (son of the prominent Philadelphian Robert Purvis) and Dr. Benjamin A. Bosemon of New York both had voting records similar to the McKinlays'. They voted conservatively on all issues except civil rights and, in the case of the Charleston representative Bosemon, the political hegemony issue in the 1868 special session.

With minor exceptions, the northern free blacks were consistently among the most radical coalitions. Lawyers like George Lee of Massachusetts, William James Whipper of Pennsylvania, and Robert B. Elliott are representative of this group. Most of the black ex-slaves—regardless of income or property holdings—voted rather consistently with the radicals. Some slave-born mulattoes like Robert Smalls were also radical, but others like Charles M. Wilder, who was later named postmaster of Columbia, and Wilson Cooke, a tanner from Greenville, tended to take moderate and sometimes conservative positions on most issues.

There were exceptions, of course. The times were too volatile, the situation too novel for political behavior to be dictated entirely by the ghosts of the slave regime. Personal ambition or unique political circumstances could give rise to ambiguities and deviations. Robert De Large, for instance, whom the press and his peers considered a conservative, actually voted with the radical bloc on the financial policy issues of 1868 and 1869. It is very likely that De Large's position on these issues was influenced by the fact that he was chairman of the ways and means committee and thus floor manager of most of the Scott administration's financial legislation. Very probably the conservative ideological tendencies suggested by his social status and background and confirmed by his positions on political issues were mitigated by his special political role in the new regime.

Undoubtedly, these legislative alignments largely reflected the interaction of competing forces and influences on the free mulatto class of South Carolina. Although they were a minority among the Negro legislators, they controlled a disproportionate number of the leadership positions.

For example, four out of eight Negro congressmen were of free mulatto origins, as well as eight of twelve Negro committee chairmen in the first House of Representatives (1868-70). They were young men who had been shaped primarily by the antebellum free mulatto class, but they had come of age in a radically altered society. Some had served in the Union Army; others had allied themselves with the new agencies of social change created after the war, such as the Freedmen's Bureau and the northern missionary societies. It is not unlikely therefore that their political attitudes were a product of both their antebellum up-bringing and their postwar experiences. After all, unlike the brown class of Jamaica which had sought its political salvation separate from the black masses, the South Carolina bourgeoisie had taken the lead in organizing the freedmen into an effective political force. Of course, given the overwhelming political majority of the black ex-slaves, they hardly could have done otherwise.

The tension remained nevertheless between the ideology of their class and the peculiar role in which the South Carolina browns found themselves. It was not yet clear whether this tension and those divisions of which Cardozo warned at one of the first conventions of the Republican leadership would imperil their success. The overwhelming Republican victories of 1868 and the successful black power movement of 1870 seemed to promise ultimate success to South Carolina's Negro leaders in securing the freedom and justice for which they struggled and suffered. But this promise, like many others, would soon prove an illusion.

Chapter Seven

Black Leaders and Black Labor: An Unexpected Failure

The attempt to make black men American citizens was in a certain sense all a failure, but a splendid failure. It did not fail where it was expected to fail.

—W. E. B. Du Bois, *Black Reconstruction*

Reconstruction in South Carolina was a political failure. Of course, there were some notable successes: the establishment of a public education system, and the general process of democratizing a state which had been infamous for the lack of popular participation were significant achievements. Most significant of all, perhaps, was the fact that Reconstruction postponed, if not entirely forestalled, the development of an apartheid system of racial and economic relationships of the dimensions prefigured in the Black Codes.

Nevertheless, Republican government ultimately failed in its two most important tasks—the task of staying in power, and the task of using that power to solve the most critical problems of its constituents. After a fleeting moment of experimentation, blacks were consigned to a special caste in America's class society. Politically they were gradually reduced to a nonentity. Economically they were bound by new and insidious devices, such as debts, poverty, and convict lease, to sell their labor in a buyer's market. Socially they became America's untouchables.

Of course, black South Carolinians did not bear this oppression alone; the bright promise of emancipation had soured in other reconstructed states as well. But South Carolina was unique, because if political Reconstruction should have succeeded anywhere, ostensibly it should have succeeded in the Palmetto State. South Carolina had a black majority from 1820 to 1930, and in the middle of the Reconstruction period (1875) that majority rose to over 60 percent. This state placed more black leaders in elective office than any other southern state. Yet the legislative accomplishments of this brief interregnum do not match the actual or potential power of that leadership. Various explanations are offered to explain the political disaster in the election of 1876, but few have explained the failure of the Republican leadership to use its full power for the social and economic advancement of the black masses during the years preceding 1876. Indeed, if anything the party seemed to be retrogressing during the last two years of Republican rule. Rather than advancing measures to further social change in South Carolina, Negro leaders found themselves struggling, sometimes unsuccessfully, to defeat the socially reactionary legislative initiatives of their own Governor Chamberlain.

But what did black leaders accomplish during the pre-Chamberlain years of 1868 through 1874 to promote the welfare of their constituents? Their work in establishing a modern, generally progressive and comparatively democratic constitution has been highlighted and commended by most scholars, but considerably less attention has been given to the legislative program after that date, except for the railroads, bond issues, and related activities. The fact is that the major legislative conflicts among Republicans developed around the latter issues, and not around the social or economic legislation most relevant to the poor blacks who were their constituents. Even the few modest programs launched to assist those constituents either were unsuccessful, or were so compromised as to become ineffective. The land commission, for example, was designed to purchase and subdivide the surplus property of debt-ridden planters for landless blacks and whites. But it was placed in the charge of an arrogant, corrupt, and inept administrator who perpetrated several fraudulent and costly transactions. The effort to replace this director involved the commission in new frauds which left its resources further depleted and its capacity to make significant land-reform initiatives severely limited.[1] A public school system was established, but again it was so badly administered that its impact on illiteracy never reached its potential.[2] Of course, there was success in the establishment of a state normal school and a scholarship program which opened up the state university to impecunious blacks. There was also progress in opening public accommodations to blacks, though the custom of segregation in many other aspects of social life remained largely unchanged and unchallenged.[3]

1. See Carol K. Bleser, *The Promised Land: The History of the South Carolina Land Commission, 1869-90* (Columbia: University of South Carolina Press, 1969), pp. 47-58.

2. See statement of Laura Towne in Willie Lee Rose, *Rehearsal for Reconstruction: The Port Royal Experiment* (Indianapolis: Bobbs-Merrill, 1964), p. 389; also see Martha Schofield to Daniel H. Chamberlain, May 29, 1876, Governor Daniel H. Chamberlain Papers, South Carolina Archives, Columbia.

3. A South Carolinian [Belton O'Neal Townsend], "South Carolina Society," *Atlantic Monthly*, XXXIX (June, 1877), 676.

On the whole, one is left with the impression that black freedmen, armed with an overwhelming electoral advantage, had a tremendous opportunity but failed to act to satisfy their most critical needs. Given this very uneven performance of the Republican government, how does one characterize the Republican leadership's performance during Reconstruction? Indeed, how does one characterize the Negroes who constituted the single most numerous group within that leadership? The most persistent image of the latter is that of a largely poor, working-class group, or representatives of the working class. In a sense, the crystallization of this image is represented in the work of W. E. B. Du Bois, who characterized the Reconstruction as "a vast labor movement" and marvelled that "poverty was so well represented," seeing in this "certain tendencies toward a dictatorship of the proletariat."[4] Indeed, this attempt to impose a not entirely crystallized Marxian interpretation on Reconstruction politics brought Du Bois a great deal of criticism; consequently, many of his other insights have been ignored.

In one such insight he qualified his description of the black leadership class as representatives of the black proletariat; he observed that the group was intelligent, but "not at all clear in its economic thought." He recognized that "on the whole, it believed in the accumulation of wealth and exploitation of labor as the normal method of economic development."[5] It failed to unite black and white labor "because black leadership still tended toward the ideals of the petty bourgeois."[6] He believed, nevertheless, that their participation and leadership in the incipient national black labor movement was proof that this orientation was undergoing a change as a result of pressure from the legislators' poor working-class constituents.[7]

And indeed, pressure there was from constituents—but the pressure groups never effectively harnessed the political process to serve their ends. At least twenty bills purporting to govern the relationship between planters and laborers were introduced during the period of Republican rule, yet very few of these measures ever became law, and none seemed to have protected farm laborers satisfactorily. Their legislative histories are tangled; often there were no roll calls, and extant reports of the legislative progress of the proposals are filled with unaccountable gaps at critical junctures. But a pattern is apparent from the information that does survive. Black legislators introduced legislation designed to surround the laborer with a variety of legal protections against capricious eviction,

4. W. E. B. Du Bois, *Black Reconstruction . . . in America, 1860-80* (New York: Harcourt Brace, 1935), p. 391.
5. *Ibid.,* pp. 350-51.
6. *Ibid.,* p. 352.
7. *Ibid.,* pp. 351, 361.

fraud in the division of the crop, and the accustomed dictation by planters of many non-economic aspects of his life. These legislative initiatives were bottled up in hostile committees in many instances, compromised through drastic amendments in others, and killed outright on not a few occasions. Those few proposals that successfully traversed this political gauntlet to become laws offered little protection to the laborers, and in some cases merely legalized their oppression.

Within days of the inauguration of Republican rule in South Carolina and the convening of the special session of the 1868 legislature, State Senator Benjamin F. Randolph introduced a "Bill to enable laborers who work under contract or otherwise to recover pay for their labor when said contract is not complied with." The judiciary committee, chaired by D. T. Corbin (who was also U.S. district attorney for South Carolina), reported unfavorably on this bill on July 22; this report was adopted, thereby defeating the bill. But a short time later a second bill was introduced by William Beverly Nash under the title, "A Bill to define the law of contract for hire." Supporters of this measure sought to bypass the hostile judiciary committee by referring it to a special three-man committee, but were defeated. Senator Randolph then moved to force the judiciary committee to report within a specified period. This effort was also unsuccessful, and no bill reached the floor of the Senate during the special session. Among this stalled legislation was a "Bill to protect laborers and persons working under contracts on shares of the crops" which had passed the House, but was postponed in the Senate until the session beginning the following November.[8]

The latter bill, or at least one bearing its title, did pass during the regular session of the legislature and was approved by Governor Scott on March 19, 1869. That this new law intended no radical changes in the legal status of farmworkers vis-à-vis the planters is clear, however, from the action taken on it during the session. At the end of February Alonzo J. Ransier, chairman of the special committee in the House to which it was referred, reported "A bill to establish an agent to supervise contracts, and to provide for the protection of laborers working on shares of the crop," which had originally been introduced by William H. Jones. In committee the bill had been drastically altered, and all references to the appointment of contract agents were dropped in the revised text. A new title was appended which read simply "A bill to protect laborers and persons working under contract on shares of crops." When this revised bill was taken up on March 3, Thaddeus K. Sasportas offered the following substitute for the first two sections.

8. *Journal of the Senate of the State of South Carolina, Being the Special Session of 1868* (Columbia: J. W. Denny, 1868), pp. 70, 158, 402.

Section 1. That any person or persons entering into contracts as laborer's, consideration for which labor is a portion of the crop, are hereby declared to be co-partners, with all rights, privileges and emoluments guaranteed to corporations by existing law, in said crop, and no further.
Section 2. That a claim for labor, whenever performed, shall constitute a lien having a priority over all other liens. All Acts and parts of Acts inconsist [*sic*] with this Act be, and the same are hereby, repealed.[9]

Claude Turner, a Democratic member, moved to postpone the whole matter indefinitely. Robert B. Elliott moved that the bill and the substitute be tabled in order to take up out of its regular order a "Bill to define contracts for laborers, and for other purposes." Elliott's motion was approved 33 to 10, but action on the second bill was postponed to take up the Port Royal Railroad Bill.[10]

The bill to define contracts for laborers was evidently the same proposal Senator Nash had introduced during the special session which had been continued to the regular session. However, Nash's bill had been altered in Whipper's judiciary committee with the following very critical substitute for section five of the original measure:

Section 5. Employees absenting themselves from labor without the consent of their employers, except in case of sickness, or on public days, or the usual holidays, shall forfeit his or her pay *for the week or month,* as the case may be, for which he or she was hired; Provided, however, That any persons attending public meetings shall forfeit only at the rate of their wages for the time lost.[11]

This substitute, by which a laborer could be docked for up to a month's wages for one day's unexcused absence, was adopted on March 11 when consideration of the labor bill resumed. It was passed and sent to the Senate on March 16. Subsequent actions on the bill are unclear, but it was postponed until the following session and, apparently, allowed to die quietly.[12]

Meanwhile, the bill written by Ransier's special committee had passed the House and Senate and had been approved by the governor in March, 1869. Judging from the content of the new law, however, the title—"To protect laborers"—was a misnomer, since in its practical application the planters would receive more "protection" than the farmworkers. The bill required that all contracts between laborers and landowners be "witnessed by one or more disinterested persons, and at the request of either party,

9. *Journal of the House of Representatives of the State of South Carolina,* 1868-69 (Columbia: J. W. Denny, 1869), p. 426.
10. *Ibid.,* pp. 427-28.
11. *Ibid.,* pp. 345-46.
12. *Ibid.,* p. 562.

duly executed before a Justice of the Peace or Magistrate, whose duty it shall be to read and explain the same to the parties." The document must clearly set forth the conditions of work, including the time, wages, or shares. The division of shares must be made immediately after harvest and before the crop was removed to market, and either party could require that a "disinterested party" arbitrate the division. If the two parties to the contract failed to agree upon an arbiter, then the local magistrate would decide the division. In the latter case the contracting parties would have to share equally the fees of the magistrate, except where one of them was guilty of fraud.

The above portions of the act undertook the task of regularizing the labor arrangements initiated under the Freedmen's Bureau in the postwar period. There was obviously an attempt here to avoid the creation of a state bureaucracy to supervise planter-worker relations, as was intended by State Representative Jones in the provision for the appointment of contracting agents in the original bill. This new version merely formalized the principle of arbitration, preferably out of court, but always on the initiative of one of the contracting partners. Thus it assumed a theoretical equality of planter and worker, and the ability and willingness of the latter to assert these rights against the man from whom he rented not only his fields, but also his house. The laborer was assumed to be an independent contractor in dealings with the man who supplied not only his seeds, tools, and wherewithal to make his crop, but the very food and clothing on which he and his family would survive while he awaited the harvest and division of that crop. Certainly the third section, which optimistically granted the laborer "a prior lien" on the crop and affirmed his right to sue to recover it, was based on such petit bourgeois assumptions.

But to the extent that the legislators made planter and worker equal before the law in principle, they also put the worker at a distinct disadvantage in certain other respects. Prior to the division of the crop, the planter was entitled to recover the advances made to the worker during the season.

> When such division has been made, each party shall be free to dispose of the several portions as to him or her or them may seem fitting: *Provided*, That if either party be in debt to the other for any obligation incurred under contract, the amount of said indebtedness may be agreed upon by the parties themselves, or set apart by the Justice of the Peace or Magistrate, or any party chosen to divide said crop or crops.[13]

This provision gave a legal sanction to the planter's lien on the crop, which prefigured the southern agricultural system of the late nineteenth century in which such debts became a potent tool for controlling labor.

13. *Acts and Resolutions of the General Assembly of the State of South Carolina, Passed at the Regular Session of 1868-69* (Columbia: John W. Denny, 1869), p. 228.

Perhaps the legislators should not be held responsible for failing to foresee the end product of this planter's lien, but the discriminatory penalties established for violators of the law were obvious to all. For violating the terms of the contract, or fraud in its implementation, the planter could receive a fine of not less than fifty dollars and not more than five hundred. The disinterested third party could receive a similar fine, or one month in jail.

> If the offending party be a laborer or laborers, and the offence consist either in failing willfully and without just cause to give the labor reasonably required of him, her, or them, by the terms of such contract or contracts, or shall fraudulently make use of or carry away from the place where the crop or crops he, she, or they, may be working are planted, any portion of said crop or crops, or anything connected therewith or belonging thereto, such person or persons so offending shall be liable to fine or *imprisonment*, according to the gravity of the offence, and upon proof to conviction before a Justice of the Peace or a Court of competent jurisdiction.[14]

And so the law to protect laborers regularized the procedures for making contracts, but punished violations committed by the planter with fines, and those committed by the worker with jail.

Evidently the discrepancies between the intent and the result of the new law were observed by laboring men in the state, for new legislation was urged at the next session of the General Assembly. The 1869-70 session was preceded by increased tensions among some elements of the working class which introduced new political considerations into the struggle, but with no more satisfactory results than the year before. In the fall of 1869 the black longshoremen of Charleston struck successfully for higher wages. Shortly after that settlement, the painters' union went out for more pay.[15] These events, along with the two national labor conventions held by blacks in January and December, 1869, spurred the call for a state labor convention to meet on November 24, 1869.

Like its national counterpart, this state labor convention tended to be dominated by Republican politicians.[16] The call for the state convention was signed by two Republican legislators, Benjamin F. Jackson of Charleston and William Beverly Nash of Richland.[17] When the convention delegates were elected at the county labor caucuses, the laborers tended to turn to politicians for representation. Aside from the deference to their

14. *Ibid.*, p. 229. Emphasis added.

15. *Daily Republican,* October 7, 27, 1869.

16. For discussion of the national convention, see Du Bois, *Black Reconstruction,* p. 361; and Sterling D. Spero and Abram L. Harris, *The Black Worker: The Negro and the Labor Movement,* reprint ed. (New York: Atheneum, 1969), p. 32.

17. *Daily Republican,* October 29, 1869.

political leaders evident in this tendency, the fact that they could be represented by their county's political delegation at little or no extra cost appears to have been a factor in the latter's selection.[18] After all, the legislature would be in session, so there would be no travel expenses or accommodations to be concerned with. At the convention itself, however, the predominance of the politicians became a bit too overbearing when Robert B. Elliott was elected president and several other politicians were nominated for the remaining offices. After some discussion, the latter nominees declined in favor of workingmen. Thus, Robert C. De Large declined to serve as vice-president in favor of T. F. Clark, head of the Longshoremen's Union, and Alonzo J. Ransier yielded in favor of the head of the Painter's Union.[19] Nevertheless, Elliott continued as president and Thaddeus K. Sasportas as secretary.

About three hundred delegates attended the convention. While the business committee drew up resolutions, each county delegation reported on working conditions in its area. Finally, the business committee, chaired by State Representative Benjamin F. Jackson, reported a resolution calling upon the General Assembly to enact legislation which would establish a labor commissioner in each county to supervise contracts between workers and planters. Another resolution was passed unanimously which asked the legislature to refuse any further aid to railroads and to purchase land and resell it to small farmers instead. A memorial was prepared for presentation to the legislature requesting: (1) that laborers have a "preferred lien" on the planter's land; (2) that the governor appoint contract commissioners in each county; (3) that laborers' suits for wages have precedence on court calendars; (4) that a person be appointed in each county to select jurors; (5) that lands sold for debts should be in tracts not exceeding fifty acres; (6) that specifications be prescribed for planters' due bills; (7) that a nine-hour day for skilled labor be established, and (8) that taxes on the sale of cotton and rice be abolished.[20]

Benjamin F. Jackson, the A.M.A. missionary who had been active in the convention's deliberations, was also the chairman of the House labor committee. Therefore, he introduced and reported to the House a bill embodying the petition of the labor convention's memorial. This bill was reported to the floor in January, 1870; in the debate Jackson, De Large, Wade Perrin, and William C. Morrison defended it against the attacks of Tomlinson and Whipper. Disillusioned memories of the Freedmen's Bureau agents who supervised contracts between planters and their laborers in the early postwar period seem to have hung over the debates.

18. *Ibid.*, November 17, 1869.
19. *Ibid.*, November 25, 1869.
20. *Ibid.*, November 27, 1869.

Referring to the Bureau, Tomlinson charged that the bill would put "task masters" over the workers. He insisted that "if these men were able to be citizens, they were able as well to manage their own affairs." Whipper opposed the bill because a similar one had been passed in the last session, only to become a dead letter in practice.[21]

The tenor of the debates indicated that House sentiment was against any labor bill for that session, observed the *Daily Republican* reporter.[22] The sponsors had the measure recommitted to the labor committee for revision to meet the criticism made in debate. But meanwhile James Henderson, an ex-slave farmworker from Newberry County, introduced a bill on January 8 to provide a labor contract agent in each county to monitor and enforce contracts between planters and workers. These agents were to be appointed by the governor, and it would be their duty "to furnish all persons wishing to contract with proper forms, showing clearly the obligations of employers and employees." They would maintain copies of every such contract at the county seat and arbitrate all disagreements, except in such cases as required legal interference through the courts. This proposal received the endorsement of the *Daily Republican* editor, who had taken a generally radical position on the labor question and the strikes of the previous fall.[23] But Jackson's labor committee reported unfavorably on this bill and recommended a substitute proposal in its stead. George Lee of Charleston moved to strike the enacting clause of the Henderson bill, presumably to clear the way for consideration of the committee's revised proposal.[24]

The substitute bill, now entitled "A bill to provide for the better protection of labourers under contract for services," was oriented more toward the establishment of traditional legal mechanisms for workers than the Henderson bill. It sought to amend the labor act passed during the previous session by providing that a contract would become null and void when either party violated its provisions (an amendment presumably to the advantage of the innocent party). It granted a ninety-day lien on crops to laborers, whereas the existing statute did not specify a time limit. It corrected the discriminatory penalties for planter and worker by prohibiting criminal prosecution of laborers for failure to keep the contract. It also provided a mechanism whereby workers could receive free legal aid to prosecute suits against their employers for violation of their contract. However, some of these latter provisions were quickly sacrificed by Elliott and Jackson during the ensuing debate in an apparent

21. *Ibid.,* January 12, 1870.
22. *Ibid.*
23. *Ibid.,* January 17, 1870.
24. *House Journal,* 1869-70, p. 183.

effort to save the rest of the bill.[25]

The debates reveal that some of the animus toward the labor committee's bill grew partly out of the general feeling that the state should not attempt to regulate such matters, and partly out of the feeling that this proposal implied that laborers were too ignorant to regulate their own affairs. A basis for the feeling was certainly supplied by the preamble of the bill, which declared that workers had been victimized because of their ignorance. Therefore, "the Committee believes it to be the duty of the State under the circumstances upon principles which all Christian people recognize as of binding force, to extend its protection to all such as compose our laboring population, and guard them as wards of the public, so far as necessary, until the time, it is hoped not far distant, when having progressed sufficiently, they shall be capable of managing the ordinary affairs of life themselves." [26]

From the pious tone of this preamble one must suspect that it was written by Jackson, the minister and A.M.A. missionary. Whipper, the lawyer, moved to strike the enacting clause of the bill simply to elicit some debate, he claimed, for he favored the general features of the bill. He was unalterably opposed to the paternalistic preamble, however, and urged that the language referring to laborers as public wards be stricken. "I trust those words will never go upon any statute book of the state," he fumed. "I know that men of the largest business capacity are sometimes taken advantage of. The fact that some few persons are defrauded does not at all demonstrate the fact that the people as a class are not able to take care of themselves." [27]

Reuben Tomlinson, a former Philadelphia abolitionist and bank clerk, opposed the bill in its entirety for reasons similar to Whipper's but with a stronger emphasis on free enterprise.[28] In his view, the very existence of any law would imply the workers' incompetence to manage their own affairs. "I believe in labor unions. But they can be effective only when gone into by free will. There has been a great deal of talk that the General Assembly must do something for the laboring people of the State. But I don't believe it is in the power of the General Assembly to do anything except to give them equal rights before the law." [29]

John Feriter, a white Republican native from the up-country, confirmed his northern colleagues' laissez-faire views and insisted that legislation

25. *Ibid.*, p. 351.
26. *Daily Republican,* February 3, 1870.
27. *Ibid.*, February 8, 1870.
28. For information on Tomlinson's background, see Rose, *Rehearsal for Reconstruction,* p. 78.
29. *Daily Republican,* February 8, 9, 1870.

in this area would perpetuate a dependence on the legislature. "Nobody has ever been able to legislate in regard to labour," he lectured the House. "The law of supply and demand must regulate the matter. . . . The quicker the people of the State learn how to transact their own business the better." Furthermore, he was concerned about the fact that laborers were migrating to the Gulf States and producing a scarcity which would raise wages.[30]

One cannot determine with any degree of assurance the extent to which these speakers represented the thinking of other legislators who also opposed the bill, and the motives for scuttling the bill in the end are somewhat obscured. But the distinctive voting patterns on the two roll calls on the labor issue suggest the legislators' motives and, given other evidence, might permit some inferences to be drawn from their performance on this issue.

The first roll call was ordered on February 5, when the labor committee's substitute passed its second reading by a vote of 57 to 9. The second occurred when George Lee's motion to kill the Henderson bill was approved, 43 to 20. Therefore, 86 percent of those voting favored the substitute, with only five Democrats, three white Republicans, and one Negro voting against it. On the Henderson bill, however, only 60 percent of the Negroes (as compared with 90 percent of the white Republicans) voted against the proposal—i.e., for Lee's motion to strike the resolving clause. However, the opposition included many House leaders, such as Robert B. Elliott and Robert C. De Large, along with more conservative Negroes like Henry W. Purvis, Philip Ezekiel, and Charles M. Wilder. The voting patterns of the Negroes by prewar origin and color indicate that those representatives closer to working-class blacks—that is, the black ex-slaves—tended to favor Henderson's bill, which promised direct assistance to resolve labor problems, rather than the legalistic and complex procedures favored by their freeborn and mulatto colleagues. With 50 and 60 percent of those voting on the bill identified by color and origins, respectively, only 11 percent of the freeborn compared to 48 percent of the slave-born, and 18 percent of the mulattoes compared to 35 percent of the blacks voted for Henderson's bill. When the categories of origins and color are combined, it is evident that black ex-slaves gave the bill its heaviest support and freeborn mulattoes its stiffest opposition. Thus, the voting behavior of the legislators on these two roll calls on the labor issue follow the pattern discerned in other roll calls during the early sessions of the legislature, when free mulattoes and black ex-slaves were found at the opposite ends of a conservative-to-radical continuum. Such opposition suggests that social class influenced political behavior.

30. *Ibid.,* February 9, 1870.

Of course, a division along lines of prewar status and color does not prove that open class antagonism was reflected in this vote. Indeed, one would not expect such class conflict to be openly expressed, or possibly even honestly perceived by the participants. After all, these legislators, whatever their origins, color, or class, depended upon the poor black farmworkers to keep them in office. But the failure of the legislature to enact meaningful labor laws certainly suggests an underlying failure of purposefulness, a failure of perception, a lack of urgency in acting on the critical needs of those constituents. Legislation involving other economic issues, such as banks, bond issues, and railroads, had experienced much less frustration, being pushed along with more tenacity and skill than those relating to the common laborers. One is forced to the conclusion that while it did not cause this failure to legislate successfully for the working class, the considerable social and cultural distance between many of these legislators and their constituents must have contributed to that failure.

The forty-seven Negro legislators who were either elected from or resided in Charleston County are admittedly not a *random* sampling of the Negro leadership cadre for this period, but Charleston County offers the distinct advantage of extant and well-maintained tax records for the 1870's, in which the property holdings of two-thirds of these forty-seven men are recorded.[31] In addition to this convenience, it is also evident that the twenty votes of the Charleston delegation were critical to the success of any legislation in the General Assembly. The median value of property of the legislators in this sample was $1,000: five men were listed as owning neither personal nor real property; ten others paid taxes on property valued at less than $1,000, and eleven on property valued at between $1,000 and $5,000, four on property worth $5,001 to $10,000, and one was taxed for property worth $14,000.[32]

Twenty-one of these men were paying taxes on real estate, and while

31. These legislators were found in the Charleston county auditor's tax duplicates for 1868, 1870, 1871, 1874, and 1877 located in the Charleston County Treasurer's Office. Information was also taken from the Charleston county probate records in Office of the Probate Judge, Charleston. The following are legislators found in these records: Benjamin A. Bosemon, Joseph H. Rainey, Richard H. Cain, Robert C. De Large, William Glover, William H. W. Gray, Hezekiah H. Hunter, John B. Wright, Nathaniel T. Spencer, George Lee, Florian Henry Frost, Edward Mickey, Samuel E. Gaillard, William McKinlay, William J. McKinlay, John Vanderpool, Abraham Smith, Julius Tingman, William R. Jervay, Aaron Logan, William E. Elliott, Peter Bright, Edward Petty, A. P. Ford, H. Z. Burchmeyer, Stephen Brown, William J. Brodie, Martin F. Becker, William A. Grant, Richard Nesbitt, and Charles F. North.

32. Burchmeyer, North, Grant, Brown, and Brodie are listed as paying no tax on property. William McKinlay, Gaillard, De Large, and Hunter were taxed on property valued at between $5,001 and $10,000. William J. McKinlay was taxed on $14,388 in real property.

some of them were legitimate farmers, others appear to have been land speculators. Some had properties in the country, a significant proportion of which was arable soil and under cultivation. For example, William R. Jervay's 136 acres in the Stephens district included 30 acres under cultivation, housed six buildings and several farm animals.[33] A similar situation could be found with William H. W. Gray's 25 acres in St. John's.[34]

On the other hand, a fair number of them appear to have been real estate speculators. This can be inferred from the fact that they held large sections, often in scattered sites in country districts, which were largely undeveloped, having much of the land covered with woods and few or no buildings or farm animals listed. This appears to have been the case with the 100 acres in the possession of Aaron Logan in St. Thomas, Samuel E. Gaillard's property at St. James Goose Creek, and George Lee's wooded lot in Summerville.[35]

The practice of investing accumulated capital in land had roots in the prewar period, when this was one of the few capital ventures open to the mulatto bourgeoisie.[36] The McKinlays, *père* and *fils*, were the wealthiest Negro politicians; much of their wealth, aggregating to $40,000 for the collective family estate and consisting primarily of investments in rental properties around Charleston's Fourth Ward, came from real estate purchased before the war.[37] The McKinlays also invested heavily in the stocks and bonds of their city and state and in the new, largely black-owned Enterprise Railroad.[38] Bosemon, Louisa Ransier (wife of Congressman Alonzo J. Ransier), George Lee, and Florian Henry Frost also invested substantially in these same issues, especially the Enterprise Railroad.[39] Frost had a part interest in a sloop, the *Martha Raven,* in addition to his other investments.[40]

One suspects then that these people were, or aspired to become, a part of the emerging capitalist class of postwar Charleston. The economic temper was optimistic, boomed by various schemes for an east-west rail

33. Assessments of Real Estate, 5th District, Charleston County, 1874, p. 37, Charleston County Treasurer's Office.

34. Assessments of Real Estate, 7th District, 1870, p. 185.

35. Assessments of Real Estate, 5th District, 1877, p. 48.

36. See the second chapter. See also Ivy Marina Wikramanayake, "The Free Negro in Ante-Bellum South Carolina" (Ph.D. dissertation, University of Wisconsin, 1966), p. 144.

37. See "Table Showing the Number, Construction, Owner, Occupant and Ward Location of Every House in the City," *Census of the City of Charleston, South Carolina for the Year 1861,* comp. Frederick A. Ford (Charleston: Evans & Cogswell, 1861), pp. 50, 71.

38. William McKinlay Estate Papers, Office of Probate Judge, Charleston.

39. Wills, Book Q, 1879-88, Charleston County; George Lee Estate Papers; Florian H. Frost Estate Papers, Office of Probate Judge, Charleston.

40. Florian H. Frost Estate Papers.

link which would usher that port city into a new era of prosperity. While their capitalist allies in the Republican party built railroads across the continent, some of the Negro leaders launched kindred ventures on a smaller scale in Charleston. A few weeks after they failed to get a labor bill through the General Assembly, a group of prominent Negro politicians succeeded in their effort to launch the Enterprise Railroad, a horse-drawn freight streetcar line which was set up to move goods in and out of Charleston harbor. All but one of the officers and directors were Negro. Richard H. Cain was president of the company; William James Whipper, vice-president; Alonzo J. Ransier, secretary; William R. Jervay, corresponding secretary; and William McKinlay, treasurer. The twelve-man board of directors included Joseph H. Rainey, Benjamin A. Bosemon, William J. Brodie, Charles Hayne, Thaddeus K. Sasportas, John B. Wright, Henry J. Maxwell, Lucius Wimbush, Robert Smalls, William E. Johnston, and Samuel Johnson. The incorporators were to subscribe $13,000 of the capital stock of the company.[41] Some of the incorporators were publicly attacked because their rail line would throw the black draymen out of work.[42] The road was established, however, and paid a handsome profit to its investors; it was still in use in the 1880's.

Other ventures of a similar nature were not so entirely black-controlled as the Enterprise Railroad. William J. McKinlay, Samuel E. Gaillard, William R. Jervay, and others incorporated the Charleston and Sullivan's Island Railroad in 1874 to run from Christ Church Parish to Moultrieville and connect Charleston with some of the outlying islands.[43] And in the spring of 1870 William McKinlay and Charles M. Wilder were elected to the board of directors of the South Carolina Bank and Trust Company.[44]

Other factors—more suggestive than demonstrative—point to the class consciousness of these men. Personal possessions are identified in the tax ledgers, and they often hint at a lifestyle that is clearly more middle than working-class. There appear in these ledgers the carriages, pianos, organs, and jewelry of people that have or seek a cultivated ease, charm, and elegance suggestive of an emerging bourgeoisie. Of course, the nouveau (as distinct from the traditional) bourgeoisie often reflected a certain lack of polish, the gaucheness expected of those who were only recently ushered to a new social level. The relish of ostentatious display evident in State Representative Sammy Green as he sped through the sandy streets of Beaufort with his thousand-dollar barouche and team exemplifies

41. *Daily Republican,* March 24, 1870.
42. See Hezekiah H. Hunter's attack on Richard H. Cain: *Daily Courier,* August 8, 1871.
43. *News and Courier* (Charleston), March 25, 1871.
44. *Daily Republican,* May 16, 1870.

not only the cruder side of these aspirations, but the growing distance between Green and his constituents as well.[45] In this case, as in many others, the social distance was not reflected in a concurrent political distance, for Green was generally identified with the extreme radical bloc in the legislature throughout his career. It merely points up the fact that what one expects to find here is not an iron law for the prediction of political behavior from social class, but something more subtle.

Certainly, the subtleties of the situation were not lost on some of the more perceptive observers of South Carolina society and politics. In a lengthy article in a Beaufort paper, a native white Southerner, obviously from the planter class, surprisingly favored the Civil Rights Bill of 1875 which was then being debated in Congress. The writer, who signed himself "W," declared that whites need not concern themselves with the Civil Rights Bill, for it would only benefit the educated class among the blacks and would serve to ally them even closer to the upper-class whites. He lectured his readers on emerging class and racial patterns in the state which would operate to maintain that status quo.

> Among them will be found two classes whose conditions will be so distinctive that their own lines of demarkation will be as wide and as well defined as that which exists between the more cultivated and refined of the white race and those less trained and cultured of either. The one will consist of such as are as highly intelligent and educated as they are capable of; the other of such as are untutored and degraded as the need of such advantages makes them. In proportion to the advantages embraced by the first will their pride and conservatism be increased.[46]

"W" went on to conclude that the Civil Rights Bill could never reconcile these two antagonistic classes among the Negroes, and thus the various constitutional amendments and civil rights laws would never be pushed beyond the "naturally constituted barriers of taste and prejudice." The Negro bourgeoisie would prevent such eventualities, because it would seek to maintain its own social distance from the black masses. The writer felt that the experience of the past few years in Beaufort had certainly established that point, for there "where the colored element predominates there have been the fewest demonstrations of a desire upon their parts to assume any unwarranted position. . . . " Thus the whites could expect to find allies among the Negro bourgeoisie.

> From the educated and intelligent of the colored race whose home is to be amongst us we confidently predict so much conservatism and so much exclusivism among themselves that any effort to make use of them to enter-

45. *Port Royal Commercial,* March 26, 1874.
46. *Beaufort Tribune,* March 31, 1875.

tain ill-blood among the races will prove futile. From the ignorant and vicious of the same race there need be no fear of other than an enforced obedience to the natural order which society is constituted according to organic law which man neither made nor can alter.[47]

The racial and economic prejudices of "W" are clear, and his interpretation of the postwar social scene was with respect to his class self-congratulatory, if not self-serving. But his comments cannot be dismissed as mere wishful thinking, for they might have been based on observable phenomena. At least one of his Beaufort neighbors was a perfect example of the nexus between the solidification of class interests and an evolving political ideology. Thomas Hamilton was a Republican, although he was often a maverick on partisan issues. During the 1875-76 session Hamilton had a fairly radical voting record on fiscal issues but was clearly conservative on those relative to political and social reform that came to a roll call vote.[48] His views are expressed more clearly and directly, though, in a speech to striking rice workers in 1876.

My friends, the longer I live and pursue my avocation as a planter the more am I impressed with the knowledge that our interests are identical with the owners of these plantations. Surely, if they are not prosperous, how can they pay you wages? You complain now that you don't get enough for your labor, but would you not have greater cause of complaint if you destroy entirely their ability to pay you at all? I am a rice planter, and employ a certain number of hands. Now, if my work is not permitted to go on, how can I gather my crops and pay my laborers, and how can my laborers support their families? They are dependent upon their labor for support; they are not calculated for anything else; they can't get situations in stores as clerks; they can't all write, nor are they fitted for anything else. There is but one course for you to pursue, and that is to labor industriously and live honestly.[49]

In the critical election of 1876, Hamilton, whose comments prefigured the anti-labor, capitalistic, accommodationist philosophy of Booker T. Washington, abandoned the Republicans for Wade Hampton to complete the overthrow of Republican government, the last hope of justice—though perhaps a misplaced one—for those rice workers whom he addressed in the summer of 1876.

The rhetoric of some of Hamilton's colleagues was more pro-labor, but their accomplishments were no less pro-planter. That the 1869 labor

47. *Ibid.*

48. A preliminary roll call analysis places Hamilton in the third bloc of an 8-bloc scale on "Social Reform" issues and in the o bloc of a 28-bloc scale on "Political" issues, but in the twenty-first bloc of a 23-bloc scale on "Financial" issues.

49. *Beaufort Tribune,* October 4, 1876.

law was not operating satisfactorily for farmworkers can be surmised from the fact that proposals were introduced in practically every subsequent session to remedy its defects. Most of the new laws that were passed, however, actually aided the planter much more than the worker.

Not that there were no legislative victories for the farmworker, but the practical effect of these victories was often quite different from the apparent intent. For instance, the cash-poor planters had instituted a system in some areas whereby they paid wage laborers in scrip or checks redeemable with certain local merchants. Sometimes the planter was also the merchant; in effect, he simply bartered high-priced merchandise for low-paid labor. In either case, the mark-up on prices at the company store was astronomical, and the workers got the short end of a line of credit that ultimately reached banking institutions beyond the state.[50]

In 1872 the South Carolina legislature outlawed the issuance of checks except where it was specifically provided for in the labor contract beforehand.[51] Of course, it is difficult to judge how much the loophole exempting cases where scrip was a prior contractual arrangement vitiated the effects of the law, since planters could make such arrangements a standard item in their contracts. But it is clear that the practice was continued, because it was directly responsible for the strike of rice workers in the summer of 1876. The law had been amended in March, 1875, so that scrips or checks would be prohibited only in those cases where they had to be redeemed "at some future time, or in the shops or stores of the employers." [52] Thus the key features of the system were preserved—that is, workers could be paid in scrip instead of currency, and this scrip was only redeemable for goods available at the local store at exorbitant prices.

The workers in the lowland rice areas were mostly wage laborers, and therefore the primary victims of the scrip system. They rebelled in July, 1876, with a massive and violent strike. The workers abandoned the fields and generally coerced their less resolute colleagues to do likewise. The whites declared that it was insurrection and called upon Governor Chamberlain to send in the state militia. But, facing a gubernatorial election in the fall, Chamberlain also sent "the King of Beaufort," Congressman Robert Smalls, to investigate. Smalls, who was also a commander in the state militia, reported that the militia was no longer needed, that the ringleaders had been arrested, and that the workers had just grievances against the checks system. His position (which Chamberlain also adopted) was that the workers had a right to strike, but not to prevent others

50. Robert Smalls to Daniel H. Chamberlain, August 24, 1876, Chamberlain Papers. For a description of the pervasive lien system, see C. Vann Woodward, *The Origins of the New South, 1877-1913* (Baton Rouge: Louisiana State University Press, 1966), pp. 180-85.
51. *Acts*, 1871-72, p. 216.
52. *Ibid.*, 1874-75, pp. 899-900.

from working.[53] This principle of "the right to work" was respectable enough, and certainly in keeping with the prevalent free enterprise philosophy of many Republican contemporaries. Smalls reported that the workers also agreed with his position, but evidently they were not so deluded as to believe they could win the strike following such a policy. They continued successfully to use might where right had failed to induce potential strikebreakers to adopt the better part of valor.[54] Convinced that the state government would not protect them from the violent and illegal actions of the strikers, the planters decided to settle and to abandon the checks system.[55]

One rice planter who deplored the government's vacillating course was State Representative Hamilton, who instructed the rice workers on the dangers inherent in such action. "I consider it a great misfortune that an example was not made of those persons who were tried a few days ago for whipping and otherwise maltreating laborers who were disposed to work, for it emboldens others to repeat that which may be repeated too often, and until all patience and sympathy is exhausted." [56]

While the legislators' efforts to regulate the use of checks failed to prevent the strike or protect the workers, their accomplishments on another labor-related issue were more successful. In 1872 a bill was passed which regulated the leasing of convicts by merely providing that their labor could not be sold at rates less than those current for comparable labor, and that the proceeds must go to the state.[57] Two years later the leasing of convicts to private parties was outlawed altogether, and such use of inmates was restricted to state projects.[58] During the 1875-76 session Governor Chamberlain's attempt to revive the practice of leasing to private concerns was defeated.[59] Thus, although the system of convict lease was instituted under Republican government, it was also terminated by that government.

Unfortunately, this was one of the few entirely pro-labor accomplishments in nine years of Republican rule. On March 19, 1874, an "Act for the better protection of landowners and persons renting land to others for agricultural purposes" was passed. This law established for planters a preferential lien on one-third of the crop against the rental of the land

53. Telegram, William Stone to Daniel H. Chamberlain, May 24, 1876; telegram, Charles J. Calcock to Chamberlain, May 26, 1876; telegram, Henry Fuller to Chamberlain, August 23, 1876, Chamberlain Papers.

54. Telegram, Henry Fuller to Daniel H. Chamberlain, August 23, 1876, *ibid.*

55. Robert Smalls to Daniel H. Chamberlain, August 24, 1876; telegram, J. M. Crofut to Chamberlain, September 13, 1873, *ibid.*

56. *Beaufort Tribune,* October 4, 1876.

57. *Acts,* 1871-72, pp. 38-39.

58. *Acts,* 1873-74, p. 601.

59. *House Journal,* 1875-76, pp. 513-14.

or advances to farmworkers during the season.[60] In December, 1876, after an election which brought an end to Republican hegemony in South Carolina, two legislatures convened in Columbia, one Democratic and one Republican, both claiming to be the legitimate representatives of the people. In the course of this heated dispute over the political future of the state, the economic future of black laborers received a fatal blow. Almost as an afterthought, the laws which had given laborers a lien on the crop of the planter were quietly repealed.[61] This was done not by the Democratic Wallace House, but by the Republican Mackey House. It was not, in the end, such a splendid failure after all.

60. *Acts,* 1873-74, p. 788.
61. *Ibid.,* Regular Session, 1876-77, p. 226.

PART FOUR

UNMAKING A REVOLUTION

Chapter Eight

A Mortal Combat: The Flaw in Republican Hegemony

Daniel H. Chamberlain left his office early on April 11. It was eleven o'clock when he stepped into a waiting carriage and was driven to his quarters by his friend James G. Thompson, the conservative Republican editor of the *Union-Herald*. They drove almost unnoticed through the anxious noonday crowds on Gervais Street. The crowd's air of expectancy was directed more toward the imminent arrival of the circus than toward the departure of the state's last Republican governor of the nineteenth century.[1]

Indeed, Chamberlain's quiet departure was almost an anticlimax. The end had come the day before, when President Hayes had ordered the removal of federal troops from the State House with all the high-noon drama of a theatrical production. The troops marched away literally to the cadence of the City Hall clock's tolling of the noon hour.[2] With this symbolic withdrawal, Republican domination of South Carolina politics ended—almost exactly nine years after it had begun—and South Carolina's black majority ceased to be a major political force literally overnight. An electoral majority of twenty to forty thousand had been overturned, and an ever increasing black domination of the legislature had been reversed. Yet the Democratic party, so soundly beaten in four previous contests that many of its major figures had openly despaired of even fielding a full ticket in this election, had possessed only a bare skeleton of organizational structure just a few months earlier.[3] How could they have won so complete a victory?

The determining elements of the Republican defeat are difficult to fathom. The causes traditionally accepted—the betrayal in Washington, the violent intimidation of Negro voters, the dramatic revitalization of a formerly apathetic white minority—are simply not sufficient to explain

1. *News and Courier*, April 12, 1877.
2. *Ibid.*, April 11, 1877.
3. See letter of ex-Governor B. F. Perry, *News and Courier*, December 1, 1875.

the party's collapse. Certainly the federal role in the April drama at the State House has been overrated, or at the very least has overshadowed key local events.

The election results showed Hampton the winner, with 92,261 over Chamberlain's 91,127. However, there had been obvious frauds in three Democratic counties, including one, Edgefield, where the Democratic majority exceeded the total white voting population by more than 2,000. With these disputed counties excluded, the count stood Chamberlain, 86,216 and Hampton, 83,071. But when the Republican state board of canvassers decided to exclude the disputed counties, their authority to do so was disputed by the Republican-elected state supreme court, which subsequently jailed the board members for contempt. Meanwhile, the board of canvassers had issued election certificates to 59 Republicans and 57 Democrats in the House, but none for the eight disputed seats from Edgefield and Laurens. The Republican and Democratic representatives met and organized separately; the former elected E. W. M. Mackey as their Speaker, and the latter, William H. Wallace. Consequently, there were two distinct houses and two governors in Columbia, both claiming to be legally elected. However, as matters stood neither House had a quorum and neither could conduct business effectively.[4]

But only a quick and decisive resolution of this conflict could save the Republicans. Time depleted their strength with key defections and betrayals, while the Democrats grew stronger. Four Republicans—three of them Negro—defected to the Wallace House.[5] The Republican-appointed superintendent of the state prison refused to honor a pardon issued by Chamberlain. Meanwhile, Hampton asserted his executive authority by granting pardons which were upheld by a Republican-elected circuit judge and sustained by the state supreme court. The Republican courts issued restraining orders forbidding the banks to honor drafts of the Republican administration. The Democrats demonstrated their increasing de facto authority by collecting more than $100,000 in taxes during the following spring.[6] The very fact that both Chamberlain and Hampton were called to Washington to confer with newly inaugurated President Rutherford B. Hayes in March signaled the Republicans' ul-

4. For a general narrative of events, see Francis B. Simkins and Robert H. Woody, *South Carolina During Reconstruction* (Chapel Hill: University of North Carolina Press, 1932), pp. 516-41. The Republicans contended that a quorum consisted of a majority of the 116 undisputed delegates. See Chamberlain's interview with Redpath in Walter Allen, *Governor Chamberlain's Administration in South Carolina: A Chapter of Reconstruction in the Southern States* (New York: G. P. Putnam, 1888), p. 459.

5. The three Negro defectors were Thomas Hamilton of Beaufort, John Westberry of Sumter, and Nathaniel B. Myers of Beaufort.

6. Simkins and Woody, *South Carolina During Reconstruction*, p. 535.

timate defeat; Hayes's decision to withdraw federal protection from the Republican administration merely formalized a fait accompli.

Martin W. Gary's highly publicized rifle companies and their violent intimidation of Negro voters were a key element in the Democrats' campaign strategy, but similar conditions had been overcome in the 1868 and 1870 campaigns.[7] Besides, whichever set of election results one chooses to countenance, they both demonstrate the essential failure of this strategy. The Republicans voted at a record pace in 1876, their turnout exceeding the previous high in 1870 by at least a thousand votes.[8] And although the revitalization of the white voters was certainly a major factor in the Democratic victory, they remained, nevertheless, a minority.

Indeed, the Republican defeat in South Carolina was forged well before the dramatic maneuvers of the dual governments in Columbia, and even before the '76 campaign itself. To a large extent the defeat was forged by Republicans themselves. One might say it began shortly after the '74 ballots were counted and Republicans celebrated their victory, for it grew out of the deep divisions that developed during the administration of Daniel H. Chamberlain, the '74 victor. Of course, the party's entire history had been one of continuous factionalism—but never to this extent, never to such depths that only a superficial unity could be attained in a time of crisis. The desertions of its legislators and judges at critical junctures while the party was fighting for its political life point up the fundamental failure of the Republicans to unite their disparate forces and to create a political culture in which solidarity was a virtue. This lack of party discipline was demonstrated in the perennial tendency of defeated candidates to bolt the party—a phenomenon viewed with horror by John Morris, an agent of the Republican National Committee, during the very first campaign of the Republican decade. "If our party was so much divided in any northern state I should predict defeat, overwhelming defeat. But here I think all can be quieted except the split in the Charleston district, and a victory won." [9]

Morris's confidence in a Republican victory in 1868 was based on the overwhelming black majority which he felt would not be significantly affected by wrangling among some of the leadership. Similarly, the bolts of succeeding years would involve primarily issues of patronage and personal power. These defections were generally headed by political out-

7. See Governor Scott's speech before a mass meeting in Washington, D.C., on the virtues of a well-armed militia in overcoming Klan terrorism. *Daily Republican*, March 26, 1870.

8. The Republican vote in the four previous gubernatorial elections had been 69,693 (75%) in 1868, 85,071 (62%) in 1870, 71,383 (66%) in 1872, and 79,531 (54%) in 1874. The black percentage of the population in the 1875 state census was 62.

9. John Morris to William Claflin, September 14, 1868, William E. Chandler Papers, Library of Congress.

siders attempting to get inside; therefore, the basic party machinery was not critically disrupted. In 1874-76, however, the division was precipitated by the administration itself, and the result was a partial dismantling of the party machinery because the initiative on legislative policy and the control of patronage was in the hands of the chief bolter, Governor Daniel H. Chamberlain. Ironically, this tremendous power had been built into the governorship as a measure of self-protection, but now it would be used to thwart the black majority and ultimately to destroy their party. Therefore, the lack of party unity which John Morris perceived in 1868, the lack of cohesion on legislative policy evident even in the early legislative sessions, the ultimate constitutional limitation on the actual power and control that the black legislative majority could exercise—all these weaknesses, though not decisive in themselves, reached a critical stage under Chamberlain's administration and left the party unable to respond to the Democratic challenge in 1876. The governor's policies, motives, and attitudes were crucial in shaping the political environment in which these general weaknesses grew unexpectedly into tragic flaws and ruptured the Republican coalition.

Chamberlain had come to South Carolina in 1866 after service as a lieutenant in the 5th Massachusetts Cavalry, a regiment of Negro volunteers. Like many Northerners, he came with visions of becoming a great planter on the abandoned lands in the Sea Islands, but he failed at this and turned to politics instead. He was elected to the constitutional convention in 1868 from the Berkeley District (merged in 1868 with Charleston County) and later to the post of attorney general.[10] At various times in his early career, Chamberlain was identified with the conservative or bolting factions of the Republican party. He was a vice-president of the Democratic-controlled Taxpayers Convention in 1871, and he had been widely touted as the prime candidate of the bolters' faction in the state nominating convention of 1872. However, after Franklin J. Moses won the nomination for governor that year, Reuben Tomlinson, a close political ally of Chamberlain's, got the nod from the dissident Republican faction.

Ironically, Chamberlain won the *regular* nomination in 1874 and was himself the victim of a bolt in which a faction of the Republican party allied itself with the Democrats. A fusion ticket offered Judge John Green for governor and the irrepressible Martin R. Delany for lieutenant governor. Both Green and Delany had been defeated in the regular party convention by Chamberlain (72 to 40) and Richard H. Gleaves (97 to 11), respectively.[11] Green was a white native who had been elected to a circuit judgeship by the Republican legislature in 1868 in its effort

10. For a biographical sketch, see Allen, *Chamberlain's Administration,* pp. 524-26.
11. *Union-Herald,* September 15, 1874.

to mollify white Conservatives; he had been nominated for attorney general on the Independent Republican ticket in 1872. Delany was a prominent and influential black spokesman, but he had never run for or held an elective office and had been spurned in all his efforts to obtain federal and local appointive offices from President Grant and Governors Scott and Moses, despite the fact that he had campaigned tirelessly for all these men.[12]

The Green-Delany ticket was supported by Democrats who generally recognized the futility of nominating a straight Conservative ticket. The Independent ticket was rumored to have also received the private support of President Grant. The rumor is certainly plausible, in view of the fact that the Customs House appointees generally supported the Green ticket, and there is indirect evidence that Grant at least considered the prospect of throwing his support to the Conservatives in this election. Francis W. Dawson, editor of the *News and Courier*, was a primary architect of a scheme whereby Grant would unload the South Carolina Republicans and secretly support General James B. Kershaw, a Democrat, for governor. Through James Conner, later to become attorney general in Wade Hampton's administration, a group of Democrats—George Trenholm, a wealthy Charleston merchant, Hugh Magrath, the ex-Confederate governor of the state, and Dawson—negotiated with Grant's aides for three weeks prior to the state Republican convention in 1874. At one point the terms of an agreement seemed to have been successfully concluded, as Dawson wrote in an ecstatic note to his wife, who was recuperating from an illness:

> God is very good to us. [Here comes?] your note announcing your wonderful gain of [weight] & with that a letter from my friend in Washington saying: "The Administration is pledged to carry out the programme indicated in your (my) last note to me, *the entire substance of which has been submitted* to the Pres. and the principal *members of the Cabinet,* & their approval obtained. xx if this will not decide the question oft. Moses Chamberlain & Co it will be because they are stronger than the ___?___ nation." [13]

Evidently part of the deal was that the national administration would denounce Chamberlain, who was then the leading candidate for the Republican nomination. On September 3, Dawson waited anxiously for the first indication that the pledges would be kept, for the administration's Washington newspaper was to begin this campaign in the next edition.[14] The denunciations never came, however, for it seems that Senator Patter-

12. Victor Ullman, *Martin R. Delany: The Beginnings of Black Nationalism* (Boston: Beacon Press, 1971), pp. 419-20.

13. Francis W. Dawson to his wife, August 29, 1874, Francis W. Dawson Papers, Perkins Library, Duke University, Durham, N.C.

14. Francis W. Dawson to his wife, September 3, 1874, *ibid.*

son got to Grant and foiled the entire plot. It was clear by September 18 that "The jig is up at Washington. Gen. Conner, our ambassador, telegraphed from Long Branch today 'Grant is thoroughly committed to Chamberlain. I can accomplish nothing.' I am disappointed, but it was the Southern outrages & Patterson's lying which did the business." [15] Dawson was soon to change his mind about Chamberlain, against whom he had intrigued so desperately, and whom earlier he had found to be no different from the despised Moses.[16]

Ironically, both political parties ran on an anti-Moses, reform platform in the 1874 general election. The Independents, the most genuine fusionist movement to develop in South Carolina, came within 12,000 votes of defeating the regulars in the gubernatorial contest, and they won Charleston County with its bulging twenty legislative seats. Independent Republicans and Democrats held a total of fifty-four seats in the House, while in the Senate there were eight Independents and seven Democrats for a combined strength of fifteen.[17]

The Conservative press was ecstatic at the election outcome and the prospect that a coalition of Democrats and dissident Republicans might be able to control the General Assembly. Their enthusiasm eventually abated, however, as it became increasingly obvious that the electoral coalition would not long survive the legislative campaigns. After experiencing its closest election and sustaining its heaviest legislative losses to date, the Republican party became more cohesive than at any time since the first legislature of 1868-70. (See Figure 2.) Much of the change can be attributed to the increased unity of white Republicans, and to the reduced conflict between the white and black majorities on critical votes.[18] It is probable also that the Republicans were shaken by the dramatic changes in the House membership. They were still in the majority, with seven out of every ten members—but this was considerably less than the nine out of ten they had enjoyed in 1868. There were ten fewer Negro members than when they had last met (1873-74), and five fewer than at the beginning of the decade. But the most dramatic change may have been among the white Republicans, who were reduced from almost a third of the House membership in 1868 to less than one-sixth by 1874. Ironically, these losses may have contributed to the increased Republican cohesion: the white Republicans who lost were those most likely to oppose

15. Francis W. Dawson to his wife, September 8, 1874, *ibid.*
16. Francis W. Dawson to his wife, August 2, September 13, [November] 1874, *ibid.*
17. *News and Courier,* January 2, 1875.
18. The black majority was opposed by most white Republicans on only 16% and 20% of the "critical" roll calls in the legislative sessions of 1874-75 and 1875-76, respectively. See note 4 in the sixth chapter.

the black majority, because they had come from counties in the up-country and midland areas most vulnerable to Democratic attack.

Strangely, the increased cohesion of the Republican legislators was not reflected in the party as a whole. It actually grew more divided during this period, and the hostility of respective factions often threatened to break into open violence. Perhaps a key to this anomaly is the fact that the conflict was not so much between legislative factions as between the General Assembly and the executive. Much of this intraparty conflict developed as a result of the policies of Governor Chamberlain, who consciously sought to destroy the existing Republican alliances and to create a new coalition with elements of the former Democratic regime. But Chamberlain could conceive and almost succeed in executing such a policy only by winning the support of elements of the Negro bourgeoisie and the Democratic leadership. This attempt is reflected in the legislature, where, despite the shifting alignments, one can see the fundamental division between Chamberlain's allies and the Republican majority.

It is not entirely clear why and when the governor conceived this scheme to betray his recent supporters and embrace his late enemies. Possibly Chamberlain recognized the thinness of the regulars' 3 percent margin of victory; or perhaps he had, as he said, planned all along to carry out his campaign pledges of reform. In either case, his particular interpretation of the reform platform clashed sharply with that of key Negro leaders. Chamberlain, after all, had not been the first or the most outspoken advocate of reform. Fresh from his celebrated speech in support of the 1875 Civil Rights Bill in Congress, Robert B. Elliott had emphasized the necessity of cleaning house during the months preceding the 1874 convention. He had tried to impress his black colleagues with their special responsibility in this regard, given their electoral majority. And in an earlier speech to a Washington audience he had warned that revolutions do indeed go backward.[19] Unlike Chamberlain, however, Elliott's reform policy was geared to preserve the old alliance with the national Republicans, rather than to forge a new one with South Carolina Democrats.

But whether Elliott and the black regulars were any more or less sincere than Chamberlain in their advocacy of reform is ultimately irrelevant to the events that transpired during those two years. The notion that the Democrats would have conceded control of the state to a reformed Republican party any more readily than to a corrupt one is very dubious, to say the least. The evidence is stronger for the proposition that more Democrats would have acquiesced in a policy of fusion and political

19. Peggy Lamson, *The Glorious Failure: Black Congressman Robert Brown Elliott and the Reconstruction in South Carolina* (New York: W. W. Norton, 1973), pp. 147, 183-88; *Port Royal Commercial,* March 5, 1874.

coexistence if a strong and united Republican party had made hopes of a straight-out victory appear illusory.

Meanwhile, the spectre of a resurgent national Democratic party, a party which had already won control of the U.S. House of Representatives in 1874, boded ill for the South Carolina Republicans. Only four of the former Confederate states were still under Republican control by Christmas, 1874; one of these—Mississippi—would succumb within a few months. Mississippi's 1875 election would be characterized by the same violence and economic intimidation used in South Carolina a year later. The dilatory response of the Grant administration to the Mississippi Republicans' plight hardly assuaged the anxieties of their Palmetto State counterparts.[20]

If the Negro leadership read these events as ominous, then one could expect them to adopt a strategy of self-defense. If they were to defend themselves against an onslaught similar to that in Mississippi, they must seek to protect their constituents from political and economic intimidation. They must consolidate their control over the state and local bureaucracy and the courts. However, a legislative body is ill designed to take the initiative in such matters and must ultimately rely on the executive. But the governor's plans, as Elliott and his colleagues soon learned, were quite opposite their own. Indeed, Chamberlain quickly launched a vigorous campaign of retrenchment in governmental spending and bipartisanship in his appointments to local offices which put him on a collision course with the Negro leadership. During the 1874-75 session he vetoed twenty acts of the legislature, including the appropriations bill. He insisted on holding taxes below 11 mills in 1874-75 and below 8¼ mills in the 1875-76 appropriations. He attempted to cut the salaries of all public employees by one-third, and to cut back services in every phase of government. He unflinchingly branded his Republican opponents in the legislature as thieves, corrupters, and profligate squanderers of the public purse. His programs were absolutely essential if the confidence of the white tax-paying citizens was to be restored, he insisted.[21]

However, a closer look at many of the measures championed by the governor reveals a more complex situation than the one portrayed by Chamberlain and the Democratic press, that is, "reformers" versus "corrupters." Chamberlain's key theme of "even-handed justice to all people"

20. Mississippi's Reconstruction government was overturned in 1875 by a coordinated application of violence, economic intimidation, and fraud against Negro Republicans. When Governor Adelbert Ames requested federal troops to restore order, President Grant refused his support. The "Mississippi Plan," as it was called, became a model for South Carolina Democrats in the 1876 election. See Vernon Wharton, *The Negro in Mississippi, 1865-90* (Chapel Hill: University of North Carolina Press, 1947), p. 193.

21. For example, see Chamberlain's response to attacks against his party loyalty in open letter to Senator Morton of Indiana, *News and Courier,* January 28, 1876.

seems to have almost invariably added up to more justice for white taxpayers and less for the poor. Of course, his titanic battles with the legislature on the tax bills oftentimes reduced, as even his key allies admitted, to a simple matter of facesaving and a demonstration of power.[22]

But often the difference was one of absolutely contradictory emphasis, indicating that the two sides were appealing to two very different constituencies—Chamberlain to the white taxpayers, and his opponents to the poor blacks. In order to conform to his recommended slash in the expenditures of public institutions, the governor proposed drastic changes in their operation. The lunatic asylum was to be cut from $65,000 to $40,000 by admitting only the violent or those who "require medical treatment" and sending those who were "simple, harmless idiots and imbeciles" to the county poorhouses.[23] The state penitentiary's appropriation was to be cut from $40,000 to $20,000 by reinstating a system of convict lease whereby workers were hired out to private employers to fill work gangs on plantations and in industries. The state university was to be cut from $43,000 to $30,000 and its nature fundamentally altered. It was now almost entirely black and annually granted a scholarship to one poor student from each county; however, it should be reorganized and the state should "abandon the attempt to keep it up on the basis of its old days." The college professors would be replaced with northern schoolmarms. After all, said the governor of all the people: "We only want a good high school." [24]

The state appropriation for public schools should be cut by one-fourth to encourage more local initiative in supporting them. The appropriations for the state normal school and the agricultural college should be halved. The state scholarship system should be terminated at an early date. The salaries of the school commissioners should be cut in half, and the office given to men who did not have to depend on its salary for a living. "What a travestie it is to see men filling the office of school commissioner, to pass upon the qualifications of school teachers, when they can barely write their own names. The duties of the office could be faithfully discharged by devoting three days in each month to a supervision of the schools, and many thrifty, honest and intelligent citizens could be found who would undertake the work for a merely nominal salary—many for no salary at all." [25]

More and more Chamberlain's language echoed the Democrats; more and more his proposals seemed destined to drive Republicans out of office

22. *Ibid.*, January 29, 1876.
23. *Ibid.*
24. *Ibid.*
25. *Ibid.*

and replace them with Democrats or white conservative Republicans. Certainly his image of public officials motivated merely by the "honor" of office, men who could work for half salary, or nominal salaries, or indeed, no salaries at all, fitted the wealthy planter or the middle-class professional more than the average local black Republican officeholder. Given Chamberlain's relationship with Francis W. Dawson, editor of the *News and Courier,* one suspects that the paper's editorial may have reflected the governor's motive in proposing these cuts: "Cutting down the pay and preventing stealing will go farther to lessen the number of candidates than anything else. And that is what we want to get at—that public offices, such as that of Governor, shall be sought for the honor, and that minor officers, such as Treasurers and Comptrollers shall be competent and trustworthy *business* men, not political chieftains. . . . The goal to aim at is the extinction of the class of professional politicians."[26]

Chamberlain's legislative initiatives were not generally successful because most Negro legislators opposed them. However, the governor's program did spark divisions within the party and among Negro legislators in particular. These divisions were similar but perhaps more sharply defined than those evident in the earlier legislatures of 1868-72. The Democrats were generally cohesive, while Republican unity was shattered. For example, the proposal to elect rather than appoint county auditors and treasurers secured unanimous support from the Democrats but divided Republicans almost in two. A roll call on this issue during the 1875-76 session produced a 51-28 vote in favor of the bill, with Democrats voting 25-0, and Republicans 26-28. Negroes, dividing down the middle, were 20 for and 22 against.[27]

Similarly, the proposal to change the rules for admission to the state lunatic asylum so as to reduce the population there was initially passed 43 to 23. Here 17 of 19 Democrats voting on the issue supported the governor's proposal, as compared with 26 of 47 Republicans. But Negro legislators split 21 to 16 in favor of the revised admission standard.[28] Fewer Negroes supported the governor's proposal to return to the practice of leasing convicts. However, an early test vote on this issue during the 1874-75 session was favorable to Chamberlain when 22 Republicans joined 24 Democrats to pass the measure 46 to 42. Twelve of Chamberlain's Republican supporters were Negroes.[29]

Apparently Negro leaders were successful in reversing many of these

26. *Ibid.,* February 4, 1876. Emphasis added.

27. *Journal of the House of Representatives of the State of South Carolina, 1875-76* (Columbia: Republican Printing Company, 1876), p. 167.

28. *Ibid.,* p. 293.

29. *House Journal,* 1874-75, p. 626.

initial legislative successes, for none appear to have become law. However, they had much less control or success in the area of patronage. The governor's appointment policies were probably more crucial to the immediate political future of the state than his legislative policies. Having recently experienced a close election and expecting a tough challenge in the next one, with uncertain national support, the party's leaders might be expected to strengthen their hold on the state and local judiciary, which might be called upon to decide critical election challenges. But, like most other reconstructed governments, the South Carolina Republicans had concentrated tremendous patronage power in the governor's office. This was done when the political future was uncertain, as a way to increase their control of the local bureaucracy in those counties that could not be won at the polls. This system worked well under normal circumstances because the governor was as dependent on the county leadership as they were on him. The governor had the constitutional authority, but in practice power was shared.

The Chamberlain years were not normal circumstances, however. Patronage, an instrument by which any governor could develop a personal constituency, was used to build a new political alliance. Consequently, in several counties the governor moved to replace Republican officeholders with Democrats. He received fulsome praise for these actions from Democratic correspondents and in the Democratic press, especially the *News and Courier*. By the spring of 1875 Chamberlain had overcome Dawson's initial suspicions and become his close and secret friend. Dawson became a key adviser on appointments and political strategy.[30] It was Dawson, for example, who suggested the most politically appropriate candidates for appointment from South Carolina to the National Centennial Committee. "As to the Centennial appointments I will co-operate with you most fully," Chamberlain wrote. "I like your idea and your selection. We want to make the appointments from that class who can do some good,—And that of course will require the larger part to be from the Conservatives, but that is no objection with me."[31]

Chamberlain's policies gained the personal praise of Democrats throughout the state and pledges from them of political support.[32] But the newfound supporters often demanded a high price: "Give us Good Government & we give you our suffrage be we called what we may,"

30. "You know we must not be *too good* friends," the governor jested with Dawson: Chamberlain to Dawson, June 24, 1875. See also Daniel H. Chamberlain to Francis W. Dawson, January 27, June 9, 1875, and May 22, 1876, Dawson Papers.

31. Daniel H. Chamberlain to Francis W. Dawson, October 11, 1875, *ibid.*

32. A. W. Moore *et al.* to Daniel H. Chamberlain, December 6, 1875, Governor Daniel H. Chamberlain Papers, South Carolina Archives, Columbia.

promised a dry goods merchant from Laurens. "Remove half the Trial Justice in our County give us a good *Jury Commiss* Commis of Election Juage of Probate & fill with good men."[33] Chamberlain apparently fulfilled some of these demands, as in the case of those made by the merchant from Laurens. A "gentleman" *was* appointed jury commissioner in Laurens, and hope for law and order in the county was thereby revived.[34] At times, though, the expectations which the governor had aroused in the Democrats were even greater than he could fulfill.

> In regard to the Marion appointments I do not understand that I made any pledges which I have not kept. And I scarcely think Ch. Johnson thinks so. What I have done I have done from a desire to do the most good ultimately. My friends in Marion ought to understand that unless I throw away all my influence with my own party there I must so manage things as to keep my hold on the party. If they are unwilling to accept my acts and interpret them in that light, then they ought not to have any confidence in me. To urge me to try to get the nomination of my party and then to denounce me for taking only a small step in that direction, and one which does no harm to them is idle. I cannot play that part. I must stop, or I must act in such a way as a sensible politician would act. I have no complaint from Ch. Johnson. The Conservatives now have an unusual number of Trial Justices in Marion—four perhaps five out of the nine. And none of the Republican Trial Justices are bad either.[35]

Such a balance was difficult to maintain, for even conservative Republicans like Thomas Hamilton attacked the governor for "selling out the Republican party to the democrats."[36] It appeared to Hamilton that the lowest Democrat had more influence with Chamberlain than a Republican of the highest position. Democrats flooded the governor's office with complaints and charges of incompetence or corruption. Some of these were obviously completely groundless, like the attempt to have the jury commissioner of Williamsburg removed because his bond was inadequate. Senator Stephen A. Swails had signed this particular bond, and when he forwarded documentation of its adequacy to the governor, he was enraged. "I have no doubt he [the informant] expected a removal on his mere statement, there is no question about it the Democratic party expect you to do anything they wish and in these exciting times many men in our own party make the declaration to the effect that you will do what they wish."[37]

33. Albert Dial to Daniel H. Chamberlain, December 1, 1875, *ibid.*
34. Albert Dial to Daniel H. Chamberlain, January 3, 1876, *ibid.*
35. Daniel H. Chamberlain to Francis W. Dawson, May 22, 1876, Dawson Papers.
36. *Beaufort Tribune,* May 5, 1875.
37. Stephen A. Swails to Daniel H. Chamberlain, January 8, 1876, Chamberlain Papers.

Certainly the single most dramatic and divisive action taken to demonstrate his new policy was Chamberlain's refusal to sanction the legislature's election of William James Whipper as judge of the important Charleston circuit. A relative of the prominent abolitionist Whipper family of Philadelphia, William's political career had been as stormy and controversial as his military service. In the army he had been court-martialed twice, once for gambling and again for insulting a white lieutenant.[38] He was elected to the 1868 constitutional convention and to the legislature from Beaufort in 1868-72 and 1875-76. During his first stint in the legislature he was chairman of the judiciary committee, and he later served on the committee on ways and means. But Whipper was just as often out of power as in. He leveled charges of corruption against Governor Scott in 1871 and led the unsuccessful effort to have him impeached.[39] In the gubernatorial elections of 1872 and 1874 he ran on the bolters' ticket and went down to defeat.

For a number of years Whipper had sought a judgeship. He was beaten by Jonathan J. Wright for a seat on the state supreme court in 1868 and again in 1872. He ran for the circuit judgeship of the Charleston district in 1874, but Chamberlain made a special trip to the Republican caucus to denounce him as incompetent and morally unfit for the position. On the following day he was defeated by Judge J. P. Reed, a white Democrat, by a vote of 73-56.[40] Since this election had been for the unexpired term of the deceased incumbent, another election was held the following year to fill the full four-year term.

During the interval, relations between the governor and the Negro Republican leadership had deteriorated considerably, especially those between Chamberlain and House Speaker Robert B. Elliott. Their relationship had begun as one of necessary mutual support, if not cordiality. Elliott had supported Chamberlain for the governorship, and the latter had supported Elliott for the speakership against many of the same coalition of Democrats and Independents who were later his allies. During the 1875-76 session, Elliott sought to secure Whipper's election despite the governor's public opposition. It may well be that his were merely personal political motives, but one can logically presuppose more global concerns. The election of Whipper was really a challenge to the long-term policy of electing Democrats or apostate Democrats to the major state judgeships. Aside from the fact that Republican lawyers may well have

38. William James Whipper, Pension File Certificate No. 721218, Civil War, RG 15, NA; also see Case MM2038, May, 1865, Box 662, Records of the Judge Advocate General, RG 153, NA.
39. *Daily Courier,* December 7, 1871.
40. *Union-Herald,* December 12, 1874.

grown restive with this policy of political self-denial, it was also unproductive in light of the hostile actions of some of these judges and unwise in view of the changing electoral picture. Lukewarm Republicans or former Democrats would certainly be a liability in a closely fought campaign. In any event, Elliott appears to have maneuvered to schedule the judicial elections while Chamberlain was out of town on a speaking engagement in Greenville. Then he and other Negro leaders exhorted a Republican caucus on the preceding night to vote a straight party ticket in the judgeship elections. Consequently, a coalition of the supporters of Whipper, ex-Governor Franklin J. Moses, and P. L. Wiggin managed to elect all three to their respective judgeships by a comfortable two-to-one margin.[41]

Whipper's election can be attributed largely to the Negro leadership's reaction against Chamberlain's appointments policy. Practically every speaker supporting these nominations invoked the necessity for strict party unity. At the caucus Speaker Elliott had declared that he would measure each member's Republicanism by his vote on this issue. Nevertheless, Elliott did "warmly" advocate the reelection of one Conservative judge. But partisan feeling was at its peak, and Samuel Bampfield retorted that he had nothing against the man Elliott had recommended except that he was a Democrat. He declared that the Republican party was "on the verge of a terrible crisis," and "an out-and-out Republican judiciary was all that could save it from utter annihilation." "Only when the day shall come when a Republican cannot be found will I vote for a Conservative," declared Senator Johnston, a fusionist candidate in the previous election. Indeed, Whipper had been defeated for this same judgeship the previous year by a combination of Democrats and Independent Republicans. That coalition was now smashed beyond repair. For example, only three of the Independent Republicans of the Charleston delegation voted against Whipper on this second occasion. One of the three, Richard Nesbitt, declared a few weeks after the election that although he had voted against Whipper, it was "the duty of all Negroes to insist that Whipper takes his seat." [42]

A great deal had changed during the intervening year. As it became increasingly clear that Chamberlain's policy of reform and anti-corruption was his platform for seeking a rapprochement with the Democrats, and that he was using the power of the governor's office, especially patronage, to build a power base outside the regular party, some of his former supporters became restive. Shortly before the Whipper election H. Z. Burchmeyer, a Negro Independent from Charleston, reportedly declared "that the sooner the negroes consolidated as a man, and took the govern-

41. *News and Courier*, December 17, 1875.
42. *Ibid.*, January 3, 1876.

ment in their own hands the better for them, and the better for the State." [43] Similar sentiments were attributed to W. G. Pinckney, another Negro Independent from Charleston. "He thought that organization with the Conservatives was a ruinous policy. He was there to advise a solid Republican vote. He didn't propose to ask the Democrats anything about the next election. He thought that the consolidation principle was played out." [44]

A few days after Whipper's election, which signaled the destruction of the Independent Republican movement, Chamberlain predicted the reorganization of the Democratic party as a consequence of that election. Indeed, he seemed to be obliquely calling for that reorganization as he suggested the policy the Democrats might pursue. "I do not allow myself to think that the good and honest men of South Carolina will find it impossible, because they are organized as Democrats, to give their help to whomsoever shall be best able to undo the terrible wrongs of last Thursday [the day of the election]." [45] Chamberlain obviously expected to be that leader, and he quickly took steps to secure the mantle of leadership. Making a move that was legally questionable to say the least, he refused to sign the commissions of Whipper and Moses, thereby blocking them from taking the seats to which they had been elected by the legislature. With this action he committed himself to a policy which would obviously split the party. The political significance of the decision was heralded by Dawson's journal with the headline: "Governor Has Crossed the Rubicon." [46]

During the early months of 1876 it appeared that Chamberlain's scenario for political realignment in South Carolina would be borne out by events. "The Conservatives are a unit in endorsing every one of your actions," he was informed by one political ally in Clarendon County, who further reported that Republicans in that county were evenly divided pro and con. [47] Chamberlain was endorsed for reelection at the January meeting of the Democratic Executive Committee. [48] Resolutions of support were forwarded to him from joint mass meetings of Democrats and Republicans. [49] Some of these meetings were biracial, with the "best

43. *Ibid.*, December 9, 1875.
44. *Ibid.*
45. *Ibid.*, December 20, 1875.
46. *Ibid.*, December 22, 1875.
47. William Ivey to Daniel H. Chamberlain, January 6, 1876, Chamberlain Papers.
48. F. A. Porcher, "History of the Administration of D. H. Chamberlain, the Last Radical Governor of South Carolina," Read before the S.C. Historical Society by F. A. Porcher, President of the Society (1875-88). Handwritten copy in Charleston Historical Society, Charleston.
49. "Proceedings of Mass Meeting in Chesterfield Co.," n.d., folder 39, Box 9, Letters Received, Chamberlain Papers.

elements" of the colored people endorsing his actions, according to the reports.[50]

Throughout the Reconstruction era Democrats had persisted in the belief that they could eventually split the black vote along class lines. "The effort must be made, and will be made, to retain the aid of the colored people who have sided with us hitherto, and to join to them now battalions of colored voters who are injured by high taxation, incapable officials and oppressive laws," declared an editor of the News and Courier.[51] Whites must be careful not to provoke the opposition of this element of the black vote. They must take care to point out that their opposition to Whipper is based not on color, but on competence. As proof of this the editor pointed to the conservative support for Jonathan J. Wright in his election to the Supreme Court. Of course, he did not recall that the Courier itself had viewed this support as a tactical move to ensure the election of "the lesser of two evils." At this critical time, however, they must be careful: "Only in case the Black line shall be formed, and we do not believe that the Elliotts and Whippers can form it, should the White line be formed to confront and overpower it. If you take the Radicals at their word and tell the colored people that we will have none of them, they will, in self-defence, band themselves together. Such provocation we cannot afford to give." [52]

The success of such a policy had always been difficult to assess, but there were always enough indicators to encourage the Democrats in the belief that it might eventually be their salvation. After the 1874 Charleston mayoral elections, for example, the Columbia Register thought it saw a break in the formerly solid Republican bloc. "The strength of the two parties in Charleston is about evenly balanced, with probably a small majority in favor of the Republicans; but the intelligence and independence which has characterized the more influential of the colored citizens of Charleston recently leads us to believe that their influence and support would be cast on the side of a straight-out Conservative ticket." [53] Of course, one must be careful in assessing the validity of such statements, for in the view of the white observer his black allies were always the more intelligent Negroes, possibly by virtue of the fact that they were his allies.

Nevertheless, their policy was not entirely based on wishful thinking. Prominent mulattoes from the freeborn class sometimes allied themselves with the Conservatives in local and state elections. William J. McKinlay,

50. Excerpt from Georgetown Times, January 13, 1876, folder 5, Box 10, ibid.
51. News and Courier, January 21, 1876.
52. Ibid.
53. Columbia Register, September 2, 1875.

for instance, endorsed the Conservative ticket in the 1874 election and advocated an alliance between Negroes and Democrats.[54] Furthermore, the statistical correlation of voting behavior with socioeconomic background evident in earlier legislatures suggests an underlying class schism among Negro legislators. While a similar statistical analysis of the 1874-75 legislature is not feasible, there are strong indications that this type of schism continued and was relevant to many of the more important issues posed during these later sessions. Because of our inability to fully identify the socioeconomic backgrounds of most of these Negro legislators, we cannot measure statistically the relationship between their political behavior and socioeconomic status.[55] Nevertheless, the twenty-nine Negro members who can be classified roughly as "upper" status appear to have been more likely to support Chamberlain and the Democrats on several key issues than were the twelve Negroes who can be designated as of "lower" status.[56]

All but three of the Independents in the House were Negro, and these formed the core of the opposition to the regular party in the early stages of the 1874 session. For instance, when Robert B. Elliott was elected speaker it was by the narrowest margin of the Reconstruction period, 62-48, with 21 Republicans joining 27 Democrats to oppose him. Of the 18 Negroes opposing Elliott, 14 were Independents. This coalition held for the vote against William James Whipper's first bid for the first circuit judgeship in 1874. By the 1875-76 session, however, this initial coalition appears to have dissolved, to be replaced by a much less formal,

54. *News and Courier*, September 29, 1874.

55. A statistical correlation of voting behavior as indicated by Guttman scale scores with Likert scales of status attributes would not be meaningful because of the lack of data on these legislators. Of the 70 Negro members in the 1874-75 session, 61% can be identified by color, 58% by antebellum origins, 53% by both, but only 33% by color, origins, and income or wealth (the factors for the social status index).

56. The status categories defined here are roughly comparable to those developed in the sixth chapter. Mulatto color *or* free origins, and evidence of real property ownership are used to define the upper group, while a lack of property, and black color *or* slave origins defines the lower group. Where there is no evidence of property ownership, evidence of professional or artisan occupation is used to classify the legislator as being of higher than average status. There were 30 legislators classified as upper status: Jacob C. Allman, William J. Andrews, Samuel J. Bampfield, H. Z. Burchmeyer, Joseph D. Boston, Andrew Curtis, John Freeman, Hastings Gantt, Thomas Hamilton, Samuel Greene, R. M. Harriett, William A. Hayne, Richard H. Humbert, Thomas E. Miller, Shadrack Morgan, Samuel Keith, Nathaniel B. Myers, Hercules Simmons, Aaron Simmons, Paris Simpkins, Jackson Smith, William Simons, James Spencer, William Scott, John Westberry, Thomas Richardson, William M. Thomas, John Vanderpool, Robert B. Elliott, and William James Whipper. There were twelve lower-status legislators: Sampson Bridges, Peter Bright, Simon Coker, Samuel Doiley, John Gibson, Reuben Gaither, Mitchell Goggins, Richard Nesbitt, James Peterson, W. G. Pinckney, Joseph Thompson, and James M. Young.

less stable bloc of conservative-leaning legislators. This conservative Negro bloc seldom exceeded twenty votes, but when added to the four to six conservative white Republicans and the thirty-four Democrats it could constitute a winning coalition, especially since the radical-moderate Republican voters were seldom all present.

While the make-up and voting behavior of this bloc was by no means constant, there was a significant core of members. William J. Andrews, a mulatto merchant from Sumter, was much more likely to be found voting with the Democrats than with his own party. William A. Hayne of Marion County was the brother of Henry E. Hayne, Chamberlain's secretary of state. A mulatto born in South Carolina of free parents, William spearheaded several conservative proposals during his tenure as a legislator. Jacob C. Allman, a mulatto evidently of slave origins, also represented Marion County, where he owned a moderate-sized farm. Most constant of all perhaps was John Westberry of Sumter, a slave-born mulatto and small farmer who defected to Wade Hampton's camp during the election crisis of 1876.

Of course, it should be noted that these men represented midland counties which had been sharply contested in past elections. This factor may have influenced their political postures. However, other Negro members who often voted with them had no such influences. Neither William Harriett, a West Indian–born merchant from Williamsburg, nor John Freeman, a freeborn mulatto artisan from Charleston, nor Thomas Hamilton, a black rice planter from Beaufort, was subject to any serious Democratic challenge. By virtue of some combination of antebellum origin, color, or income these men were of higher social status than their fellow legislators.

Taking a sample of fifteen roll calls on which Governor Chamberlain had announced a position and on which a nearly unanimous Democratic vote can be used to define the conservative pole, one discovers that members of the upper status group were most likely to favor the Chamberlain-Democratic side. Two of these roll calls were on a Chamberlain proposal to limit admissions to the state lunatic asylum; five involved the proposal to lease convicts to private employers; one was the 1875 election of Whipper as a circuit judge. The other measures had been publicly endorsed by the governor, directly or indirectly. The latter group included a proposal to elect county treasurers and auditors rather than have them appointed by the governor, a bill to limit the sale of seed cotton, and a proposal to allow counties to enact fence laws.[57]

57. This selected sample of fifteen roll calls includes those votes on the issues that were politically significant, with a high proportion of legislators participating, and a solid Democratic opposition. Five of these roll calls were from the 1874-75 session: January 26, 1875,

When the proposal to elect county auditors and treasurers came to a vote, Speaker Elliott relinquished the chair in order to condemn the bill. The ultimate effect of the legislation was to concede these key offices to Democrats in several counties, Elliott instructed his colleagues. And given the recent threats of a taxpayers' revolt, it was not politic to surrender the main offices responsible for collecting and disbursing taxes to the opposition.[58] When a test vote on this issue developed later in the session, however, more than half of the upper-status group ignored Elliott's warning and voted in favor of the bill. Their performance contrasted sharply with the lower-status sample, 80 percent of whom voted to kill the legislation. Similarly, despite the partisan pressure favoring Whipper's election to a judgeship in December, 1875, sixteen Negroes voted for other candidates. Half of these were from the upper-status group, four were lower-status, and four cannot be classified.

The other roll calls in this sample can be classified as social reform rather than strictly political issues. The attempt to limit admissions to the lunatic asylum curtailed a social service to the poor. Permitting the leasing of convicts, restricting the sale of seed cotton, and requiring the fencing of livestock were all measures perceived as inimical to the interests of poor black farm tenants. When the proposal on the lunatic asylum came to a vote in January, 1876, twenty-one Negroes joined seventeen Democrats to pass the bill. Of the Negro supporters, 57 percent were from the upper-status sample, as compared with only 18 percent from the lower-status group. Similarly, only twelve Negroes supported convict lease, but all of them were from the upper-status group. The restriction of the sale of seed cotton to daylight hours and only by "reputable" persons was opposed by 54 percent of the lower-status group, but supported by 53 percent of the upper-status group. Of the Negroes voting for the fencing law, eight were upper and three lower status.[59]

Pass H181 to 3rd Reading (Elect Co. Auditor), 56-47; February 27, 1875, Pass S147 to 3rd Reading (Regulate Sale of Seed Cotton), 44-29; March 10, 1875, Indefinitely Postpone H244 (Convict Lease), 42-50; Table H244, 44-42; Pass H244 to 3rd Reading, 47-41. (*House Journal*, 1874-75, pp. 326, 546, 625-26.) The other ten roll calls were from the 1875-76 session: December 13, 1875, Indefinitely Postpone Motion to Strike Enacting Clause of H670 (Elect Co. Auditor), 51-28; December 16, 1875, Elect Whipper 1st Circuit Judge, 63-27-50; December 17, 1875, Pass H622 (Fence Law), 40-42; January 24, 1876, Indefinitely Postpone H801 (Lunatic Asylum), 19-40; Pass H801, 43-23; Pass Sec. 1 of H783 (Sale of Seed Cotton), 32-21; January 21, 1876, Reject H788, 38-47; January 25, 1876, Indefinitely Postpone H783, 44-39; February 28, 1876, Concurrent Resolution to Lease Convicts, 27-42; Strike H875 (Convict Lease), 41-29. *House Journal*, 1875-76, pp. 167, 194-95, 210, 294, 278, 303, 512, 513-14.
58. *News and Courier*, December 15, 1875.
59. For comments on the political significance of these measures and the manifest opposition of many black constituents, see *ibid.*, December 1, 2, 13, 1875.

Probably the behavior of these legislators and the actions of more prominent Negro leaders of similar backgrounds were sufficient to encourage Chamberlain and some Democrats as to the ultimate likelihood of splitting the Negro leadership and, through them, the black vote. So when prominent mulatto leaders like Congressman Joseph H. Rainey endorsed Chamberlain's actions in the Whipper election, it seemed again that the policy of encouraging such a realignment along class lines would bear fruit.[60] Indeed, Chamberlain had privately referred to Francis L. Cardozo, the secretary of the treasury, as his "wisest and truest adviser." [61] And Cardozo had predicted or even welcomed a realignment of the political parties seven months before the Whipper election. Giving an interview to a Democratic reporter, he commented on the significance of the legislative session of 1874-75 which had just ended.

> . . . there have been several mortal combats (politically speaking) between the better and worse elements of the Republican party, and in every case the good element, with the aid of the Conservatives, have routed their opponents, horse, foot, and dragoon. You can readily perceive, therefore, that this has been the turning point of Republicanism and good government in South Carolina. If the Republican party had proved itself unable to shake off the deadly incubus of corruption and imbecility that had hitherto controlled it in this State, its doom was certain, and it would have died a natural death in 1876. It was because of my confidence in its inherent vitality, and in the ability of some of these men in its ranks to correct these evils, that I did not favor the bolt last fall, and I think that you and the political party that you represent will now admit that it was providential that the bolt did not succeed.[62]

Cardozo went on to praise their Democratic allies as "disinterested and patriotic." He admitted that he had personally antagonized his fellow Negro leaders because of his "manner"; presumably he meant that his dignity and restraint had been interpreted as haughtiness. He pictured himself as something of a king-maker. Dismissing Chamberlain's implication in the shady dealings of the Scott administration as "errors of judgment," he described how he met with him to obtain absolute assurances of his future policies and then worked for his nomination and election.[63]

Cardozo's statement reveals some of the subtleties of the growing split between Republican factions. Unlike the previous biennial bolts, this antagonism was not motivated by mere jockeying for personal power or patronage. Though the ostensible issue was the usual one, corruption, the animus seems to have gone deeper. When Cardozo spoke of some

60. *Columbia Register,* January 14, 1876.
61. Daniel H. Chamberlain to Francis W. Dawson, February 8, 1875, Dawson Papers.
62. *Aiken Tribune,* April 10, 1875.
63. *Ibid.*

leaders being antagonized because of his manner, he described the antago- nism of long standing as causing the opposition to his nomination as state treasurer in 1872. Likewise, in a letter to Dawson the governor insisted that his policies were not motivated by mere political opportunism or backroom deals, but grew out of personal convictions.[64] His declaration is believable. Although his correspondence proves that Chamberlain was not oblivious to political concerns in developing his policies, his motiva- tions were far more complex than mere power hunger or (as one observer insisted) presidential ambitions.[65]

Because the capacity of the Republican party and the Negro majority to respond effectively to the coming election crisis was ultimately depen- dent on the governor's actions, Chamberlain's motives and the reason why his perceptions of the political scene deviated so sharply from those of many of his black contemporaries are important. Reminiscing about this period in later years, the governor revealed a racial bias which may have affected his earlier policies. His historical assessment was similar to ex-Governor Scott's a quarter-century earlier, and to those of William Dunning and other historians of the coming decades. He could see now that the 1867 Reconstruction acts were plainly "a frightful experiment, which never could have given a real statesman who learned or knew the facts the smallest hope of success." Statesmen knew that self-govern- ment requires experience and mental and moral character, while he found the Negroes of 1867 "an aggregation of ignorance and inexperience and incapacity." He practically condoned the Democratic campaign of terror and violence as the only choice between lawlessness and misrule. He called out federal troops to suppress the Ku Klux Klan in 1876, but he defended the Klan in 1901: "Any observer who cared to see could see that it flourished where corruption and incapacity had climbed into power, and withered where the reverse was the case." Far from being bitter, Cham- berlain now felt the overthrow of the Reconstruction governments in the South was inevitable. He felt that the wisest federal policy for the twentieth century would be to commend the Negro to his southern neigh- bors and employers. Charity should be eschewed, for it would rob the Negro of his incentive. Negro youths should be shunted into manual education, rather than the higher education for which they presumably were not fitted.[66]

64. Daniel H. Chamberlain to Francis W. Dawson, May 15, 1875, Chamberlain Papers.
65. A South Carolinian [Belton O'Neal Townsend], "The Political Condition of South Carolina," *Atlantic Monthly*, XXXIX (February, 1877), 182.
66. Daniel H. Chamberlain, "Reconstruction in South Carolina," *Atlantic Monthly*, LXXXVII (April, 1901), 483. Cf. Robert K. Scott to Richard H. Gleaves, newspaper clipping, "Reconstruction Scrapbook," South Caroliniana Library, University of South Carolina, Columbia.

Of course, one cannot be certain whether Chamberlain's racism in his doting years had not been kindled *after* his political career in South Carolina. Certainly the attitude of the country as a whole seems to have undergone such a change. But on the other hand, since there had always been a stratum of racist attitudes just beneath the surface of the national consciousness even in the most liberal times, it may well have been the same with Chamberlain. After all, the policies he urged on the federal government in 1901 with respect to entrusting the future of the Negro to his southern employers and discouraging higher education of Negro youth were similar to the policies he had advocated as governor of South Carolina in 1875, when he had urged the legislature to turn the state university into a high school and put public offices in the hands of wealthy landowners. But in any case, proof that Chamberlain was a racist would not be sufficient to explain his actions. No doubt many of the closest political allies of blacks were no less racist.

Chamberlain's particular attitudes do indicate that his black constituency was culturally alien to him, and that this affected his political actions. As a student at Harvard and Yale he had strongly supported the *idea* of equal justice for the black slaves and had identified with the Garrisonian abolitionists.[67] And, like many other abolitionists, he must have experienced some cultural disorientation upon coming to South Carolina to deal with blacks not as a cause, but as people on a day to day basis, as equals.[68] A man of culture and learning, he found himself isolated by politics from the "best" southern society, isolated with his black cultural inferiors. It was no secret among the whites of South Carolina's upper class that the governor desperately wanted their acceptance.[69] Chamberlain's policies as governor soon won him the social position he desired. He was toasted by "fashionable associations" and "lionized everywhere." [70] He was invited to speak to the Charleston Chamber of Commerce and before white colleges throughout the state; he was flattered by invitations to fashionable dinners and prestigious social events of the Charleston upper class.

It was to one of these prestigious societies that Chamberlain sent a message containing his most vehement and defiant denunciation of the Whipper election, and certainly his most racist interpretation of the

67. Allen, *Chamberlain's Administration*, pp. 524-25.

68. See reactions of missionaries in Willie Lee Rose, *Rehearsal for Reconstruction: The Port Royal Experiment* (Indianapolis: Bobbs-Merrill, 1964), pp. 165-66; Laura Towne, *Letters and Diary of Laura M. Towne Written from the Sea Islands of South Carolina, 1862-84,* ed. Rupert Sargent Holland (Cambridge: Riverside Press, 1963), p. 20.

69. F. A. Porcher, *D. H. Chamberlain the Last Radical Governor* (n.p.); [Townsend,] "Political Condition of South Carolina," p. 182.

70. [Townsend,] "Political Condition of South Carolina," p. 182.

significance of that election. On the day when he announced his refusal to sign the commissions of Whipper and Moses, Chamberlain sent a telegram to the New England Society of Charleston apologizing for his absence as the guest of honor at their fifty-sixth anniversary dinner.

> I cannot attend your annual supper to-night; but if there ever was an hour when the spirit of the Puritans, the spirit of undying, unconquerable enmity and defiance to wrong ought to animate their sons, it is the hour, here, in South Carolina. *The civilization of the Puritan and the Cavalier, of the Roundhead and the Huguenot, is in peril. Courage, Determination, Union, Victory, must be our watchwords. The grim Puritans never qualified under threat or blow. Let their sons now imitate their example.*[71]

The implication that Anglo-Saxon civilization was imperiled by the black leviathan in South Carolina was not hyperbole to Chamberlain; his public posture is reflected in his private correspondence. He seems to have genuinely imagined himself to be, quite literally, a *white* knight leading the crusade against the black cultural heathen. On the day of Whipper's election, the governor had been in Greenville giving a lecture on the classics to a local college. Months later he found this fact very significant and brought it to Dawson's attention: "Sometimes when themes are wanted, and you have leisure, I want you to notice my Greenville address on the Classics. I value it chiefly, if you will allow me to be frank, for its testimony to the calming and strengthening influence of letters in a man who is forced into a rough and tumble fight with men who never heard of Socrates or Cicero. I wrote it under circumstances which *you* well remember. It will give you a fair text for a little sermon, perhaps, on the value of liberal education."[72]

In Chamberlain's eyes the schism in the party was not only political, but cultural as well. His opponents had no conception of their role in the great history of western civilization as he had. They did not value its cultural traditions, its idealism and values, its philosophy, as he did. Surely this was cause enough for "union of the forces of intelligence and honesty against the common enemy."[73]

This crusade was often characterized as a war between the forces of honesty and those of corruption. Chamberlain's sincerity is not in doubt—just his perception, his perspective. The fact that there was corruption at all levels in South Carolina's Reconstruction government cannot be gainsaid. No doubt Chamberlain was appalled at the apparently tolerant attitude of many black leaders toward this corruption. For example, during the 1872 Ku Klux Klan hearings in Columbia, State Repre-

71. *News and Courier,* December 23, 1875.
72. Daniel H. Chamberlain to Francis W. Dawson, April 20, 1876, Dawson Papers.
73. Chamberlain, "Reconstruction in South Carolina," p. 479.

sentative Henry Johnson, a black ex-slave from Fairfield County, was asked by a Democratic congressman whether Republicans would not buy votes as well as Democrats (who had been accused earlier). "I believe both will do it," replied Johnson thoughtfully, "but they do it for different ends. I believe the democrats would buy votes to get into power in order to take away our rights. Republicans, I believe, might buy them if they feared they were getting beat without it, but after the Republicans get in we know that they would not take away our rights, for it is from the republicans that we have got all our rights." [74]

Johnson's attitude was a pragmatic one; unlike Chamberlain, he did not see the issue in black and white, but in subtle grays. For Johnson the corruption issue should never be allowed to overshadow the key issue—the survival of black freedom, which could only be ensured by a Republican government. There is evidence that some of his black colleagues held similar views.[75] The black legislators had been initiated into the political process in an era when corruption was an ingrained feature of political life. The charge of corruption had itself become a political ploy to discredit one's enemies, serving a purpose somewhat like the charge of communism in more recent times. Besides, there was well-publicized corruption in the national government and prominent Democrats were likewise tainted by frauds. Martin W. Gary and M. C. Butler, two of the key leaders of the redemption of '76 and members of the Hampton government in the years after Reconstruction, were both implicated in well-documented frauds during this period.[76] That the Democrats' peccadilloes did not gain as much publicity as those of the Republicans can be traced in some measure to the Democrats' control of the press—at least, of that part with the greatest circulation. One Democratic journal that did report the corrupt activities of Gary and Butler was privately censured by its colleagues, and a reporter for the *Daily Courier* was fired for attempting to expose those frauds.[77] So to many Republicans there must have been little to choose between the Democrats and their own party on the corruption issue. The key issue remained one not of corruption, but of power.

74. *Testimony Taken by the Joint Select Committee to Inquire into the Condition of Affairs in the Late Insurrectionary States,* Volume I: South Carolina (Washington: Government Printing Office, 1872), p. 326.

75. For example, some legislators apparently took bribes *after* they had voted for a bill they would have voted for anyway. See discussion of corruption in the sixth chapter.

76. "Copies of Extract of Testimony and Exhibit 1, Lysander D. Chilos *et al.* vs. W. E. Everett *et al.,* Supreme Court, City and County of New York," September 23, 1875, Dawson Papers.

77. See letter of correspondent William G. Tyson to editor, *Daily Courier,* November 25, 1871.

Evidently many Democrats saw the issues in terms similar to Johnson's. As one observer put it, the native Democrats were satisfied with Chamberlain's reform efforts, but they wanted to have "government under their own auspices" to obtain influence in Washington and latitude at home. "They interpreted the election of a Democratic majority in the national House of Representatives and the white victories in Mississippi and other southern states as the resurgence of southern Democrats as a national power." [78] One faction of the Democrats saw the internal conflicts of the Republicans as "the entering wedge" which they hoped would split the party in two. The "good" side would then see its "interest" and duty to "act in conjunction with the great Democratic party of the country, which is now riding into favor with a velocity unequaled by the triumphs of any political party that ever existed in this country." [79] Democrats had won five governorships in the North in 1874, and now only three southern states remained in Republican hands in 1876. An influential sector of the Democratic leadership rejected Dawson's scheme to cooperate with conservative Republicans and determined to go into the fall campaign on a straight-out Democratic ticket. The only fusionism they approved was having Republicans vote for Democrats.

An important element in their strategy was the dissension among the Republicans. One of the straight-out leaders, A. P. Aldrich, was reported to have declared before a delighted Democratic audience that he was determined "to keep Chamberlain and some of the carpetbaggers, fighting, till they eat each other up all but the tails, and that he would keep the tails jumping at each other, until Southern raised gentlemen slide in to office and take the reins of government." [80]

It seemed during the spring and summer prior to the election that the Republicans would indeed "eat each other up." During the closing days of the 1875-76 session several Negro leaders, apparently fearful of what Chamberlain might do during the election campaign, urged that the General Assembly simply take a recess rather than adjourn *sine die.* The Assembly could be reconvened by the president of the Senate or the Speaker of the House after a recess, whereas the governor would have to call them into special session if they adjourned. William James Whipper in the House and Senators William Beverly Nash, Henry J. Maxwell, and William H. Jones were major proponents of the recess gambit. The black senator from York, better known as "Red-Hot" Jones, was livid in his anger at Republican opponents of the recess maneuver:

78. [Townsend,] "Political Condition of South Carolina," p. 182.
79. *Columbia Register,* August 8, 1875.
80. Samuel Jones to Daniel H. Chamberlain, August 13, 1876, Chamberlain Papers.

These cowards don't know what this resolution [the resolution to adjourn rather than recess] means; it means the selling out of the Republican party in this State; it means the removal of every Republican County officer in the State, and unless you bow in humble submission to the would be Dictator of the State, every man's political head will be chopped short off. You know this, and yet you are too cowardly and weak-kneed to take a recess and be ready and able to meet again at any moment when danger is at hand.[81]

The recess tactic was eventually defeated, no doubt because of the strong opposition of Speaker Elliott, who split with his friend Whipper on this issue.[82] For his part, Whipper may have seen such a tactic as offering him a counterweight against the governor in his fight to obtain his commission. When it was rumored that Whipper would attempt to take his seat as judge of the first circuit by force, Chamberlain issued a proclamation declaring that force would be resisted with force.[83]

The intraparty strife continued on the brink of open violence throughout that spring. When Republicans met in Columbia to elect delegates to the national convention, the meeting came close to ending in bloodshed. It seems that there was a great deal of confusion over the credentials of delegates and points of order over the chairman's ruling.

Several delegates were on the floor calling for the roll and raising points of order. Judge Mackey sprang to his feet and said to the president: "The question is not whether you will recognize us, but whether the convention will recognize you." Mackey, amidst intense excitement added: "We meet here today, face to face and eye to eye the banded robbers that have plundered the State." Swails, rushing up to Mackey, said: "Who do you mean?" Mackey replied: "You are one of them, and to-day we send all of you to everlasting defeat. You have come here to trample on the honest people of South Carolina. We can send you all to jail, and we mean to do it." Elliott now came face to face with Mackey, the two being separated only by the desk, and asked Mackey who he meant. Mackey, his strident voice raising above the din, said: "You are one of them; you are their head and front." Elliott said: "You're a liar," and, drawing a pistol moved around the desk to get at Mackey, who with his hand on his weapon, awaited events. Tables were upset in all directions, a chair was brandished over the head of Chamberlain, who sat unmoved. The delegates huddled around Elliott on one side, and Mackey on the other, and the confusion was heightened by the hysterical screams of Mrs. Elliott, who was in the hall. [Senator] Patterson made for the door. [Collector] Worthington, with his hand on his pistol, kept on the

81. *News and Courier,* January 27, 1876.
82. *Ibid.,* January 31, 1876.
83. Daniel H. Chamberlain to C. C. Bowen, August 21, 1876; Chamberlain to Edward J. Cain, August 21, 1876; Cain to Chamberlain, August 28, 1876; E. W. Brady to Chamberlain, n.d. [June, 1876], Chamberlain Papers.

edge of the crowd, which drifted to one corner of the hall. Whittemore, looking very pale, rapped vainly for order.[84]

This amazing scene, which occurred only seven months before the 1876 election, represents the depths to which dissension had brought the Republican party. The Democrats were also divided, though not as seriously and certainly not as violently, so when this scene transpired there was still a possibility that a fusion movement would emerge. Late in the summer W. H. Reedish of Orangeburg wrote Chamberlain that events could still go either way. "I confess there seems to be a dissatisfied element in both parties, but what will be the result cannot at this time be told." [85] But even as Reedish wrote, events had already caught up with the fusion policy as a violent clash forced the issue.

Formed in 1872 primarily out of Edgefield County, Aiken County was located opposite the Georgia border across from Augusta. Although the 1875 census shows that blacks held a comfortable majority of the population of about 5,000, the county had voted for Judge Green, the fusion candidate, in the 1874 election. Edgefield and Aiken counties had a long history of violence in general and racial violence in particular, especially during 1875-76.[86] There was a black militia company in Aiken which had been organized under Governor Scott in 1870, but it had never been very active. In 1876 the company grew to about eighty members and began regular drills again. On the Fourth of July the commander, one Doc Adams, was drilling his company on a little-used street when two whites, Thomas Butler and Henry Getzen, demanded to pass, insisting that the company was blocking the street. Adams argued that the street, which was about 150 feet wide, was sufficiently broad for their carriage to pass the company. After a heated exchange Adams gave his men orders to open ranks and the whites passed. However, Butler and Getzen made a complaint to the trial justice, Prince Rivers, and a warrant was issued for Adams's arrest. During his trial Adams was further charged with contempt of court, and the trial was continued until the following Saturday, July 8. Meanwhile, former Confederate General M. C. Butler went to Augusta and brought 200 men and a cannon to Hamburg. He demanded that the militia company surrender its arms. The militia barricaded itself within its barracks and refused, and the men were fired on by the whites. During the exchange one of the whites was killed. The attackers then assaulted the building with the cannon they had brought from Augusta, and the blacks inside fled the building.

During the ensuing melee blacks were rounded up, and five were shot down in cold blood.[87]

This outrage settled the issue of the basis on which the campaign of '76 would be waged. Chamberlain, shocked and dismayed, wrote a strongly worded letter to South Carolina Senator T. J. Robertson which was subsequently made public.

> Shame and disgust must fill the breast of every man who respects his race or human nature, as he reads this tale. To me, in my official capacity wherein, as you will testify, I have done my utmost, at no little risk of personal and political detraction from my political friends, to remove abuses and rest a good government and harmony to our people, the occurrence of such an appalling example of human passion and depravity comes as a deep mortification and discouragement. What hope can we have when such a cruel and blood-thirsty spirit avails in our midst for its hour of gratification? Is our civilization so shallow? Is our race so wantonly cruel? [88]

The *News and Courier,* which printed an editorial supporting Chamberlain as late as July 7, split with him on the Hamburg massacre which had occurred the very next day. Dawson rejected the idea that the riot was politically inspired and condemned Chamberlain's request for federal troops: "We have supported Governor Chamberlain's reform measures, and we have frankly expressed our opinions of the Hamburg riot, but we must protest against any move that wears the appearance of taking advantage of a local disturbance to prop up the waning fortunes of South Carolina Republicanism." [89] All summer the *News and Courier* had urged the Democrats to nominate a full ticket—except for the governorship, for which the paper supported Chamberlain. But on August 10, a few days before the Democratic convention, the paper endorsed Wade Hampton for the Democratic nomination.[90]

The Democratic executive committee had decided on this August convention date in a meeting just four days after the Hamburg incident; this decision was itself a defeat for the cooperationists, who had urged a meeting date after the Republican convention so that they could wait and see if the Republicans renominated Chamberlain before deciding on their ticket. But some prominent cooperationists had already abandoned this policy after Hamburg. "I think the unhappy affair at Hamburg will be made such use of in the canvass that no alternative would probably have been left us than to 'take it straight,' " surmised James B. Kershaw,

87. Attorney General Stone to Daniel H. Chamberlain, July 12, 1876, Chamberlain Papers.

88. Daniel H. Chamberlain to T. J. Robertson, July 13, 1876, *ibid.*

89. *News and Courier,* July 18, 1876; quoted in Simkins and Woody, *South Carolina During Reconstruction,* p. 488.

90. *News and Courier,* August 10, 1876.

a former fusionist. "At all events it is a luxury once more to be able to put forward the men we like best." [91] The Democrats nominated a Confederate war hero, General Wade Hampton, for governor on a ticket that included for attorney general James Connor, Dawson's agent in Washington in the '74 negotiations with President Grant. Thus the Democrats were united. They had resolved their "dissatisfactions," put together the best organized and most efficient campaign they had ever mounted, and through intimidation of whites as well as blacks moved purposefully toward overthrow of the Republican regime.

Meanwhile, events had also forced the Republicans into a reconciliation of sorts. Blacks of all political persuasions came together to protest the Hamburg massacre to the American people.[92] But even this extreme crisis could not resolve the deep scar left by internecine struggles over the past two years. Several months before Hamburg it appeared that Chamberlain would be renominated by the party because of strong pressures from the White House on key leaders like Robert Smalls and Senator Patterson.[93] Despite these moves toward reconciliation, Chamberlain still held his erstwhile enemies at arm's length. Thirteen days before Hamburg, when his attention was drawn to reports in the *Baltimore Gazette* and the *New York Herald* that he had been reconciled with Patterson, he told Dawson that this was a serious threat to his fusionist ambitions and dictated a strong denial which he asked the editor to send to the Associated Press.[94]

The nomination of Wade Hampton all but crushed Chamberlain's hopes of running a fusionist campaign. It also reduced any room for maneuvering within his own party's convention that September. But apparently the Negro leaders were also too weak or too divided to block Chamberlain's renomination. Although he was renominated for governor, Robert B. Elliott, the man Chamberlain regarded as one of his primary opponents, was nominated for attorney general. The man with whom he had twice clashed over the authority of his office, Richard H. Gleaves, was renominated for lieutenant governor. Apparently Chamberlain not only found the ticket distasteful; also he feared that if reelected, his power during the second term would be seriously curtailed. Years later he

91. *Ibid.,* July 28, 1876, quoted in Simkins and Woody, *South Carolina During Reconstruction,* p. 489.

92. *An Address to the People of the United States Adopted at a Conference of Colored Citizens Held at Columbia, S.C., July 20 and 21, 1876* (Columbia: Republican Printing Company, 1876).

93. *Beaufort Tribune,* January 19, September 13, 1876; William Harrison Shirley, Jr., "A Black Republican Congressman During the Democratic Resurgence in South Carolina: Robert Smalls, 1876-82" (M.A. thesis, University of South Carolina, 1970), p. 14.

94. Daniel H. Chamberlain to Francis W. Dawson, June 25, 1876, Chamberlain Papers.

described the situation as one in which the "reformers" were thrown back into alliance with the "rascals"; as a consequence, he believed a Republican victory would have given "redoubled power to leaders who had been temporarily discredited."[95] Evidently he did not feel that his renomination was an indication of his power; rather, under the circumstances he saw it as an expedient act of acquiescence by the party chieftains he had opposed.

One can only wonder how much Chamberlain really wanted to win this election, given the fear that reelection might have actually weakened his control of his party. Certainly he had based his entire administration and his political future on the strategy of creating a personal constituency among the Democrats and uniting these with the conservative Republicans to carry the gubernatorial race and elect a legislature which would be friendly, if not necessarily Republican. This strategy exploded at Hamburg, and he was left with a party that was splintered and despondent. The words that appear most frequently in his correspondence from Republicans in 1876 were "discouraged," "apathy," "disappointed," and "dissatisfaction." Colleton was a critical swing county which Chamberlain had carried by a margin of less than 5 percent in the 1874 election. Republican party leaders there were "most disappointed and dissatisfied with your keeping a man in office who is opposed to you and your party in this country. They say and very properly too that it is no encouragement for them to work for you and carry this county for you—while you keep such men in office," one leader lamented.[96] "We hope by judicious management to carry our county this year, but in order to do so, it will be necessary to unite all our forces. There was last year, and it still exists, a good deal of dissatisfaction in the upper part of the county. We had proposed among ourselves to have Mr. Littlejohn appointed a Trial Justice believing ourselves and having assurances of others immediately concerned, that this would heal all breach in our ranks in that section and we then present a solid front to our opponents," urged Representative Junius S. Mobley of Union County. If Littlejohn were not appointed, he warned, "it will make wider and more uncontrollable the breach of our party." Littlejohn was not appointed. Union County went to Hampton in 1876.[97]

From Laurens, one of the disputed counties in the 1876 election, came another warning. "I think the whites are made no better by your changes in the Jury Commissioner. They say they cared but little for the Jury

95. Chamberlain, "Reconstruction in South Carolina," p. 482.

96. James W. Grace to Daniel H. Chamberlain, June 22, 1876, Chamberlain Papers.

97. Junius S. Mobley to Daniel H. Chamberlain, March 30, April 20, 1876, ibid.

before and less now. Laurens on the whole seems to be getting no better. I am at last discouraged and thinking about resigning." [98] Republicans had carried Laurens with 61 percent of the vote in 1874. They lost it to Hampton by a margin of over 1,000 votes in a disputed count in 1876.[99]

Not only did the generally low Republican morale affect the campaign effort itself, but it was a critical factor during the months after the election when Chamberlain and Hampton were attempting to strengthen their claims to the governorship by demonstrating a de facto control of the state. Hampton's victory in that struggle was probably a key factor in Hayes's decision to withdraw federal troops. Hampton's Red Shirts forced Republican local officials to resign their offices, and other officials whom Chamberlain himself had appointed acted with the Democrats.[100]

Another element of Chamberlain's policy which returned to haunt the Republicans at a critical time was the issuing of state arms to the white rifle clubs. After being harassed by the "red shirts" during his speaking tour in August, the governor had abandoned any attempts to canvass the state until just a few weeks before the election, after federal troops had been deployed.[101] In a similar situation, when campaign violence threatened in 1870, Governor Scott had mobilized the black state militia and enforced order long enough to carry the election. But under Chamberlain's policies the militia, a constant irritant to the whites, had been allowed to retrogress and in some instances had been disarmed by the governor. In most cases they were very poorly armed and possessed almost no ammunition.[102] Meanwhile, Chamberlain had already been warned in the annual report of the Negro adjutant general, Henry W. Purvis, that state arms were in the hands of white rifle companies that were not a part of the state militia, and that this constituted a danger to the government.[103] Evidently most of these arms had been issued to these rifle companies during the Moses administration. In answering Democratic requests for more arms, the governor replied that personally he would "be pleased to grant" their requests, but that he had no authority to

98. J. W. Rice to Daniel H. Chamberlain, January 3, 1876, ibid.

99. Simkins and Woody, South Carolina During Reconstruction, p. 515.

100. James M. Young to Daniel H. Chamberlain, December 9, 1876; Anson Merrick to Chamberlain, December 16, 1876; William F. Myers to Chamberlain, January, 1877, Chamberlain Papers.

101. Simkins and Woody, South Carolina During Reconstruction, p. 502.

102. Thomas E. Miller to Daniel H. Chamberlain, September 17, 1875, Chamberlain Papers.

103. Henry W. Purvis to Daniel H. Chamberlain, October 13, 1874, Military Affairs Reports, "Green File," South Carolina Archives.

issue more arms. However, he assured them that he would not recall the arms already issued.[104]

On July 22, 1876, the attorney general decided that the governor did indeed have the power to authorize the organization of the rifle clubs.[105] Whether Chamberlain used this authority to organize and arm more white rifle clubs is unclear. He did issue a proclamation on October 7 disbanding these clubs after their purpose in the election campaign became obvious. However, the memoirs of one of these groups, the Carolina Rifle Club of Charleston, indicates that they were armed with guns obtained from the state arsenal, and that they remained armed well after the fall elections. Incredibly enough, their minutes also contain a copy of a letter from Reuben Tomlinson, the Republican election commissioner in Charleston, asking that the club be ready to assemble *armed* on election day to assist in keeping the peace.[106]

Therefore, not only had the state militia been rendered ineffective as a result of the governor's policies, but the arming of the Democratic rifle clubs had been indirectly encouraged, countenanced, and in some cases directly assisted. This proved to be a crucial error, because during the months when he was challenged by Wade Hampton's shadow government, Chamberlain had no means of enforcing his will except through the army. Given his racial views, it is doubtful that he would have mobilized the black militia anyway. Nevertheless, this dependence on federal arms proved fatal in the end. Hampton, on the other hand, made appointments and supported those appointees in the exercise of their powers of office with his "unofficial," allegedly disbanded rifle clubs.

Reports poured into Chamberlain's office during the critical winter months complaining of the usurpation of power by Hampton's trial justices.[107] Other Republican officeholders either refrained from taking sides or flatly refused to obey Chamberlain's orders. When Chamberlain asked that a detachment of the Columbia city police be deployed to protect the State House because of the threat of a Democratic attack, Mayor John Agnew hedged and insisted that the police remain under his command. In a separate letter written that same day, he announced the withdrawal of his official bond from key officers in the Republican

104. Augustine Smythe to Daniel H. Chamberlain, August 20, 23, 1875; Robert Hemphill to Chamberlain, August 25, 1875; Walker R. Jones to Captain J. W. Gray, November 26, 1875; Jones to Hemphill, August 17, 1875; Charles Bruce to Chamberlain, June 1, 1876, Chamberlain Papers.

105. William Stone to Daniel H. Chamberlain, July 22, 1876, Chamberlain Papers.

106. Irwine Walker, "Carolina Rifle Club," Reconstruction Pamphlets, South Caroliniana Library.

107. James Vorn to Daniel H. Chamberlain, January 9, 1877; W. J. Mixson to Chamberlain, January 4, 1877, Chamberlain Papers.

administration, Treasurer Cardozo and Attorney General Dunn.[108]

Chamberlain and Hampton were summoned to Washington at the end of March to discuss the South Carolina situation with the newly inaugurated President Rutherford B. Hayes. This conference was merely a formality, for the national Republican party had already made its peace with southern Conservatives.[109] But in truth the betrayal by Hayes merely confirmed events at the local level. The fact was that during the critical months of January and February Wade Hampton had won the battle for power in South Carolina. He had wisely refrained from any open violence against the state capitol which would inevitably end in an attack on the troops of the U.S. government. Instead, the violence was confined to the hinterland as Democrats slowly asserted control, town by town, in much of the state outside the heavily black lowland areas. These towns were patrolled by armed "Hampton Guards," and in some blacks were forced to submit to a curfew. Those who resisted were beaten, women and children as well as men.[110] Hampton appointed trial justices and tax collectors who held court and collected taxes. Thus, when Chamberlain was asked by President Hayes to submit his views on the results to be expected upon the withdrawal of U.S. troops, he had to admit that after eight years in power the Republican government could not sustain itself without the army: "My next objection to the withdrawal of the United States forces from the Statehouse is that such withdrawal at the present time, pending the decision of the question of validity of one or the other of the two Governments will be a practical decision in favor of my opponent. By this I mean that my opponent is at this moment fully prepared, in point of physical strength, to overthrow the Government which I represent." "Why is this?" the Governor asked rhetorically. "The cause is honorable to the political party which I represent. They are law-abiding; they are patient under the infliction of wrong; they are slow to resort to violence, even in defence of their rights; they have trusted that a decent regard for law, a decent respect for the rights conferred by the Government of the United States, would restrain their opponents from the violence which has now overtaken them." [111]

What he meant was that these constituents were just ordinary, long-suffering niggers and could not possibly be expected to resist the aroused

108. John Agnew to Daniel H. Chamberlain, December 6, 1876, *ibid.*

109. See C. Vann Woodward, *Reunion and Reaction: The Compromise of 1877 and the End of Reconstruction* (Boston: Little, Brown, 1951).

110. J. Townsend Rafra to Daniel H. Chamberlain, April, 1877, Box 17, Chamberlain Papers.

111. Daniel H. Chamberlain to U. S. Grant, March 31, 1877, quoted in Allen, *Chamberlain's Administration*, p. 476.

anger of "the civilization of the Puritan and the Cavalier, of the Round-head and the Huguenot." Three months later in a letter to William Lloyd Garrison he said as much. He could now state for the record that his "defeat was inevitable under the circumstances of time and place which surrounded me. I mean here exactly that the uneducated negro was too weak, no matter what his numbers, to cope with the whites." [112] This seems, at the very least, to be a most ungracious assessment of a people who had quite literally waded through blood to deliver a record vote for him, a people who by the thousands had lost jobs and homes as a result of their steadfast and unflinching political loyalty.[113] Surely this was the ultimate perversion of historical fact. After all, it was Chamberlain who had contributed so much to the ultimate dismantling of that political machine which had enabled "the uneducated negro . . . to cope with the whites" during three previous elections.

But in this letter the former governor insisted that he would not change anything he had done as chief executive, and that he could look back on his administration with "pride and satisfaction." His sole regret was his decision to run on the same ticket with his arch-enemy and that chief corrupter, Robert B. Elliott, he confided to Garrison. In fact, he had resolved not to accept the nomination of governor on a ticket with Elliott. He was actually on his way to the convention hall to "throw up the nomination," confident that his resignation would not be accepted and that Elliott would be kicked off the ticket instead. "I had actually risen in my office to go into the hall for this purpose when I was met at the door by a dozen or more of my most devoted colored supporters who came to congratulate me on *the surrender of Elliott in seeking to stand on a ticket with me!* I was disarmed of my purpose and relinquished it." But there were new consolations. His family was now relieved of the burden of his public life, and he could "now lead a life better suited to my tastes and probably to my talents." [114]

Those tastes and talents led Chamberlain into the practice of corporate law in New York City. His future contact with South Carolina, after the messy political indictments following the Cochran committee's fraud investigation, involved a brief return as receiver for the bankrupt South Carolina Railroad. In contrast, the roots which his chief antagonists had developed in South Carolina appear deeper, for by and large they stayed

112. Chamberlain to Garrison, June 11, 1877, *ibid.,* p. 504.

113. See [Townsend,] "Political Condition of South Carolina," p. 186; William Meeker *et al.,* "Petition from Middle and Low Castle Township," December 7, 1876, Chamberlain Papers.

114. Chamberlain to Garrison, June 11, 1877, quoted in Allen, *Chamberlain's Administration,* p. 504.

to rebuild the party. Robert B. Elliott remained politically active in South Carolina until 1881, when he moved to New Orleans. William James Whipper settled in Beaufort, where he finally secured a judgeship in that county's probate court.

Perhaps the respectable associations of a Wall Street lawyer *were* more suited to Chamberlain's taste than the leadership of a political organization born out of the aspirations of ex-slaves. He could look back on it all in 1882—from Munich, ironically—and believe that, despite the violence, it had all turned out for the best.

> I believe now that with peace, even if it has been in some sense the peace of the sword at first, prosperity will come to the State. Time is the all-healer. The negro is remitted to work, and the white man to power. These, with honest administration and low taxes, will keep the peace, and time will heal the wounds and blot out even the scars of old strifes. The great resources of the State, her great permanent staples, the indomitable spirit of our people—which you even, native as you are, do not know so well as I do—will bring a noble future to South Carolina.[115]

So five years after he had ridden down Gervais Street at high noon, leaving the power of his office and the hopes of his constituents behind, Chamberlain could take a perverse joy in seeing his program and his policies not only vindicated, but implemented by a Democratic administration. Low taxes, honest government, the white man in power, and the negro at work—were not these after all the great goals of his administration? Was not this its noble epitaph?

115. Daniel H. Chamberlain to B. O. Duncan, August 25, 1882, *ibid.*, p. 506.

Chapter Nine

A Rope of Sand: An Epilogue of the Reconstruction Era

As the bell at Columbia City Hall tolled twelve, signaling the removal of federal troops from the State House and the end of federal support for Republican government in South Carolina, the correspondent for the *News and Courier* declared that Republican rule was dead, never to be reborn.[1] A less biased observer would probably have found more drama than sense in that declaration. It was true that the Democrats now controlled the governorship and the executive offices, but their control over much of the governmental machinery was clearly marginal where it existed at all. The Republicans still had fifty-five uncontested seats in the House against sixty-nine for the Democrats. In the Senate they held eighteen of the thirty-three seats and, in addition, a Republican presiding officer. The death of Chief Justice Moses left two Republicans (although one had favored Hampton's suit in the election controversy) on the state supreme court, one of whom was black. At the circuit court level, six of the eight judges were Republicans. Two of the congressmen were black, and only one of the Republican U.S. senators would face reelection before 1878.

Thus, our neutral observer would probably have dismissed the *News and Courier* correspondent as a poor prophet. Based on the evidence, he would have drawn a different scenario for South Carolina politics for the coming two years. Surely the Republicans, seeing the fruits of their dissension, would be forced into greater unity by this setback. By emphasizing strict party discipline and voting as a bloc in the legislature, they should be able to block or compromise the more damaging parts of the Democratic program. Through hard-nosed and astute politicking they should be able to deal with some of the splinter factions already developing among the Democrats.[2] With strong leadership they should hold together

1. *News and Courier,* April 11, 1877.
2. See divisions that began to develop between Hampton and the Gary-Tillman wings of the Democratic party almost immediately after the election. William J. Cooper, Jr., *The Conservative Regime: South Carolina, 1877-90* (Baltimore: Johns Hopkins Press, 1968), pp. 45-83.

until the 1878 elections and wage a more unified campaign.

On April 10, 1877, such a scenario would have seemed tenable to any unprejudiced observer. But it did not happen. It was the *Courier*'s reporter, not our hypothetical observer, who predicted subsequent events correctly. Two years later an editor of the *News and Courier* would look back on the Republican debacle of 1877 with amazement. "Never was political victory more sudden or more complete!" he declared.[3] Speaking before a Republican convention at the end of the decade, Robert B. Elliott would confirm the editor's assessment of the situation in 1877. The Republican party had crumbled, he said, "like a rope of sand." [4]

It is clear that the ruthless and vigorous action of Democrats contributed significantly to the demise of Republicanism during the 1880's; but Republicans contributed to their own destruction, just as they had in the election of 1876. Hampton convened a special session of the legislature in April, 1877, and the Democrats immediately resolved that Republicans who had met with the Mackey House must take an oath purging themselves of contempt before being seated. Being high-principled but politically naive, two Republicans resigned in protest and one refused to take the oath. Two others were expelled outright. Moving like a juggernaut, the Democratic majority arbitrarily vacated seventeen Charleston County seats and scheduled new elections for June. The Republicans failed to contest that election, and the seats were filled by Democrats, their ticket including three Negro Democrats for window-dressing. The Republican bloc of fifty-five was now slashed to thirty-seven (two of them white), or less than three in ten.[5]

Meanwhile, this pattern of Democratic power plays and Republican hara-kiri was repeated in other areas of government. In the Senate the special session began with eleven Democrats outnumbered by eighteen Republicans and presided over by a black Republican, Richard H. Gleaves. But Gleaves resigned upon Hampton's installation as governor, thereby allowing Hampton's lieutenant governor, W. D. Simpson, to take the chair. As the new presiding officer, Simpson wasted no time in swearing in the four contested Democratic senators-elect, bringing their total to fifteen seats.[6]

During the spring special session two Republican legislative measures were repealed: the act providing pensions for the widows and families of victims of political violence, and the act providing scholarships to enable

3. *News and Courier,* August 7, 1868.
4. *Ibid.,* September 3, 1880.
5. *Ibid.,* November 28, 1877; George Brown Tindall, *South Carolina Negroes, 1877-1900* (Columbia: University of South Carolina Press, 1952), pp. 16-17. For failure of Republicans to contest the Charleston election, see *News and Courier,* June 27, 1877.
6. Tindall, *South Carolina Negroes,* p. 17.

poor students to attend the state university. But most important was the resolution to establish a joint committee to investigate the alleged corruption of the previous administrations. At Governor Hampton's urging, the chairmanship of the committee was given to a white Republican from the up-country, Senator John Cochran of Anderson. Little more than a score of people were charged as a result of these vigorous and extensive investigations, and only three were ever convicted in court, Francis L. Cardozo, Robert Smalls, and L. Cass Carpenter. All were later pardoned as a result of a reciprocal agreement with the federal government to drop charges against Democrats indicted for the Hamburg massacre and other violence during the election of 1876.[7] Nevertheless, some Republican legislators were apparently intimidated by the investigations and threat of prosecution, and they submitted their resignations. When three more Republican senators resigned, the Democrats acquired an effective majority of one, since the Democratic presiding officer would vote to break ties. When the regular session convened the following November, eight more senators resigned, leaving only seven stalwart Republicans behind and Democrats in full control of both houses.[8]

Of course, it is impossible to determine now from these ex parte charges whether the resignations of Gantt and other Republican legislators were the result of their guilt or their fear that, given the determination of the Democrats to seize power by any means necessary, their conviction was certain irrespective of innocence or guilt.[9] This certainly seems to have been the case with Jonathan J. Wright's resignation from the state supreme court. A special committee had been appointed to investigate Wright, who, after Chief Justice Moses's death, was one of the two remaining members of the court. After taking secret testimony, the investigating committee resolved to impeach Wright for drunkenness. The charges had all the marks of being fabricated, and even the governor expressed little confidence in their validity.[10] In any event, Wright resigned as a result of this or other pressures, and the legislature elected Democrats to fill the two vacancies. They retained Amiel Willard, electing him chief justice at Hampton's urging in order to demonstrate their moderation

7. Evidently *News and Courier* editor Francis Dawson was an important intermediary in arranging this deal. See telegram, E. W. M. Mackey to Francis W. Dawson, April 21, 1879; telegram, Hugh Thompson to Francis W. Dawson, April 23, 1879; copy of agreement to nol pros. state and federal cases, Le Roy F. Youmans to L. C. Northrup, April 22, 1879, Francis W. Dawson Papers, Perkins Library, Duke University, Durham, N.C.

8. *News and Courier,* November 28, 1877; cf. Cooper, *Conservative Regime,* p. 25.

9. See Joel Williamson, *After Slavery: The Negro in South Carolina During Reconstruction, 1861-77* (Chapel Hill: University of North Carolina Press, 1965), pp. 414-16.

10. Tindall, *South Carolina Negroes,* pp. 17-18.

to the nation and as repayment for Willard's support of Hampton during the election crisis.[11]

Temporarily ignoring those constitutional concerns they had expressed about the Whipper election during the previous year, the legislature cleared the eight circuit court benches of Republican judges except for Thomas J. Mackey and A. J. Shaw, who had defected to Hampton during or immediately after the election. Consequently, all the major institutions of state government—legislative, executive, and judicial—were now under undisputed Democratic control.

Ironically, the powerful system of gubernatorial patronage which the Republicans bequeathed them was now utilized to solidify Democratic control at the local level. County auditors, treasurers, assessors, trial justices, jury commissioners, and under special circumstances even elective officers like the county commissioners served at the governor's pleasure. Leaving the rough stuff to Martin W. Gary and his Red Shirts, Hampton had insisted throughout his campaign that the civil and political rights of blacks would not be violated under his administration. He reaffirmed his intention to pursue a liberal policy with respect to the race question upon becoming governor. He appointed prominent blacks, including Richard H. Gleaves and Martin R. Delany, as trial justices. According to a recent survey, Hampton appointed a total of eighty-six blacks to office during his two years as governor. Many Republicans were pleasantly surprised by Hampton's policies and publicly praised him for them. Former Governor Robert K. Scott, for example, declared that Hampton had appointed more blacks during his first term than he himself had in 1868-70.[12] Of course, Scott neglected to point out that his performance was indeed a poor benchmark and had led directly to the open revolt of the black leadership and a demand for more appointments.

It is clear, too, that Hampton's appointments did not conflict with the Democratic party's fundamental tenet that in South Carolina the white minority would always rule the black majority. The black appointments were confined to the minor local offices and did not include any key county positions, like auditor or treasurer. Blacks were also excluded from the critical election machinery, since only one black was appointed to a county board of elections.[13] Wade Hampton seemed more interested in creating the *image* of liberality than its substance. In a Greenville speech, Hampton spelled out the principles of his race policy. In essence, he described a policy based on the illusion of color-blindness. He promised blacks a fair *procedure* in the selection of officers, not actual *representation*

11. See Cooper, *Conservative Regime,* pp. 50-53.

12. Tindall, *South Carolina Negroes,* p. 22.

13. *Ibid.,* pp. 22-23.

of their constituents in government operations. And he left no doubt that the criteria for selection were qualities in which any white man "who deserved to be called a white man" should be superior to a black competitor.

> We propose to protect you and give you all your rights; but while we do this you cannot expect that we should discriminate in your favor, and say because you *are* a colored man, you have a right to rule the State. We say to you that we intend to take the best men we can find to represent the State, and you must qualify yourselves to do so before you can expect to be chosen. Proper qualification is necessary in all cases, and the white man who is afraid to enter the race upon such terms, does not deserve to be called a white man.[14]

Hampton's policy was shaped not out of political expediency alone, but derived in part from his own self-regard, the ethos of noblesse oblige. In his own mind, after all, he was the black man's patriarch and could represent and protect black interests much better than they could themselves. This attitude is fairly represented by the comments in a *News and Courier* editorial on the selection of a Democratic ticket for the Charleston County special election of 1877. The convention had painstakingly allocated the seventeen legislative seats among various professional and ethnic groups in an elaborate display of fairness. The Germans, Irish, lawyers, doctors, and workingmen were all allocated certain numbers of seats. In some respects the distributions had deviated from what the *News and Courier* had previously advocated, and among these deviations it noted that the number of black representatives (three) was smaller than what the editors thought appropriate. But the editor dismissed this discrepancy as being of little practical effect after all. "Upon the fair number of colored candidates we do not lay so much stress because every one of the seventeen members from Charleston will represent the colored people." [15] Thus, while great care should be taken to represent lawyers, doctors, and Germans, anyone could be counted on to represent blacks.

Democrats took steps to make certain that they would have the exclusive privilege of representing South Carolina's black citizens. The election of 1878 was the first test of the permanence of their overthrow of Republican rule; the tactics of 1876 were invoked again, with violence, fraud, and intimidating parades of armed Red Shirts widely used to insure Hampton's reelection.[16] In control of the government, however, the Democrats could

14. *Enquirer* (Yorkville), September 26, 1878, quoted in Tindall, *South Carolina Negroes,* p. 21.

15. *News and Courier,* June 21, 1877.

16. Tindall, *South Carolina Negroes,* p. 68; James Welch Patton, "The Republican Party in South Carolina, 1876-1895," in *Essays in Southern History,* ed. Fletcher Melvin Green (Chapel Hill: University of North Carolina Press, 1949), p. 101. For descriptions of some methods

add legal means to the extralegal ones of 1876. The legislature passed
an act in March, 1878, which abolished many voting precincts in heavily
Republican areas. This measure forced some black voters to walk twenty
miles and more to get to the polls; others had to cross rivers where the
ferries were inexplicably out of service on election day. New counties
and congressional districts were gerrymandered to neutralize the effects
of heavy black majorities in the low country.[17]

The expected renewal of the titanic struggle of 1876 did not materialize,
however. The apathy, fear, and defeatism engendered by that campaign
and President Hayes's betrayal were still pervasive in the Republican
party. Key leaders urged the delegates to the state convention in the
fall of 1878 not to contest the reelection of Hampton at the state level,
but to concentrate on the legislative and local elections instead. Most
prominent among supporters of the policy of not entering a statewide
ticket were white leaders C. C. Bowen, William N. Taft, and Senator
John Cochran. They argued that it would be a disaster to nominate
a gubernatorial candidate and other state officers, for this would inspire
the Democrats to mount an aggressive campaign. If the party endorsed
Hampton, however, and confined its activities to local contests, the Democrats might be lulled into a false sense of security and not work as hard.
Some prominent black leaders opposed this strategy and urged a full
slate of candidates. Whitefield McKinlay, Stephen A. Swails, and William
James Whipper (who was not seated at the convention) urged such a
"straight-out" policy, and it appeared that the general pre-convention
sentiment of the delegates favored it also. But other key black leaders
opposed the straight-out policy: Robert Smalls had spoken against a full
slate before the convention, although he vacillated on the issue later, and
party chairman Robert B. Elliott also opposed the straight-outs.[18]

In a move aimed either to embarrass the proponents of a Hampton
endorsement, or possibly to extract some concessions for this support,
Daniel A. Straker, a black delegate from Orangeburg, introduced a resolution to appoint a committee to secure Hampton's pledge to appoint

---

of intimidation, see U.S. Congress, House, *Cases of Contested Elections in the House of Representatives, Forty-seventh Congress, From 1880 to 1882, Inclusive* (Washington: Government Printing
Office, 1883), p. 434.

17. *Acts and Resolutions of the General Assembly of the State of South Carolina, Passed at the
Regular Session of 1878* (Columbia: Calvo & Patterson, 1879), p. 740; Patton, "The Republican
Party in South Carolina," pp. 102-3. Other legal restraints introduced in succeeding years
included a law which increased the bonds required of certain county officers in December,
1880, and, in February, 1882, a joint resolution to amend Article 8, section 8 of the state
constitution so as to add to murder and treason the crimes of "burglary, larceny, perjury,
forgery, or any other infamous crimes," among offenses warranting loss of suffrage rights.
Acts and Resolutions, 1880, p. 322; 1881-82, p. 1156.

18. *News and Courier,* August 8, 1878.

one Republican to the board of elections in each county to ensure a fair count. E. W. M. Mackey, Bowen, and Cochran opposed this motion, offering instead a resolution endorsing Hampton, condemning some of the actions of the previous Republican administrations, and pledging the party to nominate only men of recognized intelligence for office. This resolution was defeated the following day by a narrow vote, but one introduced by Whitefield McKinlay pledging the party to nominate a full slate of officers on a straight Republican ticket was defeated by a wide margin, 35-85. So the leadership had clearly turned the delegates against a straight-out policy. They simply declared in their platform, therefore, that the nomination of a full slate was "inexpedient" at that time because the conditions in the state after two years of Democratic rule made it impossible for Republican voters to organize and vote "without incurring great personal danger." [19] The delegates were content to leave the campaign in the hands of the various county organizations, issue their platform, and go home.

But two years out of power had left the county organizations in disarray and with uncertain leadership. Some prominent black leaders publicly endorsed Hampton. Dr. Benjamin A. Bosemon's endorsement was widely publicized from a statement made to a correspondent from the Springfield *Republican.* "You may quote me as expressing absolute confidence in Governor Hampton and entire satisfaction with his course," he declared. "We have no complaint whatever to make. He has kept all his pledges." [20] Jonathan J. Wright also supported Hampton for reelection in 1878.

A clear undercurrent of defeatism was evident in the statements of black leaders who had opposed the endorsement of Hampton. For instance, Fred Nix, a former state representative from Barnwell County, urged blacks to support only those local Democratic candidates that they felt they could trust. He urged the Democrats to give the Republicans a fair count and to eschew violence. Then, as if resigned to the inevitable outcome, he urged his constituents to emigrate to less hostile areas. "And then *when* we are turned out we will go to Beaufort or Liberia. We can get as much land as we want in either place, and who wants any better home than Liberia." [21]

The justification offered for not running a state ticket was that this would enable the local organizations to concentrate on electing legislators and county officers. But Republican tickets were fielded in only eighteen of the thirty-three counties in 1878, and most of these were incomplete or endorsed Democrats for key offices. Five white Democrats were endorsed

19. *Ibid.,* August 9, 1878.
20. Quoted in Tindall, *South Carolina Negroes,* p. 25.
21. *News and Courier,* August 7, 1878. Emphasis added.

on the tickets offered by Republicans in Charleston and Marion, three in Union, and two in Laurens.[22] Many Republican stalwarts became increasingly hostile to the party. Abraham P. Holmes, Caesar P. Chisolm, and William A. Driffle, all former Republican state representatives, addressed a political rally of blacks in Colleton County and advised them to vote for the Democrats. Driffle, one of the early organizers among Republicans in Colleton, declared that the party had died in 1876 and he was there to help bury it. Another speaker thought it highly unlikely that the Republicans could succeed without federal troops in 1878 where they had failed with them in 1876.[23]

Indeed, it did appear unlikely that, given the well-organized opposition and their own tactics of virtual nonresistance, the Republicans would fare well in the general elections. They did not. Only nine blacks were elected to the House, and six of these were Democrats. The three black Republicans came from Beaufort, and they were the only Republicans, black or white, in the House. Republican representation in the Senate was cut to five, three of them black.[24]

The election of 1878 nearly completed the destruction of the Republican party that had begun in 1876. Between 1878 and 1895 forty-four blacks sat in the legislature, but never more than three in the Senate or twelve in the House at any one time. Until 1890 some of those in the House would be black Democrats; consequently, the greatest representation of black Republicans was nine in 1882, but in most years it was only four. Only in the heavily black counties of Beaufort and Georgetown did Republicans maintain any consistent organization capable of electing candidates, although Berkeley County Republicans elected a senator and five representatives immediately after the county was created in 1882 and three representatives in 1890.[25]

Any remaining hopes of revitalizing the party in the presidential election year of 1880 were quickly squelched at the state convention. Again party leaders discouraged attempts to mount a full-scale campaign. Actually, the initial sentiment of the delegates was known to be overwhelmingly in favor of nominating a state ticket. Veteran Negro leaders like Henry

22. *Ibid.*
23. *Ibid.*, October 28, 1878.
24. The Negro Republican state representatives were Thomas E. Miller, Benjamin Simons, and Hastings Gantt, all from Beaufort. The Negro senators were Bruce H. Williams of Georgetown, Israel Bird of Fairfield, and Samuel L. Duncan of Orangeburg. *Ibid.*, November 7, 1878.
25. The state senator was Robert Simmons (1882-86). In 1882 the state representatives were W. G. Pinckney, James Singleton, Andrew Singleton, W. W. Beckett, and Cain Ravenel. In 1890 the representatives were Andrew Singleton, Mark P. Richardson, and Thomas H. Wallace.

L. Shrewsbury, Thomas E. Miller, and John Freeman spoke in favor of this policy. They admitted that the state ticket might not be electable but argued that it would at least maintain the Republican party organization which was now in danger of falling apart completely. Most white leaders, especially the federal officeholders like internal revenue collector E. M. Brayton, opposed nominations at the state level.[26]

The matter was referred to a special committee dominated by advocates of a state ticket. The committee not only reported in favor of making nominations, but presented a slate of officers as well. John Winsmith, an elderly native white Republican from Spartanburg, was nominated for governor, Thomas E. Miller of Beaufort for lieutenant governor, Henry L. Shrewsbury for secretary of state, and relatively obscure white Republicans for the other five offices. When objections were raised to the rather unimpressive quality of the ticket, the chairman indicated that the committee had done its best but had been unable to get more prominent Republicans to accept nominations.[27]

At this juncture Robert B. Elliott rose to oppose the policy of making any campaign at the state level that year. He spoke for a full hour and his remarks were tremendously effective, although they were basically a rehash of the arguments put forth by others two years before. The Democrats were too strong and would never yield power without a struggle. If the Republicans fielded a state ticket, their opponents would be galvanized into action and would wage a vigorous campaign. This would endanger the chances of the Republican presidential candidate in the state. No, the party must bide its time, wait until it could gain more strength, wait until the Democrats were weakened by dissension within their own ranks. Here Elliott offered a remarkable comparison between the position of the Republicans then and the Democrats during the period between 1868 and 1876, urging his colleagues to adopt the latter's tactics.

> The Convention would remember that the Democratic party have never attempted to wage a pitched battle when they saw no chance of success, but they had bided their time, and by devices of their own and divisions in the Republican ranks they had finally conquered. No one knew better than the gentleman from Charleston [John Freeman] how these divisions had been brought about, as he was a prominent leader of the Green bolt in 1874, which shook the party to centre and finally resulted in its downfall. He knew how these bolts had been organized in South Carolina until the regular party had crumbled like a rope of sand.[28]

No help could be expected from the national party, Elliott informed

26. *News and Courier,* September 3, 1880.
27. *Ibid.*
28. *Ibid.*

the delegates. If they simply waited, the Democrats would eventually disintegrate when the reason for their unity (that is, the Republican opposition) had been removed. To support this prognosis, he pointed to the independent organizations (Greenbackers and People's party) which had already sprouted in Marlboro and other counties as a result of agrarian discontent.[29]

Elliott's eloquence turned the tide once again, as strong supporters of a state ticket began to vacillate on the issue and finally decided to postpone any decision. They left the matter in the hands of the executive committee, with instructions to issue the ticket if they found it expedient to do so at some later date.[30] Elliott was chairman of the executive committee. No ticket was ever issued.

Republicans gained one seat in the House in 1880 for a new total of four and lost one seat in the Senate for a new total of two. The Democrats passed additional measures to rid themselves of the threat of a political resurgence of the black majority before the next election in 1882. One law made registration a prerequisite for voting and required voters to register in May and June in order to vote in November. The registration machinery and administration of the law were clearly designed to discriminate against blacks—especially sharecroppers, whose migratory habits were notorious. A person not registering during the specified period could be perpetually disfranchised. The law gave each county supervisor full discretion to determine who was entitled to register. A voter who was denied a certificate of registration could appeal the action, but his appeal had to be filed in writing within five days of the action and the proceedings had to commence in court within ten days after that; otherwise, no appeals were possible. Under the law various other subterfuges were possible in which the registrar gave no notice of where and when prospective voters could register, or issued defective certificates which would cause the registrant to be turned away from the polls on election day with no effective remedy for his disfranchisement.[31]

A complement to the new registration law was the so-called Eight Box Law. This measure amounted to an indirect literacy test, since it provided that separate boxes should be maintained for each office, and that voters must deposit their ballots without assistance in the correct box or they would be void. It also required that the ballots be of plain white paper with no symbols to identify the party. Furthermore, if a box contained more ballots than there were electors on the poll list, then the surplus

29. *Ibid.*
30. *Ibid.*
31. *Acts and Resolutions,* 1882, p. 1110. Patton, "The Republican Party in South Carolina," pp. 105-6.

ballots could be selected arbitrarily and destroyed. Sometimes the polling places for state and federal elections were separated by several miles. Since candidates had to arrange for the printing of their own ballots, they were sometimes disallowed for minute deviations in size, printing, or type of paper.[32]

Thus the policy urged so eloquently by Elliott and others was a miserable failure. It contributed to the complete disintegration of the Republican party and allowed Democrats time to solidify their gains. During this period the leadership cadre itself changed significantly, as veteran leaders retired, moved away, or died. Francis L. Cardozo moved to Washington in 1877 to take a position in the treasury department and later became a prominent educator in the District.[33] He was followed in 1881 by Joseph H. Rainey, who worked briefly as an IRS agent in New York after completing his five terms in Congress in 1879. After several years in the banking and brokerage business in Washington, Rainey returned to his South Carolina home in Georgetown in 1886, but died in the summer of 1887.[34] John H. White, the senator from York County, also went to Washington to take a government post in the summer of 1877, but died exactly a year later in Freedmen's Hospital.[35] Richard H. Cain completed his second term in Congress in 1879 and was elected a bishop in the A.M.E. Church. He turned his attention from politics to church work, after being assigned to organize the Louisiana and Texas districts.[36]

The Republican convention of 1880 in which he argued so eloquently, if erroneously, against the straight-out policy was Elliott's last in South Carolina. A special agent of the Internal Revenue Service at that time, he was transferred in 1881 to New Orleans, where he died three years later.[37] Indeed, 1881 was a critical year for the old leadership. Between that winter and the summer of 1882, four more founding fathers of South Carolina Republicanism died. Benjamin A. Bosemon succumbed to Bright's disease in February, 1881; Landon S. Langley of Beaufort passed away in June, and William H. W. Gray, a veteran of the assault on Fort Wagner, followed close behind in July.[38] Alonzo J. Ransier, who

32. *Acts and Resolutions,* 1882, p. 1126. Patton, "The Republican Party in South Carolina," pp. 106-7.

33. William J. Simmons, *Men of Mark: Eminent, Progressive and Rising,* reprint ed. (New York: Arno Press, 1968), p. 430.

34. *Biographical Directory of the U.S. Congress* (Washington: Government Printing Office, 1971), p. 1581.

35. Emily B. Reynolds and Joan R. Faunt, *Biographical Directory of the Senate of South Carolina, 1776-1964* (Columbia: South Carolina Archives Department, 1964), p. 332.

36. Richard R. Wright, Jr., *The Bishops of the African Methodist Episcopal Church* (Printed by A.M.E. Sunday School Union, 1963), pp. 121-22.

37. *Biographical Directory of the U.S. Congress,* pp. 855-56.

38. Benjamin A. Bosemon, Pension File Certificate No. 482344; Landon Langley, Pension

had served as a collector of internal revenue after his congressional term expired in 1875, had been reduced to common laborer jobs after 1877 and died in August, 1882.[39] Indeed, most of the black leaders, including Northerners, remained in the state and died among the constituents they had served. They were still young men by and large, but some were invalids for much of the ensuing decade and others simply turned their full attention to private business or careers outside politics. New men appeared to take their places in the party. When the Republican ticket for county and state offices was printed in 1878, only three veteran politicians were on the slate for Charleston County, two in Richland, and one in Georgetown. None of the others had previously served in state offices.[40] Of the forty-six state and federal officeholders elected during this period, only ten had served at the state level during Reconstruction.[41]

Some of the new leaders had participated in local politics during the hegemony of the Republican party, but their lack of experience at the state level may have been a crucial weakness in party organization. From whatever causes, party organization faltered in the decade after Hampton's victory. In many counties tickets were not nominated for the biennial elections. In others the tickets were largely incomplete, which in some cases represented the party's decision to endorse or simply not to oppose the Democratic contender. In some cases the county organizations appear to have merely become personal power bases serving the limited local ambitions of the county chairmen. In Georgetown, for example, George Herriott, the mulatto county chairman of the Republican party, was an architect of the fusion movement. In an agreement worked out with Georgetown Democrats in 1880, there was to be no contest of the general election. The Democrats would get the position of sheriff, clerk of court, coroner, two of the three county commissioners, and one representative. Republicans got the state senator, one representative, the probate judge, school commissioner, and one of the three county commissioners. Herriott himself held the post of school commissioner for twenty-two years.[42]

File Certificate No. 222864; W. H. W. Gray, Pension File Certificate No. 500756, Civil War, RG 15, NA.

39. Ransier was hired as night watchman at the Charleston Customs House at $1.50 per day in 1879. D. B. Thomas, Supt., to John Fraser, Acting Supervising Architect, February 25, 1879, Letters Sent, January, 1879—September, 1880, Superintendent, Charleston Customs House, RG 56, NA. Cf. Alonzo J. Ransier to Daniel H. Chamberlain, September 8, 1876, Governor Daniel H. Chamberlain Papers, South Carolina Archives, Columbia.

40. This conclusion was reached by checking the published tickets against lists from previous years. News and Courier, October 28, 1878.

41. These ten were Caesar P. Chisolm, William A. Driffle, Samuel L. Duncan, Hastings Gantt, Thomas E. Miller, William G. Pinckney, Aaron Simmons, Robert Smalls, John W. Westberry, and Bruce H. Williams.

42. Tindall, South Carolina Negroes, p. 63.

Considering the general disfranchisement of blacks in the 1880's, this does not seem to be an entirely unsatisfactory arrangement at first glance. However, when one notes that Georgetown's black population percentage was larger than Beaufort's, and yet Beaufort maintained Republican control of local offices well into the 1890's, the agreement appears less defensible. In a county where the black population was over 80 percent in 1880, the Democrats held all the key offices controlling the judicial and financial affairs of the county. The Republicans got the more prestigious positions of state senator and representative, but these were meaningless and powerless in a Democratic-controlled General Assembly.

A number of attempts at fusion on a statewide basis failed miserably during the 1880's. Even when a creditable black vote could be delivered by Republicans for a Greenbacker or People's party candidate, the white vote was seldom split sufficiently to allow any possibility of victory.[43] In 1890 and 1892 Republicans tried fusion with conservative white Democrats in a futile attempt to defeat Benjamin Tillman, a former supporter of Martin W. Gary and Wade Hampton who now capitalized on the up-country farmers' resentment of the low-country merchants in his successful race for the governorship.[44]

Tillman won a second term in 1892 by a large enough margin to enable him to push through his pet project, the referendum to write a new constitution which would disfranchise blacks forever. The governor was opposed by a large minority representing the conservative faction of the Democratic party.[45] But when the Constitutional Convention assembled in 1895, only five Republicans, all black, had been elected. Thus the chance for the coalition that Elliott had predicted in 1880 had come, but too late. By the time the fissure in the Democratic party—which was fully visible even in 1876—had matured, the Republican party and the black majority that suckled it had ceased to be viable political entities.

The party's demise was not due solely to the mistaken strategy of the party leaders, or to the fraudulent electoral tactics of the Democrats. The dissensions and sometimes violent conflicts among Republicans did not diminish after the sobering defeat of 1876. Conflict and distrust between the black and white elements of the party continued. For example, Junius S. Mobley publicly denounced the selection of whites as delegates to the national Republican convention in 1880 and exhorted his black fellow delegates to throw off the slavery to white federal officeholders who simply sought to use them to further their own careers.[46] E. W.

43. *News and Courier,* November 8, 9, 1882.
44. Tindall, *South Carolina Negroes,* pp. 15-53.
45. *Ibid.,* pp. 73-75.
46. *News and Courier,* April 29, 1880.

M. Mackey declared that the party's revival would depend on attracting white Republican immigrants to the state.[47] Because of the heavy black majority, lily-white Republicanism was never as serious a threat in South Carolina as it was in other southern states, but the tendency in that direction was evident, nevertheless.[48]

There were also continued internal dissensions among Negroes based on color distinctions. George W. Murray, a black, attacked the extremely light color of his opponent, Thomas E. Miller, in winning the party's nomination for Congress in 1892.[49] Nor was there always solidarity among Negroes against white Republicans. When the Democrats gerrymandered the 7th congressional district and conceded it to the blacks in 1882, three Republican candidates entered the competition. Two were Negro (Robert Smalls and Sam Lee) and one was white (E. W. M. Mackey). After 250 ballots Smalls threw his support to Mackey, ensuring in the process that the "black district" would be represented by a white Republican.[50]

The tendency of one Republican faction to bolt and ally with the Democrats was also a feature of Reconstruction politics which persisted into the 1880's. One such bolt involved the normally "safe" Republican county of Beaufort and the traditionally stalwart regular Republican, Robert Smalls. Smalls, who was still involved in contesting the previous election for the 7th district congressional seat held by William B. Elliott, returned to Beaufort in 1888 to run for sheriff. He was unsuccessful at the county convention controlled by his life-long political enemy William James Whipper, as were several of his political allies. A Republican faction made up of Smalls's personal and political intimates bolted the convention and formed a fusion ticket with the Democrats. On this ticket the Democrats were given the offices of probate judge, one county commissioner, one state representative, and the state senatorship; Republicans were nominated for sheriff, clerk of court, school commissioner, two county commissioners, two state representatives, and coroner.

Later Smalls was nominated for collector of customs at Beaufort; an avalanche of petitions and letters protesting his appointment and accusing him of complicity in the earlier defeat of the regular Republican slate

47. Tindall, *South Carolina Negroes,* pp. 46-47.

48. See comments on the lily-white movement *and* the success of Negro Republicans in combating it in S. W. Bennett to Whitefield McKinlay, December 17, 1902; W. T. Andrews to McKinlay, October 11, 1910, Whitefield McKinlay Papers, Carter G. Woodson Collection, Library of Congress.

49. Tindall, *South Carolina Negroes,* p. 49.

50. For fuller discussion, see Okon Edet Uya, *From Slavery to Public Service: Robert Smalls, 1839-1915* (New York: Oxford University Press, 1971), pp. 115-17; William Harrison Shirley, Jr., "A Black Republican Congressman During the Democratic Resurgence in South Carolina: Robert Smalls, 1876-82" (M.A. thesis, University of South Carolina, 1970), pp. 48-51.

were received by the secretary of the treasury. The charges included assertions that he did not campaign for the ticket, that he either did not vote, or voted for the Democratic candidates for president as well as local offices, and that he stuffed ballot boxes and used other fraudulent practices to ensure the election of the Democratic ticket.[51]

These charges were categorically denied by Smalls, and the evidence offered to support them does not appear very plausible or entirely convincing. Smalls did admit that he was opposed to the election of the county Republican ticket, however. He denied working actively for the Democrats, but left no doubt that he was pleased with the election of the fusion ticket.[52] He justified his position by making unsubstantiated ad hominem attacks against Whipper and his other opponents. They were, he said, "the lowest element in Southern politics, the Carpet-baggers and the Rum element." They were "adulterous, drunkards and gamblers, a disgrace to Beaufort and an injury to Republicanism." [53]

While it is improbable that Smalls would publicly support the Democrats when his own contest for a congressional seat was pending, it is equally improbable that he did not secretly manifest more than sentimental support for the movement. His own son-in-law, Samuel J. Bampfield, was the candidate for clerk of court on the fusion ticket and the chief architect of the movement. Smalls admitted that he had supported George A. Reed, the fusion nominee for sheriff. It is clear, too, that his accusers in this controversy were not simply "the Rum element" as he charged; rather, they included a large and diverse group of Republican citizens and politicians within and outside Beaufort County. Numbered among the protesters were former political allies like Thomas E. Miller and Julius I. Washington, along with former and current officeholders like State Representatives Joseph Robinson and F. S. Mitchell, State Senator Thomas J. Reynolds, and the party's county chairman Thomas Wheeler. There were also non-political figures like the pastor of the A.M.E. Church in Beaufort and political reformers like Macon B. Allen, the candidate for secretary of state on the Green-Delany ticket in 1874.

Finally, Smalls, who had once made the famous retort to a Democratic heckler in Congress that his integrity was vouched for by a 4,000-vote majority, was now having that integrity sharply questioned by petitions bearing the names of thousands of his constituents.[54] Indeed, most of

51. "Summary of Protests Against the Appointment of Robert Smalls as Collector of Customs at Beaufort, South Carolina," Collector of Customs Applications, South Carolina, Box 206, RG 56, NA.

52. Robert Smalls to Benjamin Harrison, May 7, 1889, ibid.

53. Robert Smalls to Benjamin Harrison, April 23, 1889; Samuel J. Bampfield and George A. Reed to Benjamin Harrison, March 25, 1889, ibid.

54. See two petitions signed by 589 and 226 citizens, respectively; "Summary of Protests," ibid.

his letters of support came from outside the state, from congressmen he had served with and prominent Northerners who vouched for his long-standing reputation for loyalty. They could not believe that the man whose name was synonymous with South Carolina Republicanism, one of the founders of the party in 1864, could betray that party.[55]

The incident was symbolic of the deterioration of the Republican party. But it was more than symbolic, for it represented the fall of the final stronghold of South Carolina Republicanism. Through Republican dissension, the Democrats won offices that they had been unable to take by other means. Of course, it is debatable whether a greater unity among Republicans, in the 1870's or the 1890's, would have produced a significantly different result in the end—that is, whether blacks would have maintained some permanent political foothold. In hindsight, the prospect of long-term black control of a state government in nineteenth-century America seems implausible. Certainly it seemed so to the black nationalist and emigrationist Martin R. Delany, who warned repeatedly that the black political majority could not survive the onslaught of white immigrants and the temporarily quiescent racial antipathy of northern whites. During the winter of 1874, shortly before his gubernatorial campaign, he lectured J. J. Wright on the facts of political life in white America. "The white race is true [to] itself; and it is useless and doing injustice to both races to conceal the fact, that in giving liberty and equality of rights to the blacks, they had no desire to see them rule over their own race. And the blacks may as well know this at once; that there is no scheme that can be laid, no measure that may be entered into, nor expense so great which they will not incur to change such a relation between blacks and whites in this country." [56]

Indeed, the weighty evidence of subsequent events makes Delany's remarks appear prophetic. Any proposition contrary to the obvious facts of the case seems implausible, largely because it must by definition be hypothetical. The facts are; therefore they could not have been otherwise. Yet, one can argue that if the Republicans had maintained control of the state government in 1877, subsequent events might have unfolded otherwise. A Republican administration strong enough to defend itself against the Red Shirts' virtual insurrection would probably have created a different set of options for the Hayes administration. It might well have encouraged more white Democrats to join the Republican party (as James L. Orr did in 1870), or to fuse with an element of it (as some of Charleston's white conservatives did in 1874). And if one accepts the

---

55. *Ibid.*

56. Martin R. Delany to Jonathan J. Wright, February 10, 1874, reprinted in *Beaufort Republican*, February 19, 1874.

notion that a Republican party capable of defending itself during and after the 1876 election would have changed the subsequent political scenario in the state, then it follows that greater Republican unity would have made a difference.

Of course, the scenario did not develop that way. Ultimately, Republican unity was—to use Elliott's simile—like so many grains of sand. Frozen into inaction by the fear of defeat, decimated by defections and deaths, the Republican leadership continued to be weakened by internal dissension over tactics and patronage. At the 1895 constitutional convention, the five black delegates were simply a forlorn reminder of the earlier Republican majority. At that convention Benjamin Tillman made certain that blacks would not regain their political majority in that century; henceforth even the blackest districts would have white masters. Lonely and isolated, the black delegates could only watch as the process of disintegration, begun almost twenty years before, was about to be completed. They could only listen as their party's death knell, begun at noon on April 10, 1877, was now stilled.

Appendix A

Sources for Biographical Data
on Negro Legislators

The biographical data on Negro legislators were taken from several sources, both primary and secondary, which are described in the Bibliographical Essay. Collating this data was an arduous task which gave rise to many ambiguous situations. The purpose of this appendix is to set forth some of those ambiguities and their resolutions, as well as to present in tabular form a summary of some of the biographical data collected. Most of the categories of data listed here, such as year of birth, place of birth, and pre- and postwar occupations, have fairly straightforward interpretations. However, some of the others necessitated decisions which should be explained. Even if other scholars should disagree with those decisions, the raw data should still be useful if the classification scheme is clear and reasonably consistent.

Identification: The manuscript census was a major source used to identify Negro legislators. It was crosschecked with other sources, however, and at least one or two items of identification (such as children's names, ages, occupations, etc.) had to match before a positive identification was assumed. Of course, there are errors in the census classifications, particularly in an area like South Carolina, with large numbers of light-complexioned Negroes. However, the chances for mistaken identification of a politician should be much less than for the general population; first, he was a prominent figure by virtue of his office, and second, most of the census takers were political colleagues.

Prewar Status: It is easier to positively identify persons of free origins than those of slave backgrounds because of extant manuscript censuses and free Negro lists. A person is classified as free if he was free before the Civil War. Thus persons who were born slaves but purchased their freedom or escaped before the war are classified as free. Persons are assumed to have been slaves if they do not appear on any of the extant "free" lists, and if there is evidence (such as the birth dates and places of their children) that they were residents of the state over an extended period during the antebellum era.

Color: Either physical appearance or heredity is used as the basis for identifying persons as mulatto or black. Since the propositions put forth in this study deal with social status, the concern here is with a social definition of color, rather than a biological one: what a person actually was is less important than how he was perceived by his contemporaries. Of course, there is still a possibility for error in these observations, but in most cases there are multiple sources to indicate color. Contrary to the usual rule in this study, classifications by "interested" observers, such as newspaper correspondents, are given priority over those of "casual" observers, such as census takers, army enlistment officers, or bank tellers.

Education: A person may have had more education than the surviving evidence shows. (For this reason this particular variable was not used in most analyses, but was confined to simply refuting the notion of widespread illiteracy.) Letters and signatures on documents are taken as evidence of literacy, and very literate correspondence is taken as evidence of common school education. Higher education is assumed only when there is direct evidence. However, the category "college" includes professional education in nonformal settings, such as reading law.

Property: The population census is one source on property holdings, but these censuses were not relied on very heavily without corroboration from the agricultural census or tax records. Actually, the population census tends not to show persons as having property when they actually did have it. Consequently, there is a possibility of an undercount in this category. Persons for whom the population census gave no indication of property and for whom no tax or agricultural census could be found were classified as "missing data" and excluded from the analysis in the sixth chapter. Other legislators who appeared on property tax lists were also excluded from the statistical analysis if the dates were not congruent.

Sources: In order to make the following exhibit less cumbersome, the sources of data have been coded. These codes are keyed to the respective primary or secondary items in the list of sources.

Keys to Table 5

CC   constitutional convention delegate
SR   state representative
SS   state senator
Cong   congressman
SST   secretary of state
ST   secretary of treasury
SJ   supreme court justice
AG   adjutant general

LG   lieutenant governor
F   free
S   slave
(S)   indicates that the classification is inferred from indirect evidence
M   mulatto
B   black
Farm O.   farm owner
Farm T.   farm tenant

CODES FOR SOURCES

PRIMARY
P1   1860 MSS Census, Population
P2   1870 MSS Census, Population
P3   1880 MSS Census, Population
P4   1850 MSS Census, Population
P5   1860 MSS Census, Agriculture
P6   1870 MSS Census, Agriculture
P7   1880 MSS Census, Agriculture
P8   Compiled Military Service Record, RG 94, NA

P9 Civil War Pension Files, RG 15, NA
P10 Registers of Signature Depositor Cards, Freedman's Savings and Trust Company, RG 101, NA
P11 Nominations Files, U.S. Customs Service, RG 56, NA
P12 Appointments Files, U.S. Internal Revenue Service, RG 58, NA
P13 Governor Daniel Chamberlain Papers, South Carolina Archives
P14 Fisk Brewer MSS, South Caroliniana Library
P15 Militia Enrollments, South Carolina Archives
P16 Registers of Free Negroes, South Carolina Archives and South Caroliniana Library
P17 Registers of Students, University of South Carolina, South Caroliniana Library
P18 American Missionary Association Archives, Amistad Research Center
P19 Singleton, *Romance of African Methodism*
P20 *KKK Hearings, 1872*
P21 Assessments of Real Estate, Charleston County, 1868-70
P22 Auditor's Tax Duplicates, Charleston County, 1871, 1874, 1877
P23 Probate Court Records, Charleston County
P24 Index of Wills, Charleston County, 1840-1927
P25 Treasurer's Tax Duplicates, Fairfield County, 1882
P26 *News and Courier* (Charleston), October 10, 1874
P27 *News and Courier* (Charleston), December 26, 1874
P28 WPA Slave Narratives
P29 *Daily Courier* (Charleston), November 27, 1868
P30 *News and Courier* (Charleston), December 9, 1875

SECONDARY

S1 Bryant, Lawrence C., *Negro Lawmakers in the South Carolina Legislature, 1869-1902; and Negro Senators and Representatives in the South Carolina Legislature, 1868-1902*
S2 Work, Monroe, comp., "Some Negro Members of Reconstruction Legislatures," *Journal of Negro History*, V (1920)
S3 Hume, Richard L., "The Black and Tan Constitutional Conventions of 1867-1869 in Ten Former Confederate States: A Study of Their Membership" (Ph.D. thesis, University of Washington, 1969)
S4 Simmons, William J., *Men of Mark: Eminent, Progressive, and Rising*
S5 *Biographical Directory of the U.S. Congress*
S6 Wright, Richard R., Jr., *The Bishops of the African Methodist Episcopal Church*
S7 Rosen, Michael, "Negro Reconstruction Office-Holders: Their Backgrounds and Beliefs"
S8 Williamson, Joel, *After Slavery: The Negro in South Carolina During Reconstruction, 1861-77*
S9 Simkins, Francis, and Robert Woody, *South Carolina During Reconstruction*
S10 Woody, Robert, "Jonathan Jasper Wright, Associate Justice of the Supreme Court of South Carolina, 1870-77," *Journal of Negro History*, XVIII (1933)
S11 Smith, Samuel D., *The Negro in Congress, 1870-1901*
S12 Reynolds, Emily, and Joan Faunt, eds., *Biographical Directory of the Senate of South Carolina, 1776-1964*

Table 5. Summary of Biographical Data for Negro Legislators, 1868-76

Name	Offices and dates	County	Prewar status	Color	Year of birth	Place of birth	Prewar occupation	Postwar occupation	Education	Value of real property	Value of personal property	Sources
Adamson, Frank	SR70-74	Kershaw	S	B	1809	SC	–	Tailor	Literate	$ 1,500	$ 130	P2,P28,S1
Adamson, William	SR69-70	Kershaw	S	M	1825	SC	–	Farm O. Minister (Methodist)	Literate	700	0	P2,P28,S1
Alexander, Purvis	CC	Chester	(S)	M	1837	SC	Blacksmith	Blacksmith	Literate	500	150	P2,P6,P15,S3
Allman, Jacob C.	SR72-76	Marion	(S)	M	1827	SC	–	Farm O.	Literate	700	50	P2
Andrews, William J.	SR74-76	Sumter	–	M	1840	SC	–	Teacher Merchant	Common	–	–	P27,S1
Artson, Robert B.	SR72-74	Charleston	–	B	1835	–	–	Tailor	Common	–	–	P10,P13,S1
Bampfield, Samuel J.	SR74-76	Beaufort	F	M	1849	SC	–	Lawyer	Lincoln University (Pa.)	–	–	P3,P16,S1,S7
Barber, George W.	SS68-72	Fairfield	(S)	B	1831	SC	–	Farm O.	Literate	600	150	P1,P2,P25,S12
Bascomb, John B.	SR70-74	Beaufort	(S)	M	1827	SC	–	Merchant	Illiterate	0	0	P2,P15
Becker, Martin F.	CC	Berkeley	F	M	1834	West Indies	Printer	–	Common	5,000	–	P2,P6,P9,P8,P22
Bishop, W. A.	SR68-70	Greenville	–	–	–	–	–	–	–	–	–	–
Bonum, John	CC	Edgefield	F	B	1822	SC	Huckster	Wood Factor	Literate	0	0	P1,P2,P22,S3
Bosemon, Benjamin A.	SR68-73	Charleston	F	M	1839	NY	Doctor	Doctor	Bowdoin College	650	365	P2,P9,P10,P13,P22,P24
Boston, John	SR68-70; 72-74	Darlington	(S)	B	1830	SC	–	Farm O.	Illiterate	196	200	P2,P6,P15,S1
Boston, Joseph D.	SR68-76	Newberry	(S)	B	1843	VA	–	–	U. of SC	–	100	P2,P17
Bowley, James A.	SR69-74	Georgetown	F	B	1844	MD	–	Teacher	Common	500	500	P2,P15,S7
Brayton, E. M.	SR74-76	Aiken	–	–	–	–	–	–	–	–	–	–
Bridges, Sampson S.	SR72-76	Newberry	(S)	B	1840	SC	–	Farm T.	Literate	0	0	P2
Bright, Peter	SR74-76	Charleston	(S)	B	–	SC	–	–	Literate	0	165	P2,P22,P23,P26

Name	Offices and dates	County	Prewar status	Color	Year of birth	Place of birth	Prewar occupation	Postwar occupation	Education	Value of real property	Value of personal property	Sources
Lee, Levi	SR72-74	Fairfield	–	–	–	–	–	–	–	–	–	P25
Lee, Samuel	CC	Sumter	S	M	–	SC	–	–	–	–	–	P28
Lee, Samuel J.	SR68-74	Edgefield Aiken	–	M	1844	SC	–	Lawyer	Professional	–	–	P23
Lilley, John	SR72-74	Chester	–	M	1844	SC	–	State Constable	Illiterate	175	160	P2
Lloyd, Joseph W.	SR70-72	Charleston	(S)	B	1840	SC	–	Carpenter	Literate	0	0	P2
Logan, Aaron	SR70-72	Charleston	(S)	B	1843	SC	–	Farm O.	Literate	600	451	P2,P6,P7,P10, P21,P22,P28
Lomax, Hutson J.	CC SR68-70	Abbeville	S	M	1832	SC	–	Merchant Farm O.	Literate	3,000	3,000	P2,P15,S1,S3
Martin, Moses	SS73-76	Fairfield	(S)	M	1830	SC	–	Farmer	–	1,000	100	P2,S12
Martin, Thomas	SR72-74	Abbeville	–	–	–	–	–	–	–	–	–	
Maxwell, Henry J.	SS68-70	Marlboro	F	B	1836	SC	Brickmason	Teacher Brickmason Lawyer	Professional	1,500	250	P2,P8,P9,P10, P16,S2
Mayer, Julius	CC SR68-70	Barnwell	S	B	1843	SC	–	Farm O.	Literate	1,000	1,000	P2,P7,P8,P15, S1,S3
Mays, James P.	SR68-70	Orangeburg	F	B	–	–	Barber	Farm T.	–	–	–	P9,S1
McDaniels, Harry	CC SR68-72	Laurens	S	–	–	–	Coachmaker	–	–	–	–	S3,S7
McDowell, Thomas D.	SR70-72	Georgetown	F	M	1827	SC	–	Civil Service	Literate	500	200	P2,P10
McKinlay, William	CC SR68-70	Charleston	F	M	1807	SC	Tailor	Tailor	Literate	c.20,000	–	P1,P2,P22, P23,S3,S7,S8
McKinlay, William J.	CC SR68-70	Orangeburg Charleston	F	M	1835	SC	–	Teacher	Common	14,388	–	P1,P2,P22, S1,S3,S7
Meade, John W.	CC SR68-72	York	S	M	1831	SC	Coachmaker	Coachmaker	Literate	50	100	P2,P15,S1,S3
Mickey, Edward C.	SR68-72	Charleston	F	B	1818	SC	Tailor	Minister (AME)	Literate	0	0	P1,P10,P22, P23,P24,S1

Name	Terms	County	Status	Color	Birth	SC	Trade	Occupation	Education	Real Est.	Pers. Prop.	Codes
Coker, Simon P.	SR74-76	Barnwell	(S)	B	1847	SC	–	Farm T.	Literate	0	0	P2,P15,S1
Coleman, Samuel	SR75-76	Chester	(S)	B	1841	SC	–	Farmer	–	–	–	P2
Collins, Augustus	SR72-76	Clarendon	–	–	–	–	–	–	–	–	–	–
Cooke, Wilson	{ CC / SR68-70	Greenville	S	M	–	–	Tanner	Minister (Methodist)	Literate	–	–	P29,S3,S7
Curtis, Andrew W.	SR72-76	Richland	(S)	B	1843	SC	–	Carpenter	Literate	500	200	P2,P11,S1
Dannerly, Abram	SR72-74	Orangeburg	–	–	–	–	–	–	–	–	–	–
Dannerly, William	SR70-72	Orangeburg	–	–	–	–	–	–	–	–	–	–
Davies, Nelson	SR73-76	York	–	M	–	–	–	Minister (Methodist)	Literate	–	–	P30,S1
Davis, James	SR70-72	Richland	–	B	1827	SC	–	Farm O.	Literate	500	200	P2,S1
Davis, Nelson	CC	Laurens	S	–	1835	SC	–	–	Literate	–	–	S3
Davis, Thomas A.	SR70-76	Charleston	–	–	–	–	–	–	Literate	–	–	S1
De Large, Robert C.	{ CC / SR68-70 / Cong71-73	Charleston	F	M	1842	SC	Barber	Freedmen's Bureau	High School	6,650	0	P1,P2,P22,P23,S3,S5,S7
Dix, John	SR72-74	Orangeburg	–	–	–	–	–	–	–	–	–	–
Dogan, Abram	CC	Union	S	–	–	–	–	Minister	Illiterate	–	–	S3,S7
Doiley, Samuel B.	SR74-76	Charleston	(S)	B	1847	SC	–	Farm T.	Illiterate	0	0	P2,P28
Driffle, William A.	{ CC / SR68-70	Colleton	S	M	1835	SC	Carpenter	Carpenter	Literate	2,000	300	P2,P6,S1,S3
Duncan, Hiram W.	SS68-72	Union	–	–	–	–	–	Farm O. / Minister	–	–	–	S12
Duncan, Samuel L.	SR72-76	Orangeburg	–	–	–	–	–	Minister	–	–	–	P10,S1
Edwards, Harvey D.	CC	Fairfield	S	B	1826	SC	–	Minister	Literate	–	–	P2,S3,S7
Elliott, Robert B.	{ CC / SR68-70; 74-76 / Cong71-74	{ Barnwell / Edgefield / Aiken	F	B	1842	–	–	Lawyer	Professional	5,500	3,000	P2,S4,S5,S11,S13
Elliott, William E.	SR70-72	Charleston	–	B	1836	SC	–	Fisherman	Literate	–	–	P10,P22
Ellison, Henry H.	SR70-72	Abbeville	–	–	1839	–	–	Farmer	–	–	–	P15
Ezekiel, Phillip E.	SR68-70	Beaufort	F	M	1827	SC	Tailor	Tailor	Literate	1,000	200	P1,P2,P10,S1
Farr, Simeon	SR68-72	Union	–	–	1835	SC	–	Farm O.	Literate	670	305	S1
Farrow, Simeon	SR74-76	Union	–	–	–	–	–	–	–	–	–	–

Name	Offices and dates	County	Prewar status	Color	Year of birth	Place of birth	Prewar occupation	Postwar occupation	Education	Value of real property	Value of personal property	Sources
Ferguson, Edward	SR70-72	Barnwell	(S)	B	1818	SC	–	Minister (Methodist) Grocer	Literate	–	–	P2
Ford, Adam P.	SR70-74	Charleston	(S)	B	1831	SC	–	Huckster	Literate	0	0	P2,P10,P22
Ford, Sanders	SS72-73	Fairfield	(S)	M	1810	SC	–	Farm O.	Literate	1,200	300	P2,S12
Foster, Rice	CC	Spartanburg	S	–	1833	–	–	Farmer Minister	Literate	–	–	P15,S3
Frazier, William H.	SR72-74	Colleton	–	B	1838	SC	–	Blacksmith	Literate	0	200	P2,P10,S1
Freeman, John M., Jr.	SR74-76	Charleston	F	M	1849	SC	–	Butcher	Literate	–	–	P2,P10,P16,P28
Frost, Florian Henry	SR70-72	Williamsburg	F	M	1846	SC	–	Teacher	Common	0	1,087	P22,P23,S1,S2
Gaillard, Samuel E.	SS70-76	Charleston	F	B	1839	SC	Millwright	Farm O. Teacher Merchant	Common	–	–	P2,P10,P14,P22,P23,S12
Gaither, Reuben D.	SR70-76	Kershaw	(S)	B	1831	SC	–	Farm T. Minister (Baptist)	Literate	0	0	P2,P6,P15,S1
Gantt, Hastings	SR70-76	Beaufort	S	B	1827	SC	–	Farm O.	Literate	1,100	–	P2,P6,P7,P10,P15
Gardner, John	SR68-70	Edgefield	–	–	–	–	–	Teacher	Literate	–	–	P15
Gardner, William H.	SR70-72	Sumter	–	–	–	–	–		Literate	–	–	S1
Gary, Stephen	SR70-72 74-76	Kershaw	–	B	1841	SC	–	Minister (Methodist) Teacher	Common	0	0	P2,S1
George, Ebenezer F.	SR74-76	Kershaw	F	–	1842	SC	–	Farm T.	Illiterate	–	–	P1,S1
Gibson, John	SR74-76	Fairfield	(S)	M	1848	SC	–	Laborer	Literate	–	–	P2
Giles, Fortune	SR70-74	Williamsburg	(S)	B	1830	SC	–	Farm T.	Literate	0	125	P2,S1
Gilmore, John T.	SR72-74	Richland	(S)	B	1837	SC	–	Laborer	Literate	0	0	P2,S1
Gleaves, Richard H.	LG 72-77	Beaufort	F	M	1817	PA	–	Lawyer	Professional	500	600	P2,P10,S8
Glover, William C.	SR70-72	Charleston	F	B	1848	SC	Butcher	Teacher	Normal	840	0	P1,P2,P8,P9,P10,P18,P22,S1

Name	Service	County	Status	Color	Birth	Birthplace	Occupation 1	Occupation 2	Education	Real Est.	Personal	Codes
Goggins, Mitchell	SR70-72, 74-76	Abbeville	(S)	B	1850	SC	–	Farm T.	Literate	–	–	P2
Goodson, Aesop	SR68-72	Richland	(S)	M	1826	NC	–	Gunwright	Illiterate	0	100	P2,S1
Graham, David	SR72-76	Edgefield	–	–	–	–	–	–	–	–	–	–
Grant, James J.	SR72-74	Charleston	–	–	–	–	–	–	–	–	–	–
Grant, John G.	SR68-70	Marlboro	(S)	M	1818	SC	Turpentine Mfg.	Gristmill Worker	Illiterate	3,500	900	P2,P5,P6
Grant, William A.	SR72-74	Charleston	–	–	–	–	–	–	–	–	–	–
Gray, William H. W.	CC, SR68-70	Berkeley / Charleston	F	B	1825	MA	Barber	Farm O.	Literate	550	0	P8,P9,P10,P21,P22,S3
Green, Charles S.	SR72-76	Georgetown	S	–	–	–	–	–	–	–	–	–
Green, John	SR70-72	Edgefield	S	–	–	–	–	–	–	–	–	–
Greene, Samuel	SR70-75, SS75-77	Beaufort	S	B	1847	SC	Fieldhand	Carpenter / Farmer	Literate	–	–	P10,P11,S12
Greenwood, Ishom	SR72-74	Newberry	(S)	B	1820	SC	–	–	Illiterate	0	0	P2
Hamilton, Thomas	SR72-76	Beaufort	–	B	1847	SC	–	Farm O.	Literate	800	–	P2
Hardy, James J.	SR70-71	Charleston	(S)	M	1840	SC	–	Brickmason	Literate	0	0	P2
Harriett, R. M.	SR74-76	Georgetown	F	M	1828	West Indies	–	Merchant	Literate	500	1,060	P2
Harris, David	CC, SR68-72	Edgefield	S	M	1816	SC	Shoemaker	Minister (Baptist) / Farmer	Literate	500	250	P2,P13,S3,S9
Hart, Alfred	SR70-72	Darlington	–	–	1834	SC	–	Farmer / Minister (Baptist) / Farm T.	–	–	–	S1
Hayes, Eben	SR68-70, 72-74	Marion	(S)	B	1820	SC	–	–	Illiterate	0	150	P2
Hayne, Charles D.	CC, SR68-72, SS72-76	Barnwell	F	M	1847	SC	Tailor	Bureau / Teacher, / Tailor	Normal	1,200	600	P2,P15,S1,S3,S8,S12
Hayne, Henry E.	CC, SS68-72, SST72-7	Marion	F	M	1842	MA	Tailor	Teacher	U. of SC	0	0	P8,P10,P14,P15,S3
Hayne, James N.	CC, SR68-72	Barnwell	F	M	1831	SC	–	Teacher / Bureau	Common	2,000	1,500	P2,P15,S1,S3,S8

Name	Offices and dates	County	Prewar status	Color	Year of birth	Place of birth	Prewar occupation	Postwar occupation	Education	Value of real property	Value of personal property	Sources
Hayne, William A.	SR74-76	Marion	F	M	1842	SC	–	Teacher / Clerk	Common	0	0	P2,P10,P11,P15,P24,S1
Hedges, Plato P.	SR70-72	Charleston	F	–	1840	NJ	–	Farmer	Common	–	–	P28
Henderson, James A.	CC SR68-70 74-76	Newberry	(S)	M	1817	VA	–	–	Literate	–	–	P2,S3
Henderson, John T.	SR70-72	Newberry	–	B	1846	SC	–	Trial / Justice	Literate	–	–	P2,P22
Holland, Gloster H.	SR70-74	Aiken	–	–	–	–	–	–	–	–	–	–
Holmes, Abraham P.	SR70-74	Colleton	–	–	1845	SC	–	Laborer	Literate	–	–	S1
Hough, Allison W.	SR72-74	Kershaw	–	B	1842	SC	–	Merchant / Teacher	Common	0	300	P2,P15,S1
Howard, A. H.	SR74-76	Marion	–	–	–	–	–	–	–	–	–	–
Hudson, Allen	SR70-72 74-76	Lancaster	–	–	1844	SC	–	–	Literate	–	–	S1
Humbert, Richard H.	CC SR70-76	Darlington	S	B	1835	GA	Carpenter	Merchant / Minister	Literate	250	100	P2,P8,P9,S1,S3,S7
Humphries, Barney	SR68-72	Chester	–	–	–	–	–	–	Illiterate	–	–	–
Hunter, Alfred T. B.	SR74-76	Laurens	S	–	1850	SC	–	–	Literate	–	–	S1
Hunter, Hezekiah H.	SR70-72	Charleston	F	M	1838	NY	Minister	Teacher / Minister (Presbyterian)	Normal	3,650	230	P10,P18,P22,P23
Hutson, James	SR68-70	Newberry	–	–	–	–	–	–	–	–	–	–
Jackson, Austin	SR74-76	Barnwell	–	–	–	–	–	–	–	–	–	P28
Jacobs, Henry	CC SR68-70	Fairfield	F	M	1815	SC	Wagonmaker	Minister / Wagonmaker	Literate	1,000	500	P1,P2,P25,S3
James, Burrell	SR68-70	Sumter	–	B	1838	SC	–	Minister (Methodist)	College	600	500	P2,P19,S1
Jamison, James L.	SR70-72 SS72-73	Orangeburg	–	B	1838	SC	–	Farm O. / Teacher	Common	500	0	P2,S12
Jefferson, Paul W.	SR74-76	Aiken	–	–	–	–	–	Minister	–	–	–	–

Name	Service	County	S/F	Race	Year	State	Occupation 1	Occupation 2	Literacy	Real	Personal	Codes
Jervay, William R.	CC SR68-72 SS72-76	Charleston	S	M	1847	SC	Domestic	Minister† Farm O.	Literate	950	550	S1,S3,S12, P2,P3,P6,P8, P9,P10,P22
Johnson, D. J. J.	SR68-70	Chesterfield	(S)	B	1825	SC	–	Minister (AME)	Literate	100	200	P2
Johnson, Griffin C.	SR68-72	Laurens	(S)	B	1834	SC	–	Farm T.	Literate	0	0	P2,S1
Johnson, Henry	SR68-70	Fairfield	S	B	1840	SC	Brickmason	Brickmason	Literate	450	200	P2,P20
Johnson, John W.	CC SR72-74	Marion	S	B	1849	SC	–	Farm T.	Literate	0	0	P2,P15,S3
Johnson, Samuel	CC	Anderson	–	–	–	SC	–	–	Literate	–	–	S3
Johnson, Samuel	SR68-70	Charleston	F	B	1821	SC	–	Minister (AME)	Literate	–	–	P10,P16
Johnston, William E.	CC SR68-69 SS69-77	Sumter	F	M	1838	SC	Cabinetmaker	Minister (AME)	Literate	150	200	P2,P8,P10,P15, S1,S12
Joiner, W. Nelson	CC	Abbeville	F	–	–	TN	–	Teacher Bureau	–	–	–	S3
Jones, A. H.	SR74-76	Charleston	–	–	–	SC	–	Laborer	Literate	0	0	P28
Jones, Charles	CC	Lancaster	S	B	1830	SC	–	Laborer	Literate	0	250	P2,P10,P15,S3
Jones, Henry W.	CC	Horry	S	B	1829	SC	Slave Preacher	Minister (AME)	Illiterate	0	100	P2,P19,S3
Jones, Paul E.	SR74-76	Orangeburg	–	–	–	SC	–	–	–	–	–	–
Jones, William H.	CC SR68-72 SS-72-76	Georgetown	F	B	1842	SC	–	Teacher	Professional	200	500	P2,S7,S12
Keith, Samuel J.	SR70-76	Darlington	–	B	1834	SC	–	Carpenter	Illiterate	600	100	P2,S1
Lang, Jordan	CC SR68-72	Darlington	F	B	1813	SC	Laborer	Farm T.	Literate	0	1,309	P2,P6,P7,S1,S3, S7
Langley, Landon S.	CC	Beaufort	F	M	1839	VT	Farm O.	Farm O. Teacher	Common	600	200	P2,P3,P8,P9, P10,P15
Lee, George H.	CC SR68-70	Charleston	F	B	1841	MA	Lawyer	Lawyer	Professional	900	1,500	P2,P23,S3
Lee, John	SS72-74	Chester	(S)	M	1837	SC	–	Postmaster	Literate	0	0	P2,S7,S12

† Jervay became a minister (Northern Methodist) after his political service.

Name	Offices and dates	County	Prewar status	Color	Year of birth	Place of birth	Prewar occupation	Postwar occupation	Education	Value of real property	Value of personal property	Sources
Brockenton, Isaac P.	CC	Darlington	S	B	1833	SC	–	Minister (Methodist)	Literate	–	–	P8,P15,P26
Brodie, William J.	SR68-70	Charleston	F	M	1840	SC	Bricklayer	Bricklayer	Literate	0	0	P2,P10,P17,P22,S1
Brown, Stephen	SR68-70	Charleston	S	B	1829	SC	–	Farm O.	Literate	1,800	1,275	P22,P26,S1
Bryan, Richard	SR70-74	Charleston	–	–	–	SC	–	–	–	–	–	–
Burchmeyer, H. Z.	SR74-76	Charleston	F	–	–	SC	–	Merchant	–	–	–	P22,P26
Burton, Barney	CC SR68-70	Chester	S	B	1834	SC	–	Minister (Methodist)	Literate	0	200	P2,P15,S3
Byas, Benjamin	CC SR70-72	Berkeley Orangeburg	F	M	1842	West Indies	–	Farm O.	Howard University	–	–	P10,P22,S1,S3
Cain, Edward J.	CC SR68-70	Orangeburg	S	B	1837	SC	Wheelwright	Carpenter	Common	–	–	P9,S1
Cain, Everidge	SR70-74	Abbeville	–	–	1842	SC	–	Farm O.	Literate	360	–	P2,S1
Cain, Lawrence	SR68-72 SS72-76	Edgefield	–	–	1845	SC	–	Farm O. Teacher	U. of SC	400	471	S1,S7,S12
Cain, Richard H.	CC SS68-70 Cong73-75	Charleston	F	B	1825	VA	Minister (AME)	Minister (AME)	Wilberforce University	3,400	500	P2,P21,P22,S3,S4,S5,S7,S11,S12
Cardozo, Francis L.	CC SST68-72 ST72-77	Charleston	F	M	1837	SC	Carpenter Minister (Congregational)	Teacher Minister (Congregational)	U. of Edinburgh	7,000	1,000	P2,P10,P12,P18,P22,S3,S7
Cardozo, Henry	CC SS70-74	Kershaw	F	M	1830	SC	–	Minister (Methodist)	Literate	1,500	2,000	P2,P15,P16,S12
Carter, Frank	SS74-76	Kershaw	–	–	–	–	–	–	–	–	–	–
Chestnut, John A.	CC SR68-70	Kershaw	S	M	1839	SC	Barber	Barber	Literate	750	150	P2,S3,S7,S8
Clinton, Frederick Albert	CC SS70-76	Lancaster	S	B	1834	SC	Domestic	Farm O.	Common	500	300	P2,P7,P14,P15,S3,S12

Middleton, Abram	Barnwell	CC	F	B	1828	SC	Tailor	Tailor / Minister (Methodist)	Illiterate	500	200	P2,P10,P15,S3
Middleton, Benjamin	Barnwell	SR72-74	F	B	1844	SC	—	Postmaster / Farm O.	Common	400	0	P2,P7,P10,P15,S1
Miller, Isaac	Fairfield	SR72-74	F	B	1833	SC	—	—	Literate	—	150	P1,P2,P25
Miller, M.	Fairfield	SR72-74	—	—	—	—	—	—	—	—	—	—
Miller, Thomas E.	Beaufort	SR74-80, SS80-82 Cong.	F	M	1849	SC	—	Lawyer	Lincoln University (Pa.)	—	—	P10,S5,S7,S12
Mills, James	Laurens	SR72-74	—	—	—	—	—	—	—	—	—	—
Milton, Syphax	Clarendon	SR70-72, 74-76	—	—	1833	—	—	Farmer	Literate	—	—	S1 / P15
Minort, Charles S.	Richland	SR72-74	—	M	1840	SC	—	Civil Service / Farm O.	Literate	1,500	500	P2
Mobley, Junius S.	Union	SR68-72	—	—	1836	—	—	Farm O.	Literate	—	—	P15,S1
Moore, Alfred M.	Fairfield	SR70-72	(S)	M	1834	SC	—	Minister	Literate	0	165	P2,P15
Morgan, Shadrack	Orangeburg	SR74-76	S	B	1846	SC	Fieldhand	Farm T.	Literate	—	—	P7,P9,S1
Morrison, William C.	Beaufort	SR68-70	F	B	1819	SC	—	Tinsmith	Literate	—	—	P2,P8,P16,S1
Myers, Nathaniel B.	Beaufort	SR70-75	—	M	1843	SC	—	Farm O.	Literate	0	0	P2,P15
Myers, William F.	Colleton	SS74-75	F	M	1848	SC	—	Lawyer	U. of SC	0	0	S2,S12
Nance, Lee A.	Newberry	CC	S	—	—	—	Domestic	—	—	—	—	S3,S7,S8
Nash, Jonas W.	Kershaw	SR68-69	—	B	1840	B	—	—	Literate	—	—	S1
Nash, William Beverly	Richland	CC, SS68-76	S	B	1826	VA	Hotel Servant	Brick Mfg.	Literate	5,000	2,000	P2,P6,S1,S3,S7,S12
Nelson, William	Clarendon	CC, SR68-70	S	B	1837	SC	—	Farm O.	Illiterate	100	159	P2,P6,S3
Nesbitt, Richard	Charleston	SR74-76	(S)	B	1840	SC	Laborer	Laborer	Literate	—	—	P2,P22,P24,P28
Nix, Frederick, Jr.	Barnwell	SR72-74	—	B	1842	SC	Wheelwright	Wheelwright	Illiterate	0	100	P2,P15,S1
North, Charles F.	Charleston	SR72-74	(S)	M	1836	SC	—	Carpenter	Literate	0	0	P2,P22,P23,S1
Nuckles, Samuel	Union	CC, SR68-72	S	—	1814	SC	Blacksmith	Farm O. / Minister	Literate	—	—	P20,S1,S3,S7
Pendergrass, Jeffrey	Williamsburg	SR68-72	(S)	B	1814	SC	—	Farm O. / Minister (Methodist)	Illiterate	600	375	P2,P6,P7,P15

Name	Offices and dates	County	Prewar status	Color	Year of birth	Place of birth	Prewar occupation	Postwar occupation	Education	Value of real property	Value of personal property	Sources
Perrin, Wade	SR68-70	Laurens	–	B	1820	SC	–	Merchant	Illiterate	0	150	P2
Peterson, James F.	SR72-78	Williamsburg	(S)	B	1842	SC	–	{Teacher, Farmer}	Common	–	–	P2,S1
Petty, Edward	SR72-74	Charleston	–	–	–	–	–	–	–	0	80	P22
Pinckney, William G.	SR74-76	Charleston	S	B	1842	SC	–	{Teacher, Farm T.}	Literate	–	–	{P2,P6,P9, P10,P28}
Pressley, Thomas	SR72-74	Williamsburg	(S)	B	1813	SC	–	Farm T.	Illiterate	0	0	P28
Prioleau, Isaac	SR72-74	Charleston	–	–	–	–	–	Teacher	Common	–	–	
Purvis, Henry W.	{SR68-70 AG70-77}	Lexington	F	M	1846	PA	–	–	{Oberlin College}	0	0	P2,P11,S7
Rainey, Joseph H.	{CC SS68-70 Cong70-79}	Georgetown	F	M	1832	SC	Barber	Barber	Literate	1,500	6,845	{P1,P2,P22, S3,S5,S11,S12}
Ramsey, Warren W.	SR69-76	Sumter	–	–	–	–	–	–	–	–	–	P8,S3,S7
Randolph, Benjamin F.	{CC SS68}	Orangeburg	F	M	1837	KY	{Minister (Presbyterian)}	{Minister (Methodist)}	{Oberlin College}	–	–	P8,S3,S7
Ransier, Alonzo J.	{CC SR68-70 LG70-72 Cong73-75}	Charleston	F	M	1834	SC	{Shipping Clerk}	Civil Service	Literate	550	–	{P22,P24,S3, S7,S11}
Reed, George A.	SR72-74	Beaufort	–	B	1815	SC	–	Minister	Literate	0	0	P2
Richardson, Thomas	{SR68-70 74-76}	Colleton	(S)	B	1841	SC	–	Carpenter	Literate	900	150	{P2; Courier (Charleston) 7 August 1868}
Riley, Henry	SR72-74	Orangeburg	–	B	1825	SC	–	Grocer	Literate	0	500	P2
Rivers, Prince R.	{CC SR68-74}	{Edgefield Aiken}	S	B	1822	SC	Domestic	Civil Service	Common	250	500	{P2,P7,P8, P9,P13,S7}
Rush, Alfred	{SR68-70 74-76}	Darlington	–	–	–	–	–	–	–	–	–	
Sasportas, Thaddeus K.	{CC SR68-70}	Orangeburg	F	M	1844	SC	Shoemaker	{Teacher, Farm O.}	Normal	–	–	{P3,P8,P10, P22,S1,S3,S7}

Name												
Saunders, Sancho	CC SR68-72	Chester	S	B	1805	SC	–	Minister (Baptist)	Literate	0	175	P2,S3
Scott, Robert F.	SR68-70	Williamsburg	F	B	–	–	–	–	–	–	–	–
Scott, William C.	SR74-76	Williamsburg	–	B	1845	SC	–	Teacher Farmer	Common	–	–	S1
Shrewsbury, Henry L.	CC SR68-70	Chesterfield	F	M	1846	SC	–	Teacher Bureau	Common	0	500	P2,P10,P15,S3
Simkins, Augustus	SR72-76	Edgefield	–	–	–	–	–	–	–	–	–	–
Simpkins, Paris	SR72-76	Edgefield	(S)	M	1849	SC	Barber	Barber Lawyer	U. of SC	600	100	P2,P11,S1
Simmons, Aaron	SR74-76	Orangeburg	S	B	1836	SC	Fieldhand	Farm O.	Literate	–	–	P8,P22,S1
Simmons, Benjamin	SR75-76	Beaufort	–	–	–	–	–	–	–	–	–	–
Simmons, Hercules	SR74-76	Colleton	–	B	1841	–	SC	Farm O.	Illiterate	1,000	0	P2,S1
Simmons, Limus	SR72-74	Edgefield	–	–	–	–	–	–	–	–	–	–
Simmons, William	SR68-72 74-76	Richland	(S)	M	1810	SC	–	–	Literate	2,000	1,000	P2,S17
Sims, Charles	SR72-74	Chester	–	–	–	–	–	–	–	–	–	–
Singleton, Asbury L.	SR70-72	Sumter	(S)	M	1845	SC	–	Blacksmith	Literate	0	0	P2,S1
Singleton, J. P.	SR70-72	Chesterfield	–	B	1819	SC	–	Brickmason	Literate	100	50	P2
Smalls, Robert	CC SR68-70 SS70-75 Cong75-77	Beaufort	S	M	1839	SC	Seaman	Pilot	Common	6,000	1,000	P2,P6,P9,P10, S4,S5,S12,S14
Smalls, Sherman	SR70-74	Colleton	–	B	1843	SC	–	Carpenter	Literate	0	0	P2,S1
Smiling, James E.	SR68-70	Sumter	F	M	1812	SC	Carpenter	Farm O.	Literate	300	200	P1,P2,P6
Smith, Abraham W.	SR68-72	Charleston	(S)	B	1833	SC	–	Shoemaker	Literate	1,400	200	P2,P6,P10, P15,P16,P22
Smith, Jackson A.	SR72-76	Darlington	(S)	M	1830	SC	–	Merchant	–	3,500	500	P2
Smythe, Powell	SR68-70	Clarendon	(S)	M	1835	SC	–	Farmer	Literate	–	300	P2,P6,P15
Spears, Butler	SR72-74	Sumter	–	M	1848	SC	Porter	Policeman	Illiterate	0	150	P2
Spencer, James A.	SR74-76	Abbeville	F	M	1850	SC	–	Teacher Civil Service	Common	0	0	P1,P2,P10, P15
Spencer, Nathaniel T.	SR72-74	Charleston	F	M	1844	SC	–	Tailor Minister	U. of SC	950	–	P2,P10,P17, P22

Name	Offices and dates	County	Prewar status	Color	Year of birth	Place of birth	Prewar occupation	Postwar occupation	Education	Value of real property	Value of personal property	Sources
Sperry, Charles H.	SR72-74	Georgetown	–	–	–	–	–	–	–	–	–	S1
Steele, Henry	SR74-76	York	–	–	–	–	–	–	–	–	–	–
Stubbs, Calvin T.	CC	Marlboro	S	B	1825	SC	–	Laborer Teacher	Common	0	200	P2,P15,S3
Sullivan, Caesar	SR72-74	Laurens	–	–	1816	SC	–	–	Illiterate	–	–	S1
Swails, Stephen A.	CC SS68-77	Williamsburg	F	M	1832	PA	Boatman	Teacher Bureau	Common	1,800	500	P2,P7,P8,P9, S1,S7,S12
Tarlton, Robert	SR70-74	Colleton	–	–	–	SC	–	Farm Laborer	Literate	–	0	–
Thomas, John W.	SR70-72	Marlboro	(S)	B	1835	SC	–	Minister (AME)	Literate	0	0	P2
Thomas, William M.	CC SR68-76	Colleton	(S)	B	1828	SC	–		Literate	0	0	P10
Thompson, Augustus R.	CC	Horry	S	B	1816	SC	–	Farm O.	–	0	0	P2,P7,S3
Thompson, Benjamin A.	CC SR68-74	Marion	(S)	M	1830	SC	–	Farm O.	Illiterate	6,000	376	P2,P6,P7,P15, S1,S3
Thompson, Joseph	SR74-76	Fairfield	(S)	M	1829	SC	–	Farmer	–	–	650	P2,P25
Thompson, Samuel B.	CC SR68-74	Richland	F	B	1833	GA	Barber	Carpenter	Literate	1,000	500	P2,P8,P9, P10,S1
Tingman, Julius C.	SR72-74	Charleston	(S)	B	1845	SC	–	Farm T.	Literate	0	0	P2,P6,P7, P22,S1
Turner, Robert	SR72-73	Charleston	–	–	–	–	–	–	–	–	–	–
Valentine, Richard M.	SR68	Abbeville	(S)	B	1822	SC	–	Farm T. Minister (Methodist)	Literate	0	0	P2,P20
Vanderpool, John	SR72-76	Charleston	(S)	B	1837	SC	–	Barber	Literate	0	0	P2,P22,P28
Viney, William M.	CC	Colleton	F	M	1842	OH	Broommaker	Laborer Minister (Presbyterian)	Literate	–	–	P8,P9,P10, S3
Walker, Dublin J.	SS74-77	Chester	(S)	B	1835	SC	–	Minister	Literate	–	–	P2,P6,S12
Wallace, John	SR70-71	Orangeburg	–	–	–	–	–	–	–	–	–	–

Name	Service	County	Status	Race	Birth	State	Occupation	Occupation	Education			Refs
Warley, Jared D.	SR70-74 SS74-76	Clarendon	–	–	–	–	–	{ Minister Farm O.	–	240	360	P6
Weldon, Archie	SR74-76	Edgefield	(S)	–	–	–	–	–	–	–	–	–
Westberry, John	SR74-76	Sumter	–	M	1840	SC	–	Farm O.	Literate	200	125	P2,S1
Weston, Ellison M.	SR74-76	Richland	–	M	1841	SC	–	Farm T.	Illiterate	0	160	P2,S1
Whipper, William James	CC SR68-72 75-76	Beaufort	F	B	1834	PA	Lumberman	Lawyer	Professional	–	–	{ P3,P8,P9, P22,S2,S3
White, John H.	CC SR68-72 SS72-76	York	(S)	B	1829	SC	Blacksmith	Blacksmith	Literate	500	600	P2,S1,S12
Wideman, Hannibal A.	SR72-76	Abbeville	–	–	–	–	–	–	–	–	–	–
Wilder, Charles M.	CC SR68-70	Richland	S	M	1837	SC	Carpenter	Carpenter	U. of SC	5,000	1,500	{ P2,P15,S1, S3,S7
Williams, Bruce H.	SR74-76	Georgetown	S	B	1832	SC	Plasterer	{ Minister (AME)	{ High School	–	–	S1,S12
Williamson, Thomas M.	CC	Abbeville	F	–	1831	SC	–	Teacher	Common	–	–	P15,S3
Wilson, James Clement	SR72-74	Sumter	S	B	1844	SC	Fieldhand	Teacher	Common	0	0	{ P2,P8,P9, S1
Wimbush, Lucius W.	SS68-72	Chester	(S)	M	1838	SC	–	Grog Seller	Literate	1,300	200	P2,S12
Wingo, Coy	CC	Spartanburg	S	–	–	–	–	–	Literate	–	–	S3
Wright, John B.	SR68-70	Charleston	F	B	1814	SC	–	Tailor	Literate	840	105	P2,P10,P22
Wright, Jonathan J.	CC SS68-70 SJ70-77	Beaufort	F	B	1840	PA	Teacher	{ Lawyer Teacher	{ Lancaster University	–	–	{ P10,S3,S10, S12
Wright, Smart	SR74-76	Charleston	–	–	–	SC	–	–	–	–	–	P28
Young, James M.	SR72-76	Laurens	(S)	B	1832	SC	–	Farm T.	Literate	0	150	P2,S1
Young, Prince	SR72-74	Chester	(S)	B	1825	SC	–	Laborer	Illiterate	0	100	P2

Appendix B

Notes on Roll Call Analysis Methods

The purpose of this appendix is to provide the kind of documentation not normally found in historical studies and which is probably of little interest to the general reader, but which students more technically inclined might find necessary to evaluate this study. Since there is sufficient material on the theory and general practice of scale analysis, it should not be necessary to repeat it here, except for a brief note to orient the reader to the method. (See specific references in the text.) Therefore, this addendum will be confined to a discussion of the specific programs and procedures used in this particular study which might assist replication of the results as well as a critical examination of the work.

Theoretical Concepts. Scale analysis was originally developed by Louis Guttman for application to sociological research, specifically to attitude questionnaires. Its purpose is to resolve the problem encountered in trying to determine if a given set of survey questions really measures a given attitude or predisposition, such as racism, social welfare, etc. If the questions are all related to a common dimension, then they can be used to construct a scale with which to measure the degree to which respondents to the questionnaire have such attitudes or predispositions. For example, one might administer a questionnaire with the following items on racial attitudes.

(1) Would you ride a bus with black people?
(2) Would you attend school with black people?
(3) Would you live next door to black people?
(4) Would you marry a black person?

These questions all tap a common dimension—attitude toward black people—and the responses should form a pattern. One would normally expect a person who responded "yes" to item number four to answer all of the preceding questions affirmatively as well. This is because the scale is cumulative—i.e., each question is more "difficult" to answer affirmatively in that it implies a greater intimacy than the preceding one or ones. Therefore there are five ideal response patterns that individuals might have to these four questions.

(1) no no no no
(2) yes no no no
(3) yes yes no no
(4) yes yes yes no
(5) yes yes yes yes

Since these response patterns are also cumulative in that the first shows the greatest racial animosity and the last shows the least, it is possible to completely describe an individual's response pattern by its position on the scale. This "score" can then be correlated with other factors, attitudes, or personal attributes.

Specific Methods of Analysis. Obviously, the application of scaling techniques to legislative roll calls is a bit more complex than the example cited above. First, the items to include in the scale have to be selected and empirically tested to see if they are related. Although these items can be statistically unidimensional in the sense that the legislators' responses to them have a strong correlation, the common dimension that they share may not be obvious in a substantive sense. For example, roll calls on tariffs, social welfare, and legislative elections may all fall on the same scale because the members voting on these issues were aligned in the same or similar patterns, but their attitudes on these issues need not be similar.

Therefore, in the application of scale analysis to roll call voting, one is more concerned with how the legislators are related to each other (that is, how they are aligned) on a set of generically related roll calls. In this particular application all the roll calls and all the legislators in a given session were subjected to an exploratory analysis using two Fortran computer programs developed by John McCarthy in his study of Congress during Reconstruction. The first program (SCALE) constructs scales of the roll calls, while the second (SCORE) ranks the members along these scales. The roll calls were then divided into three broad categories according to apparent content—economic, political, and social—and subjected to a second analysis using these two programs. The exploratory step was necessary because the title of a bill or motion does not always describe its content. For instance, the fact that the repeal of the Airlines Railroad charter in 1869-70 was actually a civil rights issue and not an economic one was not apparent until it repeatedly scaled with other civil rights roll calls, rather than with other railroad legislation. Likewise, some seemingly simple procedural questions were shown to have a common underlying dimension when they scaled with substantive issues. Therefore, the results of the exploratory scaling assisted in the identification of roll calls to be included in the three broad content categories.

Scales will generally have response patterns that do not fit any of the ideal patterns in that scale. These are considered "errors" or non-pattern votes. The preliminary scales produced by the analysis described above were "pruned" to eliminate as many non-pattern votes as possible without altering the basic character or substantive content of the scale. This pruning is achieved by first manipulating several parameters in the computer programs. For instance, in this analysis all legislators who were absent on more than half of the roll calls in a given scale were not scored and thus not included in the subsequent analysis. The number of non-pattern votes that are attributable to each roll call in a scale is provided in the SCORE printout. Those roll calls causing the largest number of errors or non-pattern votes were eliminated. A coefficient of reproducibility— the ratio of the difference between the number of votes and the number of errors, to the number of votes—of 0.90 was used as the minimum standard for each scale. The mathematical properties of the reproducibility coefficient are somewhat suspect because it tends to be inflated where the roll calls have lopsided margins, that is, large majority votes. Therefore, as a further check, a coefficient of scalability was also calculated; these values ranged between 0.52 and 0.95. (The scalability coefficient is the difference between the number of errors expected by chance and the number of errors, divided by the number of errors expected by chance. See G. David Garson, *Handbook of Political Science Methods* [Boston: Holbrook Press, 1971], p. 124.) Given the overwhelming Republican preponderance in the South Carolina legislature, the values for the coefficient of scalability are generally acceptable. The coefficients for each scale are reported in Table 6.

Roll calls that were simply repetitions of others in a given scale were eliminated. (For example, several roll calls resulting from a filibuster on the Greenville Railroad Bill in the 1870-71 session were eliminated.) Out of the 511 roll calls in the three legislative sessions studied here, 51 are included in the final six scales used in this study. (See Table 6.)

It should be clear, therefore, that a scale is simply a construct; the analyst is shaping a yardstick with which to measure attitudes and/or behavior.

Explaining the Scales. The scales alone provide a great deal of information on how the South Carolina representatives were aligned on legislation. The major purpose here, however, was to see how certain subgroups among the Negro legislators reacted to the political questions of their time. Therefore the Negro members' scores were correlated with other information on these individuals. But first the scores produced by the computer program (SCORE) were transformed into percentile scores. The percentile score used here was calculated by taking the total persons listed on a scale (Negro and white) and calculating the cumulative percentage falling in each block; this percentile score is then assigned to each member of that bloc. This procedure was used because the original score shows the position of the legislators relative to the items in the scale, that is, in the bloc of voters as defined by these items regardless of the size of the bloc. Each legislator's score will vary therefore with the number of items in the scale, which is always to some degree arbitrary. Under these circumstances it is impossible to compare one scale with another, because the substantive significance of a position on one scale may not be the same as a similar spot on another scale. Therefore, in this study the scores of the members have been calculated to show a legislator's position relative to other members voting on that scale. The score indicates whether a member was among, for example, the upper 50 or 30 percent or the lower 50 or 30 percent of those scored on a scale regardless of the number of items or their content. When one compares scores, the comparison is not of a member's position on the issues per se, but of his position on the issues *relative to the other members voting.* This particular interpretation is congruent with the definition of radical-ism-conservatism presented in the sixth chapter.

The percentile scores of the legislators are then correlated with other variables to see which had the strongest relationship and, inferentially, may have had the

TABLE 6. SCALES FOR THREE LEGISLATIVE SESSIONS, 1868-71

Motion Maker	Motion	Yeas-Nays	How lower coalition voted

SCALE 1: FINANCIAL POLICY, 1868 SPECIAL SESSION

Tomlinson	—Bill to authorize loan to redeem state debts	95-12	yea
Tomlinson	—Bill to authorize state to pay interest on debts	94-12	yea
Ransier	—Bill to authorize $125,000 loan for state	91-8	yea
Neagle	—Bill to close S.C. Bank—final passage	66-23	yea
Moore	—Indefinitely postpone motion to strike sec. 4, bill to close S.C. Bank	64-27	yea
Neagle	—Bill to close S.C. Bank to 3rd reading	55-32	yea
Neagle	—Sec. 2 of bill to close S.C. Bank	56-35	yea
Elliott	—Motion postpone resolution for financial inquiry into S.C. Bank	29-39	yea

Subjects Scored = 105   Coefficient of Reproducibility = 0.99
No. of Errors = 10   Coefficient of Scalability = 0.86

SCALE 2: REPUBLICAN HEGEMONY, 1868 SPECIAL SESSION

Tomlinson	—Ratify 14th Amendment to U.S. Constitution	108-12	yea
C. Hayne	—Motion to indefinitely postpone amendment to sec. 12 of Elections bill	78-11	yea
Feriter	—Amend sec. 1 of state militia bill	15-79	nay
Crews	—Bill to tax Kershaw Co. to support Dill's widow	66-21	yea
R. Smith	—Motion to strike sec. 12 of Elections bill	26-65	nay
Whipper	—Bill to extend time for county officers to qualify for offices	45-23	yea
Feriter	—Postpone bill to establish office of county prosecutor	31-42	nay
Jenks	—Override governor's veto of bill altering Charleston charter	41-43	yea

Subjects Scored = 114   Coefficient of Reproducibility = 0.97
No. of Errors = 30   Coefficient of Scalability = 0.62

SCALE 3: FINANCIAL POLICY, 1869-70

Senate	—Sinking Fund bill	85-12	yea
Senate	—Sec. 5 Wilmington & Carolina RR	67-8	yea
Senate	—Bill to regulate rights and powers of railroads	67-12	yea
De Large	—Indefinitely postpone motion postpone Wilmington & Carolina RR bill	58-11	yea
Committee	—Override governor's veto of Phosphates bill	77-24	yea
De Large	—Wilmington & Carolina RR bill	62-16	yea
Committee	—Wilmington & Carolina RR bill to 3rd reading	57-14	yea

TABLE 6. SCALES FOR THREE LEGISLATIVE SESSIONS, 1868-71

Motion Maker	Motion	Yeas-Nays	How lower coalition voted
Committee—Bill to redeem state bonds in gold coin		66-26	yea
De Large —Table motion to reconsider sec. 1 Gold Coin bill		67-30	yea
Committee—Sec. 1 Gold Coin bill to 3rd reading		61-32	yea
De Large —Previous question on Gold Coin bill		66-37	yea
De Large —Indefinitely postpone amendment to sec. 1 Gold Coin bill		59-37	yea

Subjects Scored = 103   Coefficient of Reproducibility = 0.96
No. of Errors = 47   Coefficient of Scalability = 0.52

SCALE 4: CIVIL RIGHTS, 1869-70

Committee—Bill to enforce U.S. Civil Rights Act		81-8	yea
Hyde —Postpone bill repealing charter of Airline RR		21-54	nay
Committee—Bill repealing charter of Airline RR to 3rd reading		48-23	yea
Senate —Repeal charter of Airline RR		42-53	yea

Subjects Scored = 99   Coefficient of Reproducibility = 0.99
No. of Errors = 2   Coefficient of Scalability = 0.95

SCALE 5: REPUBLICAN HEGEMONY, 1870-71

Crews —Resolution to impeach Judge Vernon		93-19	yea
Lee —Adopt articles of impeachment of Judge Vernon		84-14	yea
Whipper —Previous question, resolution to seat Littlefield and Singleton		63-9	yea
Crews —Resolution ordering Judge Vernon to answer charges of contempt		78-27	yea
Frost —Table resolution instructing congressional delegation to vote No on U.S. General Amnesty bill		28-69	nay
Whipper —Resolution to unseat Evans and Hough		53-25	yea
Jones —Resolution to postpone bill declaring martial law in up-country		17-56	yea
Crews —Strike enacting clause of martial law bill		70-16	nay
Mobley —Indefinitely postpone motion to strike enacting clause of martial law bill		12-70	yea

Subjects Scored = 103   Coefficient of Reproducibility = 0.98
No. of Errors = 21   Coefficient of Scalability = 0.58

SCALE 6: FINANCIAL POLICY, 1870-71

Senate —Concur bill consolidating Greenville & Columbia RR		79-20	yea

TABLE 6. SCALES FOR THREE LEGISLATIVE SESSIONS, 1868-71

Motion Maker	Motion	Yeas-Nays	How lower coalition voted
Committee—Sterling fund debt bill—Final passage		83-24	yea
Committee—Previous question Greenville RR bill		69-33	yea
Committee—Previous question sec. 12 Greenville RR		68-33	yea
Committee—Greenville RR bill to 3rd reading		66-35	yea
Committee—Sec. 5 Greenville RR to 3rd reading		60-30	yea
Myers	—Substitute amendment to sterling fund debt bill	52-47	yea
Jervay	—Table motion to postpone resolution to furnish State House	76-10	nay
Jervay	—Table reconsideration of resolution to furnish State House	77-7	nay
Levy	—Resolution for special committee to investigate expenses in furnishing State House	78-7	nay

Subjects Scored = 111
No. of Errors = 22

Coefficient of Reproducibility = 0.98
Coefficient of Scalability = 0.78

greatest influence in determining a member's voting pattern. Since some of the variables of interest, color, origins, and leadership role are nominal-level data and the percentile rank is only ordinal, a nominal-level statistic must be used. There were difficulties in applying some of the chi-square based statistics (such as phi) to this data, because many of the expected cell frequencies were too low. Therefore, lambda-b was chosen because it provides a proportional reduction in error interpretation (PRE) and requires no prior assumptions about the data. The PRE interpretation means that if a lambda value of 0.50 were obtained, then one could say that 50 percent of the errors made in predicting the value of the independent variable can be avoided if the value of the dependent variable is known. This feature is congruent with the approach taken in the sixth chapter. For example, a legislative lobbyist trying to improve his chances of predicting a member's behavior might make a similar analysis. The more information he had, the better he could determine the odds for a given voting alignment. He could never *predict* in the sense of determining a sure thing, but his information would give him something more than a blind guess. Such an analogy is more consistent with the complexity of human political behavior than classifying relationships as strong or weak as measured against an unattainable 100 percent reduction in error or some other arbitrary figure. In truth, the statistics of these relationships only make sense when the variables of interest are being compared with each other and not by trying to account for all the variability of the independent variable.

However, lambda does have the disadvantage of sometimes underestimating a relationship when one of the marginal values is extremely high, as is the case

TABLE 7. CORRELATION OF VOTING BEHAVIOR WITH STATUS AND ROLE ATTRIBUTES (Lambda-b)

Scales	Prewar origins	Color	Wealth	1870 Election margin	Leadership role	Prewar origins and color	Prewar origins and color controlling for wealth	
							Below median wealth	Above median wealth
Republican Hegemony 1868	0	0	0	0	0	0	0	0
Republican Hegemony 1870-71	0.05	0.08	0	0	0	0.16	0.40	0.27
Financial Policy 1868	0	0	0	0	0	0.04	0	0.06
Financial Policy 1869-70	0	0	0	0	0	0	0.33	0
Financial Policy 1870-71	0	0	0	0	0	0.05	0	0.17
Civil Rights 1869-70	0	0	0	0	0	0	0.20	0.10

with the data here. In the present study, however, a deliberate choice was made to favor a Type I error rather than a Type II error: the nature of the data is such that I prefer to miss a statistical relationship that is actually present than to find a relationship that is specious.

The preliminary findings of this analysis are presented in Table 7. First, knowledge of a member's wealth, election margin, or leadership role alone would not assist one in predicting his voting behavior. Similarly, knowledge of a member's origins (free or slave) or color (black or mulatto) would assist in predicting that member's voting behavior on only one of the six scales (Republican Hegemony 1870-71). However, when origins *and* color are combined and treated as one value (that is, freeborn mulatto, mulatto ex-slave, freeborn black, and black ex-slave), their usefulness as predictors is improved in two additional scales (Financial Policy 1868 and 1870-71). Furthermore, knowledge of origins and color, controlling for wealth, dramatically improves one's ability to accurately predict voting behavior and increases the number of instances in which prediction is possible. For example, if one knows a legislator's origins and color *and* the value of his property, then 40 percent and 27 percent of the errors in predicting his voting position on the Republican hegemony issue in 1870-71 can be eliminated, according to which property-holding class he falls into. Likewise, given data on property status, 33 and 17 percent of the errors in assigning him to the correct voting bloc on financial policy issues in 1869-70 and in 1870-71, respectively, can be eliminated as well. Similar effects are evident in the civil rights scale.

These findings suggested that origins, color, and wealth are interrelated and may well define a single dimension. We can make more efficient use of this data to refine our concept of socioeconomic status beyond the rough dichotomous categories—slave-free, black-mulatto, and poor-affluent. In the contemporaneous hierarchy of social attributes, the evidence shows that free was considered better than slave, mulatto better than black, and, of course, well-to-do better than poor. Given these hierarchies, it is possible to place freeborn mulatto property-holders on the top rung of the intraracial status hierarchy and poor, black ex-slaves on the bottom. We can rank an individual with respect to social status according to the degree to which he possessed the favored attributes. A scale is constructed by assigning the values one and two, respectively, to black-mulatto, slave-free, and poor-affluent; the scale scores range from a maximum of 6 for affluent freeborn mulattoes to a minimum of 3 for poor black ex-slaves. Those members for whom data are missing in any one of the three categories are deleted. This rank-ordering of the members by socioeconomic status can be correlated in turn with their voting behavior. Since the data are now at the ordinal level, Kendall's tau-b can be used rather than lambda-b; also tau shows the positive or negative direction of a relationship.

The results presented in Table 4 in the text show that the relationships varied from weak to moderate, but that they were inverse in all but one case. This means that the higher the socioeconomic status of a member, the more likely he was to vote conservatively and vice versa. Although rather weakly manifested, the pattern with civil rights legislation was just the opposite, with high-status members slightly more likely to take a radical position than those of lower status.

Table 4 also indicates that, despite the fact that they were not useful predictors of voting behavior by themselves, the members' leadership positions and the political situations in their home districts suppressed or obscured the relationship between status and voting behavior. The tendency for Negro legislators of high socioeconomic status to vote conservatively is consistently stronger among the leadership than among ordinary members, and—with one exception—among those from safe election districts as opposed to those from close districts. It appears that the leadership roles of the members tended not to mitigate, but to accentuate their inclinations to vote according to socioeconomic status. Indeed, in three instances (Republican Hegemony 1868 and 1870-71 and Financial Policy 1870-71) members of high social status tended to vote with the radicals, while leaders displayed the opposite pattern. Undoubtedly, this is correlated with the higher proportion of free mulattoes among the leaders than among the members. Meanwhile, the election margin of a representative did appear in two instances (Financial Policy 1868 and 1869-70) to suppress, and in one instance (Republican Hegemony 1868) to distort, the tendency for radical voting behavior to be associated negatively with status. In most cases, conservative voting by members from close election districts was less likely to reflect high social status than by those members representing safe districts. Indeed, on the hegemony issue in 1868, those of low status were actually more conservative than those of high status. Not their class interest, but the uncertainties of their reelection may have dictated the legislative response of these members.

One can surmise from these statistics that the most accurate predictor of a legislator's voting behavior was his socioeconomic status, as defined by his color, antebellum origins, and financial resources. While strictly political factors such as constituency pressure and party leadership had some impact, they were only secondary effects in that they obscured the influence of social status. Generally, the relationship appears to have grown stronger with each session, suggesting a hardening of the class antagonisms as the issues were more deeply contested; however, a more extensive series of analyses would be required to substantiate this impression.

Table 8 provides a summary of the individual scale scores resulting from this analysis.

TABLE 8. SUMMARY OF ROLL CALL SCALE SCORES, 1868-71

Name	1868 Special Session		1869-70		1870-71	
	Republican Hegemony	Financial Policy	Financial Policy	Civil Rights	Republican Hegemony	Financial Policy
Adamson, Frank					NS	90
Adamson, William			39	54		
Bascomb, John B.					100	NS
Bishop, W. A.	43	29	NS	23		
Bosemon, Benjamin A.	100	36	11	100	23	21
Boston, John	100	NS	100	100		
Boston, Joseph D.	100	34	100	54	79	23
Bowley, James A.			100	100	45	33
Brodie, William J.	100	38	10	100		
Brown, Stephen	43	NS	100	100		
Bryan, Richard					NS	90
Burton, Barney	100	NS	100	NS		
Byas, Benjamin					45	90
Cain, Edward J.	100	56	33	100		
Cain, Everidge					100	52
Cain, Lawrence	51	100	100	23	89	90
Chestnut, John A.	100	56	100	NS		
Cooke, Wilson	43	56	100	23		
Dannerly, William					79	90
Davis, James					79	90
Davis, Thomas A.					24	90
De Large, Robert C.	21	100	100	100		
Driffle, William	100	29	100	100		
Elliott, Robert B.	100	100	100	100		
Elliott, William E.					NS	52
Ellison, Henry H.					90	52
Ezekiel, Phillip E.	43	100	100	54		
Farr, Simeon	51	100	100	54	100	52
Ferguson, Edward					79	100
Ford, Adam P.					79	52
Frost, Florian Henry					31	21
Gaither, Reuben D.					79	90
Gantt, Hastings					79	90

Name	1868 Special Session		1869-70		1870-71	
	Republican Hegemony	Financial Policy	Financial Policy	Civil Rights	Republican Hegemony	Financial Policy
Gardner, John	100	100	39	100		
Gardner, William H.					89	100
Gary, Stephen					79	NS
Giles, Fortune					79	23
Glover, William C.					NS	NS
Goggins, Mitchell					45	52
Goodson, Aesop	100	56	100	NS	NS	90
Grant, John G.	43	29	39	54		
Gray, William H. W.	100	100	100	100		
Green, John					79	90
Greene, Samuel					79	32
Hardy, James J.					89	52
Harris, David	100	100	100	23	NS	90
Hart, Alfred					79	52
Hayes, Eben	43	100	100	54		
Hayne, Charles D.	100	56	100	100	79	32
Hayne, James N.	100	34	100	100	NS	32
Hedges, Plato P.					NS	90
Henderson, James A.	100	56	100	54		
Henderson, John T.					100	90
Holland, Gloster H.					NS	NS
Holmes, Abraham P.					NS	21
Hudson, Allen					79	90
Humbert, Richard H.					79	52
Humphries, Barney	100	38	39	100	79	90
Hunter, Hezekiah H.					45	90
Hutson, James	100	100	100	54		
Jacobs, Henry	100	56	30	100		
James, Burrell	43	56	30	54		
Jamison, James L.					89	90
Jervay, William R.	100	34	100	100	45	34
Johnson, D. J. J.	43	56	30	100		
Johnson, Griffin C.	100	100	100	100	45	90
Johnson, Henry	100	100	100	NS		
Johnson, Samuel	100	100	100	100		
Johnston, William E.	51	100				
Jones, William H.	43	100	100	100	100	100
Keith, Samuel J.					45	52
Lang, Jordan	43	100	100	100	45	NS
Lee, George H.	100	100	100	100		
Lee, Samuel J.	100	100	100	23	89	90
Lloyd, Joseph W.					NS	52
Logan, Aaron					100	NS
Lomax, Hutson J.	43	NS				
Mayer, Julius	100	34	31	NS		
Mays, James P.	43	56	100	NS		

Name	1868 Special Session		1869-70		1870-71	
	Republican Hegemony	Financial Policy	Financial Policy	Civil Rights	Republican Hegemony	Financial Policy
McDaniels, Harry	100	100	100	54	45	90
McDowell, Thomas D.					31	92
McKinlay, William	100	29	10	100		
McKinlay, William J.	100	29				
Meade, John W.	16	100	39	100	31	90
Mickey, Edward C.	100	100	100	100	79	90
Milton, Syphax					45	32
Mobley, Junius S.	51	100	100	100	45	90
Moore, Alfred M.					NS	90
Morrison, William C.			100	54		
Myers, Nathaniel B.					31	32
Nash, Jonas W.	100	56				
Nelson, William	100	NS				
Nuckles, Samuel	100	100	100	100	100	NS
Pendergrass, Jeffrey	51	100	100	100	89	52
Perrin, Wade	100	100	100	100		
Purvis, Henry W.	21	56	30	100		
Ramsey, Warren W.			100	100	45	90
Ransier, Alonzo J.	100	58	NS	100		
Richardson, Thomas	43	NS	100	54		
Rivers, Prince R.	100	100	100	NS	89	100
Rush, Alfred	NS	100	100	100		
Sasportas, Thaddeus K.	100	29	30	100		
Saunders, Sancho	51	100	100	54	79	90
Scott, Robert F.	43	100	100	54		
Shrewsbury, Henry	46	29	10	100		
Simons, William	43	36	100	24	79	90
Singleton, Asbury L.					89	93
Singleton, J. P.					NS	90
Smalls, Robert	100	100	100	54		
Smalls, Sherman					100	32
Smiling, James E.	NS	58	30	54		
Smith, Abraham W.	100	100	100	100	31	90
Smythe, Powell	100	100	39	100		
Tarlton, Robert					79	90
Thomas, John W.					79	52
Thomas, William M.	43	100	NS	100	NS	90
Thompson, Benjamin A.	100	100	100	100		
Thompson, Samuel B.	100	100	NS	NS	NS	90
Valentine, Richard M.	13	9				
Wallace, John					79	52
Warley, Jared D.					79	23
Whipper, William James	100	100	100	54	100	32
White, John H.	100	100	100	100	79	52
Wilder, Charles M.	43	56	33	54		
Wright, John B.	100	34	16	NS		

Bibliographical Essay

Manuscripts

Source materials on the lives and careers of Negro political leaders during Reconstruction are exceedingly scarce—so scarce, in fact, that biographical studies that
measure up to normal scholarly standards are difficult to find in most cases
and impossible in others. More often than not the effort to trace a manuscript
"collection" bearing the name of a prominent Negro leader will not be rewarded.
Such is the case with the Joseph H. Rainey MSS in the South Caroliniana
Library at the University of South Carolina in Columbia; aside from a brief
biographical sketch, there are only three letters of no particular significance.
The results are similar with the Leigh Whipper Papers in the Moorland Collection
at Howard University in Washington, D.C. The bulk of the materials here relate
to Leigh's theatrical career, with a few scattered legal papers from the tenure
of his father, William James Whipper, as a lawyer and probate judge in Beaufort.
There is also a biographical sketch of the elder Whipper, but it adds little to
the extant contemporary sources.

The problem confronted in this study was to discover other sources of biographical data and to apply new methods to this data in order to reconstruct
the lives and careers of these men. The research strategy involved an exhaustive
search of numerous extant lists of individuals containing biographical data,
collating and cross-checking this data for errors, and finally applying various
computer routines to develop profiles of these leaders.

The sources of biographical data used in this study are diverse and numerous,
but a few were particularly helpful and may prove so for others. The most
voluminous information came from the federal manuscript population censuses
for 1860, 1870, and 1880, which are on microfilm at the National Archives in
Washington, D.C. The population census is not very reliable for property-holding
information, however, and it should be supplemented with the manuscript censuses of agriculture, which are in manuscript form in the South Carolina Department of Archives and History. County records are an excellent source for biographical and property data, but unfortunately they are less accessible. The
Charleston county auditor's and treasurer's tax duplicates for the period 1868
to 1877 are available and maintained in good condition at the County Auditor's
Office. Lacking the financial resources or time to search out similar records in
the thirty other South Carolina counties, I had to be content with the microfilmed

records of three, Fairfield (1882), Laurens (1868, 1870, 1872), and Lexington (1868), which are at the South Carolina Archives. Also in those archives are the Registers of Free Negroes (also called the Free Negro Book) for the city of Charleston. As a measure of control and for purposes of levying a special head tax, free Negro adults were required to register annually. The registers for 1816, 1819, 1823, 1824, 1833, and 1851 were found in the South Carolina Archives and those for 1828, 1851, 1855, 1857, and 1858 are in the South Caroliniana Library. Also in the latter are the Registers of Students at the University of South Carolina, 1867-73.

Some of the most fruitful sources of biographical data were found not in South Carolina, but in the National Archives in Washington. The Compiled Military Service Records for the U.S. Colored Troops, Records of the Adjutant General's Office, Record Group 94, and the Civil War Pension Files, Records of the Veterans Administration, Record Group 15, were excellent sources for those legislators who served in the army or navy. There are microfilm indexes available for each of these record groups. The recently microfilmed Registers of Signatures of Depositors in the Branches of the Freedman's Savings and Trust Company, 1865-74, Records of the Office of the Comptroller of the Currency, Record Group 101, provided very useful, though sometimes spotty, information. This record contains the signatures and personal identification data of depositors in branch offices of the Freedman's Bank immediately after the war. Most of the depositor cards include age, residence, complexion, name of employer or occupation, names of family members, and signatures. Early records occasionally included the name of the former slave master. There is one roll of microfilm for Beaufort and three for Charleston arranged chronologically by the date the account was opened. There is now an index to the accounts which was not available for this study. Another useful source of biographical and political data in the National Archives are the various patronage files of federal agencies. The ones that proved most useful for this study were the Nominations Files and Collector of Customs Applications, Records of the Bureau of Customs, Record Group 56. Surprisingly, the Records of the Bureau of Refugees, Freedmen, and Abandoned Lands, Record Group 105, were not very helpful in collecting biographical information, but materials in the letter-press books for the Assistant Commissioner for South Carolina did help reconstruct the activities of the Negro Bureau agents.

The Amistad Research Center in New Orleans has microfilmed the records of the American Missionary Association Archives; these proved invaluable for commentary on local conditions, race relations, and the interrelationships of missionaries with freedmen and with each other, especially in the immediate postwar period. The papers of the Reconstruction governors of South Carolina are well organized but disappointing insofar as any candid discussion of political events or decisions is concerned. It is possible to reconstruct political alignments through the correspondence dealing with patronage, however. These papers are voluminous, with twenty-six boxes of the Governor Robert K. Scott Papers and twenty boxes of the Governor Daniel H. Chamberlain Papers. Other manuscript collections that proved useful were the Thaddeus Stevens Papers, volumes 5-12, and the William E. Chandler Papers, volumes 4-10, both at the Library of

Congress. The papers of the editor of the *News and Courier,* Francis W. Dawson, in the Perkins Library at Duke University, Durham, North Carolina, and the Martha Schofield Diary in the Southern Historical Collection at the University of North Carolina, Chapel Hill, were also useful. Some of the diverse sources that provided interesting perspectives on Reconstruction politics were the Fisk P. Brewer Papers at the South Caroliniana Library, and a handwritten manuscript in the South Carolina Historical Society in Charleston, of a speech entitled "History of the Administration of D. H. Chamberlain, the Last Radical Governor of South Carolina," read before the Society by F. A. Porcher, its president from 1875 to 1888.

Public Documents

Of course, the *Journals* of the House and Senate have been essential to the roll call analysis included in this study, and the *Acts and Resolutions of the General Assembly* were used to reconstruct the legislative histories of selected laws. Other public documents that were useful were: *Proceedings of the Constitutional Convention of South Carolina* (Charleston: Denny and Perry, 1868); U.S. Congress, *Testimony Taken by the Joint Select Committee to Inquire into the Condition of Affairs in the Late Insurrectionary States,* Volume I: South Carolina (Washington: Government Printing Office, 1872); *Evidence Taken by the Committee of Investigation of the Third Congressional District, Under Authority of the General Assembly of the State of South Carolina, Regular Session, 1868-1869* (Columbia: John W. Denny, 1870); *Report of the Joint Investigating Committee on Public Frauds and the Election of Hon. John J. Patterson to the United States Senate* (Columbia: Calvo & Patton, 1878). Information on Negro congressmen was easily accessible in the *Biographical Directory of the U.S. Congress* (Washington: Government Printing Office, 1971).

Newspapers

There were numerous Republican newspapers in South Carolina during Reconstruction, but they were short-lived and few copies survive. However, a rather full series of the *Daily Republican* (Charleston) and the *Union-Herald* (Columbia) are available at the Library of Congress. These dailies provide a useful counterweight to the Democratic press, but unfortunately they were not available in the formative years of the Republican party. Coming later in the period when cliques and factions had fully developed, they tended to represent various factional interests. Thus one should note that these papers are biased in more subtle and potentially more dangerous ways than the Democratic papers. A few extant Republican local weeklies help balance the perspectives of the metropolitan dailies. The *Aiken Tribune* (1875), *Walterboro News* (1873-75), *Beaufort Tribune* (1874-76), and *Beaufort Republican* (1871-73) all provide useful perspectives on state politics and often more accurate biographical information on local politicians than the Charleston and Columbia papers. The extant issues of the *Charleston Advocate* (1867), Charleston *Free Press* (1865), and *Missionary Record* (1873) were too scattered and incomplete to be very useful in this study. The Charleston *Daily Courier* (1864-73) and Charleston *News and Courier* (1873-1877) were Democratic papers, but key sources of information on daily political and social activities nevertheless. Various local Democratic weeklies, such as the *Edgefield Advertiser* (1867-72), *Chester Reporter* (1870-72), and *Greenville Enterprise* (1871-76) were helpful in ways similar to their Republican counterparts. The *Columbia Register* (1875-76) pursued a more militant editorial policy than Dawson's *News and Courier,* and thus provided an interesting contrast.

Published Contemporary Accounts

John W. De Forest was unusually sensitive and observant for a Bureau officer and provides a number of insights into the racial and intraracial relations in the South Carolina up-country in his memoir, *A Union Officer in the Reconstruction,* ed. James Croushore and David Potter (New Haven: Yale University Press, 1948). Useful in similar ways is Laura Towne's *Letters and Diary of Laura M. Towne, Written from the Sea Islands of South Carolina, 1862-84,* ed. Rupert Sargent Holland (Cambridge: Riverside Press, 1912). Alrutheus Ambush Taylor uncovered some years ago the perceptive commentary of a South Carolina native, Belton O'Neal Townsend, in three articles appearing in the *Atlantic Monthly:* "The Political Condition of South Carolina" (February, 1877), 177-94; "South Carolina Morals" (April, 1877), 467-75; and "South Carolina Society" (June, 1877), 670-84. In a very different way the post-Reconstruction perspective of ex-Governor Daniel H. Chamberlain in "Reconstruction in South Carolina," *Atlantic Monthly,* LXXXV (April, 1901), 473-84, is extremely revealing. Several sources contributed biographical data as well as an understanding of the religious proselytizing during the period. Daniel A. Payne's *Recollection of Seventy Years,* reprint ed. (New York: Arno Press, 1968) and William Henry Heard's *From Slavery to the Bishopric of the A.M.E.* (Philadelphia: A.M.E. Book Concern, 1924) were useful in that regard. The published minutes and journals of the Methodist Church, North, also provided some biographical data.

Unpublished Theses and Dissertations

John L. McCarthy's "Reconstruction Legislation and Voting Aligments in the House of Representatives, 1863-69" (Ph.D. dissertation, Yale University, 1970), helped me refine methodological approaches and techniques. The most up-to-date study of free Negroes in South Carolina is Ivy Marina Wikramanayake's "The Free Negro in Ante-Bellum South Carolina" (Ph.D. dissertation, University of Wisconsin, 1966); this work was subsequently published under the title *World in Shadow* (Columbia: University of South Carolina Press, 1974). The South Carolina Historical Association has a typescript entitled "The Brown Fellowship Society," written by G. H. Walker as a WPA project during the 1930's. The essay quotes extensively from the Brown Society's minute books. Several master's theses undertaken at the University of South Carolina provided helpful information on special topics. There were two on Reconstruction: William H. Shirley, Jr., "A Black Republican Congressman during the Democratic Resurgence in South Carolina: Robert Smalls, 1876-82" (1970), and Julian L. Mims, "Radical Reconstruction in Edgefield County, 1868-77" (1969). Several theses have been done on black religious conversion in South Carolina: Nancy Vance Ashmore, "The Development of the African Methodist Episcopal Church in South Carolina,

1865-1965" (1969); Septima Chappell Smith, "The Development and History of Some Negro Churches in South Carolina" (1942); Susan Markey Fickling, "The Christianization of the Negro in South Carolina, 1830-60" (1923); and Annie Hughes Mallard, "Religious Work of South Carolina Baptists from 1781 to 1830" (1912). Two undergraduate essays were useful in the initial stages of this project: Winthrop Brown Conrad, Jr., "Rehearsal for Redemption" (Senior thesis, Yale University, 1967); and Michael N. Rosen, "Negro Reconstruction Office Holders: Their Backgrounds and Beliefs" (Senior thesis, Princeton University, 1962).

General Works

As with the Reconstruction histories of most states, many of the authoritative works written before 1960 are marred by a generally racist or paternalistic outlook. In this category one might include: John P. Hollis, *The Early Period of Reconstruction in South Carolina* (Baltimore: Johns Hopkins Press, 1905); John S. Reynolds, *Reconstruction in South Carolina, 1865-77* (Columbia: State Printing Company, 1905); and Francis B. Simkins and Robert H. Woody, *South Carolina During Reconstruction* (Chapel Hill: University of North Carolina Press, 1932). Alrutheus Ambush Taylor's *The Negro in South Carolina During the Reconstruction* (Washington: Association for the Study of Negro Life and History, 1924) provides a corrective for these works to some extent. But the definitive work on the social and economic adjustments of the freedmen after slavery is Joel Williamson's *After Slavery: The Negro in South Carolina During Reconstruction, 1861-77* (Chapel Hill: University of North Carolina Press, 1965).

A number of special studies proved extremely helpful to the present project. Carol K. Bleser made a detailed study of the land reform problem in *The Promised Land: The History of the South Carolina Land Commission, 1869-90* (Columbia: University of South Carolina Press, 1969). Martin Abbott has detailed the activities of the Bureau in South Carolina in *The Freedmen's Bureau in South Carolina, 1865-72* (Chapel Hill: University of North Carolina Press, 1967). A number of scholars have confronted the problems of writing full-length biographies of Negro legislators with creditable results. Peggy Lamson presents a very plausible interpretation of Robert B. Elliott's origins and early life in *The Glorious Failure: Black Congressman Robert Brown Elliott and the Reconstruction of South Carolina* (New York: W. W. Norton, 1973). Okon Edet Uya exhausts local materials to reconstruct the life of Robert Smalls in *From Slavery to Public Service: Robert Smalls, 1839-1915* (New York: Oxford University Press, 1971). Unfortunately, Victor Ullman's work on Delany is less useful to scholars because he fails to note the sources of his materials in *Martin R. Delany: The Beginnings of Black Nationalism* (Boston: Beacon Press, 1971). Robert H. Woody provides useful data on the only black justice on the state supreme court in "Jonathan Jasper Wright, Associate Justice of the Supreme Court of South Carolina, 1870-77," *Journal of Negro History*, XVIII (April, 1933), 114-31.

A number of special studies either have provided a beginning point for collecting biographical data or have filled critical gaps: Monroe N. Work, comp., "Some Negro Members of Reconstruction Conventions and Legislatures and Congress," *Journal of Negro History*, V (January, 1920), 63-125; Emily B. Reynolds and Joan

R. Faunt, eds., *Biographical Directory of the Senate of South Carolina, 1776-1964* (Columbia: South Carolina Archives Department, 1964); Lawrence C. Bryant, *Negro Lawmakers in the South Carolina Legislature, 1869-1902* (Orangeburg: South Carolina State College, 1968) and *Negro Senators and Representatives in the South Carolina Legislature, 1868-1902* (Orangeburg: South Carolina State College, 1968). Of the numerous "mug books," only one was useful: William J. Simmons, *Men of Mark: Eminent, Progressive, and Rising,* reprint ed. (New York: Arno Press, 1968). Two essays by E. Horace Fitchett were seminal treatments of the free mulatto class of Charleston: "The Tradition of the Free Negro in Charleston, South Carolina," *Journal of Negro History,* XXV (April, 1940), 139-52; and "The Origins and Growth of the Free Negro Population of Charleston, South Carolina," *Journal of Negro History,* XXVI (October, 1941), 421-37. Other special studies are: C. W. Birnie, "The Education of the Negro in Charleston, South Carolina, before the Civil War," *Journal of Negro History,* XII (January, 1927), 13-21; Herbert Aptheker, "South Carolina Negro Conventions, 1865," *Journal of Negro History,* XXXI (January, 1946), 91-97; and Walter Allen, *Governor Chamberlain's Administration in South Carolina, A Chapter of Reconstruction in the Southern States* (New York: G. P. Putnam's Sons, 1888).

Local histories were generally not very useful for biographical data; but material on black politicians was found in George C. Rogers's *The History of Georgetown County, South Carolina* (Columbia: University of South Carolina Press, 1970). On the 1880's, the following works were used extensively: George Brown Tindall, *South Carolina Negroes, 1877-1900* (Columbia: University of South Carolina Press, 1952); William J. Cooper, *The Conservative Regime: South Carolina, 1877-1890* (Baltimore: Johns Hopkins Press, 1968); and James Welch Patton, "The Republican Party in South Carolina, 1876-95," in *Studies in History,* ed. Fletcher M. Green (Chapel Hill: University of North Carolina Press, 1949). Daniel Augustus Straker, a minor Negro politician, provides a first-hand commentary on the Republican party in the 1880's in *The New South Investigated* (Detroit: Ferguson, 1888).

Two general works which have particular relevance to South Carolina are the excellent treatment of the Bureau by William S. McFeely in *Yankee Stepfather: General O. O. Howard and the Freedmen* (New Haven: Yale University Press, 1968); and the provocative thesis of W. E. B. Du Bois in *Black Reconstruction: An Essay toward a History of the Part Which Black Folk Played in the Attempt to Reconstruct Democracy in America, 1860-80* (New York: Harcourt Brace, 1935). Ira Berlin's excellent *Slaves Without Masters: The Free Negro in the Antebellum South* (New York: Pantheon, 1974) was published too late for use in all but the final stage of the preparation of this manuscript, but his interpretations do not deviate materially from my own.

The comparative perspective on the social and political patterns in post-emancipation societies that is reflected in this work was inspired most by Philip D. Curtin's *Two Jamaicas: The Role of Ideas in a Tropical Colony, 1830-65* (Cambridge; Harvard University Press, 1955). Other works that confirm Curtin's findings and provide additional insights are: Anton V. Long, *Jamaica and the New Order, 1827-47* (Mona: Institute of Social and Economic Research, University College of the West Indies, Jamaica, B.W.I., Special Series No. 1, November, 1956);

M. G. Smith, *The Plural Society in the British West Indies* (Berkeley: University of California Press, 1965); Charles H. Wesley, "The Emancipation of the Free Colored Population in the British Empire," *Journal of Negro History,* XIX (January, 1934), 137-170; and Graham Knox, "British Colonial Policy and the Problems of Establishing a Free Society in Jamaica, 1838-65," *Caribbean Studies,* II (January, 1963), 3-13. Detailed studies of the economic changes after emancipation are found in Hugh Paget, "The Free Village System in Jamaica," *Caribbean Quarterly,* X (March, 1964), 38-51; Douglas Hall, *Free Jamaica, 1838-1865: An Economic History* (New Haven: Yale University Press, 1959); and Gisela Eisner, *Jamaica, 1830-1930, A Study in Economic Growth* (Manchester: Manchester University Press, 1961). Useful for background on race relations in Jamaican slave society was Orlando Patterson's *The Sociology of Slavery* (London: Macgibbon Kee, 1967). The comparative approach to the problems of freedom in Western societies was only a backdrop for this study, but I believe it will be a fruitful direction for further research.

Index

Abbeville County, 69
Act for the better protection of
landowners, 169
Act providing for widows and families of
victims of political violence, repealed,
209
Adams, Doc: and Hamburg Massacre, 199
Adams, E. J., 89
Adamson, Frank, 90n, 148
Adamson, William, 90n
Adjutant general: tenure of blacks as, 97
African heritage of Negroes, 61, 62, 90n
African Methodist Episcopal Church:
Negro officeholders in, 81, 88;
competition with northern Methodists,
88; factions within, 88
Agnew, John, 204
Aiken County, 199
Airline Railroad: bill to repeal charter of,
144
Aldrich, A. P., 197
Allen, Macon B., 222
Allen, S. C., 30
Allman, Jacob C., 189n, 190
American Missionary Association: and free
Negro teachers, 70; and recruitment of
Negro politicians, 81-87; religious bias of
missionaries, 87
Anderson County, 101
Andrews, A. B., 140n
Andrews, John, 78
Andrews, William J., 189n, 190
Army, Union: restraint of freedmen by,
13, 29-30; hostility to freedmen, 30; and
recruitment of Negro politicians, 73,
76-80, 151; mentioned, 149
Ashley River, 139

Assassination of political leaders, 30, 105,
141
Attorney general: tenure of blacks as, 97
Auditor, county: tenure of blacks as, 98;
proposal to elect, 182, 190, 191

Baltimore Gazette, 201
Bampfield, Samuel J.: education, 54;
supports Whipper, 186; as fusionist,
222; mentioned, 189n
Baptist Church: Negro officeholders in, 81,
87
Baxter, A. G., 16
Beaufort County: representatives from, 15,
215; political activism of, 28, 35, 215,
220; free Negroes in, 51, 166;
mentioned, 13, 115
Beaufort, Port of, 120
Beaufort Standard, 113n
Becker, Martin F., 76n, 163n
Beckett, W. W., 215n
Berkeley County, 215
Berlin, Ira, 60n
Bethel Church, 11
Bills. *See* Legislative bills
Bird, Israel, 215n
Black Codes: prewar, 11n; effects on free
Negroes, 19-20; content of, 20; voided
by military, 23; repealed, 24; criticism
of, 24; mentioned, 25, 152
Black officeholders. *See* Negro officeholders
Blue Ridge Railroad, 143
Bonds: legislation on, 140, 148, 153
Bonneau, Thomas S., 52
Bonneau Society, 65
Bosemon, Benjamin A.: at Colored
Peoples' Convention, 16; in Brown

McKinlay, William (*continued*)
146, 149; mentioned, 112, 163
McKinlay, William J.: property, 37n, 164,
165; antebellum origins, 71; political
behavior, 149, 188-89; mentioned, 38,
112, 163n
McKinney, William, 52
Magrath, Hugh, 177
Manumission: conditions of, 45, 63n
Marion County, 184, 215
Marlboro County, 217
Martial law bill, 142-43
Martin, James: assassination, 141
Maxwell, Henry J., 29n, 74, 76n, 165, 197
Methodist Church (North): political
influence, 80-81, 87; black politicians in,
81, 88; conflict with Southern
Methodists, 87-88
Methodist Church (South), 87, 89
Mickey, Edward, 57, 163n
Militia, 144
Miller, Thomas E., 54, 189n, 215n, 216,
219n, 221, 222
Missionaries: political influence, 13, 73;
and Negro education, 52; Negroes
among, 70, 80-90; conflicts among,
84; attitudes toward blacks, 85-86, 89;
mentioned, 151
Mississippi: election of 1875, 180
Mitchell, T. S., 222
Mitchelville, 12
Mobley, Junius S., 101, 142, 143, 202, 220
Monk v. *Jenkins,* 43
Morgan, Shadrack, 76n, 189n
Morris, John, 115-16, 175-76
Morrison, William C., 57, 76n, 159
Moses, Franklin, 54, 208, 210
Moses, Franklin J.: political opinions, 103,
124, 126, 129, 130, 203; political career,
104, 176, 177, 186; mentioned, 84, 98n,
113, 119n
Mulattoes: political behavior, 15, 16, 17,
63, 65, 76, 126, 151, 162; political
conflict with blacks, 17, 61, 126, 162;
patronage advantage, 59
Murray, George W., 221
Myers, Nathaniel B., 149, 174n
Myers, William F., 98n

Nash, William Beverly: political opinions,

17, 18, 60, 126, 132, 155, 156, 197;
antebellum occupation, 47; political
career, 108, 110n, 158
Nat Turner's Revolt, 53
National Negro Laborers' Convention,
59-60, 158
Negro Democrats, 209
Negro officeholders: numbers elected or
appointed, 1, 97, 98, 105, 125n, 189n,
211, 215, 224; power, 4, 72, 73, 96, 98,
99, 109, 110, 120; assassination, 30;
social composition and background, 36,
38, 39, 40, 43, 49, 59, 62, 70; literacy,
36, 38, 52-56; property, 36-37, 38, 112,
141n, 163-64, 165; occupations, 39
(Table 1), 47, 90n; military service, 40,
49, 76-78; cohesion and dissension
among, 58-60, 123, 138, 144, 188;
religion, 63-64, 81, 87, 88; image, 95,
98; legislative success, 100; alliances
with Democrats, 115, 174, 214, 215, 219,
221; political opinions and behavior,
126-51, 162, 186, 190, 191; and their
constituents, 163; deaths among, 218
Negro women: political role, 34-35
Nesbitt, Richard, 163n, 186, 189n
Newberry County, 142
New England Society of Charleston, 195
New York Herald, 201
New York Times, 2n
Nix, Fred, 214
North, Charles F., 163n
Northern Methodists. *See* Methodist
Church (North)
Northern missionaries. *See* Missionaries
Northerners: political recruitment of, 73
Nuckles, Samuel, 55

O'Connell, Patrick, 144
Old Brick Church in St. Helena, 13, 14
104th U.S. Colored Troop, 56
128th U.S. Colored Troop, 34, 49, 82
Orangeburg County, 15n
Orr, James L., 23, 25, 29, 37n, 68-69, 223

Painters' union, 159
Patterson, John, 120, 147, 177-78, 201
Payne, Daniel A., 53, 88
People's party (Populists), 217
Perrin, Wade, 159